Basel Abbas//Ruanne Abou-Ra1 Ancarani//Ed Atkins//Jeremy Bi George Barber//Judith Barry//R Birnbaum//Claire Bishop//Iwon Blümlinger//J. David Bolter//Bri Comay//Jonathan Crary//Edith Decker//T.J. Demos// Jean Fisher//Morgan Fisher//Hollis Frampton//Jean-Michel Frodon//Peter L. Galison//Melanie Gilligan// Mark Godfrey//Kenneth Goldsmith//Kim Gordon//Tim Griffin//Andrew Grossman//Richard Grusin//Félix Guattari//Ed Halter//John G. Hanhardt//Gary Hill// Susan Hiller//Travis Jeppesen//Shanay Jhaveri// Stanya Kahn//William Kentridge//Jacob King//Anja Kirschner//George Kuchar//Pip Laurenson//Jay Leyda//Kate Linker//Susan Lord//Sven Lütticken//Chris McCormack//Steve McQueen//Francesco Manacorda// Jumana Manna//Janine Marchessault//H.G. Masters// Karen Mirza//Kate Mondloch//Rob Mullender// Michael Newman//Nam June Paik//Johan Pijnappel// Luther Price//Yvonne Rainer//R.V. Ramani//Steve Reinke//Ben Rivers//Pipilotti Rist//Ken Saylor//Jacolby Satterwhite//Roddy Schrock//Jason Simon//Vivian Sobchack//Hito Steyerl//Ryan Trecartin//Trinh T. Minh-ha//Marcia Tucker//Andrew V. Uroskie//Woody Vasulka//Bill Viola//Ian White//Kaelen Wilson-Goldie// Akram Zaatari//Maxa Zoller//Thomas Zummer

Moving Image

Whitechapel Gallery
London
The MIT Press
Cambridge, Massachusetts

Edited by Omar Kholeif

MOVING IMAGE

Documents of Contemporary Art

Co-published by Whitechapel Gallery
and The MIT Press

First published 2015
© 2015 Whitechapel Gallery Ventures Limited
All texts © the authors or the estates of the authors,
unless otherwise stated

ISBN 978-0-85488-238-0 (Whitechapel Gallery)
ISBN 978-0-262-52810-8 (The MIT Press)

A catalogue record for this book is available from
the British Library

Library of Congress Cataloging-in-Publication Data

Moving image / edited by Omar Kholeif.
   pages cm. — (Whitechapel: documents of
contemporary art)
  Includes bibliographical references and index.
  ISBN 978-0-262-52810-8 (pbk. : alk. paper)
1. Motion in art. 2. Technology and the arts. 3.
Arts and globalization. 4. Space (Art) I. Kholeif,
Omar, editor. II. Title.
  NX650.M64M68   2015
  700'.456—dc23
                                     2015012835

Whitechapel Gallery   10 9 8 7 6 5 4 3 2
The MIT Press   10 9 8 7 6 5 4 3 2 1

Series Editor: Iwona Blazwick
Commissioning Editor: Ian Farr
Project Editor: Francesca Vinter
Design by SMITH
Allon Kaye, Justine Schuster
Printed and bound in China

Cover, Ryan Trecartin, still from *The Re'Search
(Re'Search Wait'S)* (2009–10), HD video, 40 min.,
6 sec. © Ryan Trecartin. Courtesy of Andrea Rosen
Gallery, New York

Whitechapel Gallery Ventures Limited
77–82 Whitechapel High Street
London, E1 7QX
whitechapelgallery.org

Distributed to the book trade (UK and Europe only)
by Thames & Hudson
181a High Holborn
London, WC1V 7QX
+44 (0) 20 7845 5000
sales@thameshudson.co.uk

The MIT Press
Cambridge, MA 02142
mitpress.mit.edu

Documents of Contemporary Art

In recent decades artists have progressively expanded the boundaries of art as they have sought to engage with an increasingly pluralistic environment. Teaching, curating and understanding of art and visual culture are likewise no longer grounded in traditional aesthetics but centred on significant ideas, topics and themes ranging from the everyday to the uncanny, the psychoanalytical to the political.

The Documents of Contemporary Art series emerges from this context. Each volume focuses on a specific subject or body of writing that has been of key influence in contemporary art internationally. Edited and introduced by a scholar, artist, critic or curator, each of these source books provides access to a plurality of voices and perspectives defining a significant theme or tendency.

For over a century the Whitechapel Gallery has offered a public platform for art and ideas. In the same spirit, each guest editor represents a distinct yet diverse approach – rather than one institutional position or school of thought – and has conceived each volume to address not only a professional audience but all interested readers.

Series Editor: Iwona Blazwick; Commissioning Editor: Ian Farr; Project Editor: Francesca Vinter; Editorial Advisory Board: Roger Conover, Neil Cummings, Mark Francis, David Jenkins, Omar Kholeif, Gilane Tawadros

People should know that these Phantasms are the upshot of a ponderous and refractory art

Morgan Fisher, Statement, 1975

Omar Kholeif
Introduction//Navigating the Moving Image

You are in darkness. On the small rectangle of the editing table, imagery goes by. Slightly clenched on the control, your hand feels the image. It feels, it knows, it thinks it can control the image. Yes, but for what image? In the name of what image? There were times when the hand forgot, when the image appeared almost of its own accord. A force. A frame. A gaze. Fixity made unbearable ...
– Raymond Bellour, *Between-the-Images*[1]

All media are extensions of some human faculty – psychic or physical.
– Marshall McLuhan, *The Medium is the Massage*[2]

It is nearly impossible to speak of the twenty-first century without discussing the interplay of moving images with our everyday lives. They have become, as cultural theorist Norman M. Klein has noted, cross-embedded with every element of daily life, creating an ongoing series of special effects.[3] In changed conditions, unlike those addressed by formative discussions around cinema and its relationship to the audience during the 1960s and 1970s,[4] the image today moves in a different way, in a manner that is ever more bodily in its relationship to the individual. It is embedded into walls and billboards, subway platforms and buses; the moving image is in our pockets, on our laptops, at the gym, the bar, and everywhere else in between. Its affective relationship with us – that is, the desire or enchantment induced by facial close-ups or ambient effects, what Gilles Deleuze, drawing on the philosophy of Henri Bergson, terms 'affection-images' – has become ever more enhanced.[5] The moving image has become ever more proactive in its quest to kill everything around it; unequivocally, it decimates its surroundings, obliterating whatever may have come before it, forming 3-dimensional worlds where the image of the body and the body itself are intertwined.

This is all the product of an ongoing symbiosis between life and technology. We have come into an age of ongoing digital preservation; the unending documentation of the human self has become one of the primary affective experiences of day-to-day existence, as evidenced by the norms and parameters defined by social media and smartphone technology. Arguably, the moving image has taken on a new life through its function of documenting and encapsulating round-the-clock reality; it has also embodied its own movement through the ever-growing platforms for its distribution, as evinced by the omnipresence of video-sharing interfaces.[6]

The field of the moving image is a spatial practice. The interplay of light with the physical world creates a spectacle where the world becomes a hologram of itself. Here it is subject to constant imagination and reimagination. In this milieu, artists have played a defining role in shaping the form that the moving image can take. Indeed, artists' moving-image practice, the subject of this volume, has become a phenomenon within contemporary art and culture. It interfaces with physical space and bodily presence, it materializes within autonomous architectures. It varies in scale from the immersive installation to an image on a smartphone. An expanded field with origins in cinema, performance and conceptual art, it is equally diverse in its global roots. It is a practice that crosses over from the auditorium to exhibition or performance spaces and traverses the Internet's distributed realms.

Independent from mainstream forms of cinema, it is, rather, a form that focuses on its embodiment in diverse spatial environments. Moving-image work by visual artists is activated by the context of an exhibition space, an environment, a site, an action, a performance; it is equally activated by its apparatus, its history, by bodies, by the structures and channels of its own distribution. It extends beyond the confines of a restricted material or analogue form. Debatably, it is also a practice that is bound by an inherent contradiction. On the one hand, it derives from the hegemonic mass medium of cinema, and is thus markedly more distributable than the singular, rarefied art object. On the other, it is a practice often consciously restricted from mass-market circulation, limited to a small number of editions by artists and their galleries, and in many cases requires the context of an arts institution to define its genealogy and significance.[7]

Yet, despite artists' moving-image practice having been widely adopted by arts institutions and academia, its genealogy is nevertheless subject to much debate and contention. The reasons for this are extensive; among these is the fact that early moving-image practitioners often produced work that was staged around the notion of the event – its make-up was ephemeral. So, in its genesis, documentation was poor, and thus swathes of the practice's history have been situated outside of a definable canon, whereas in today's conditions the documentation of more recent work is constantly being updated and reformulated as emerging technologies are deployed.

Moreover, the question of obsolescence has been a key concern for many artists, with the shifts in video playback equipment over the last three decades alone rendering numerous moving-image file formats out of date. This has required extensive conservation work simply to maintain the formats for existing works, often a costly and time-consuming endeavour. And it is this material concern which has historically meant that museums and private collectors have been reticent about collecting moving-image artworks. At the same time, many major museums have historically restricted moving-image work to medium-specific collections and exhibiting spaces. The 'media' or 'box' gallery was a structure that could be found at New York's Museum of Modern Art and the Whitney Museum's former Marcel Breuer building, as well as the Smithsonian Institution's Hirshhorn Museum in Washington, to cite just three examples in the United States. This has meant that a sense of ghettoization has surrounded the field of moving-image practice even when the institution has embraced it.

Nevertheless, since the turn of the twenty-first century, key shifts have taken place. Institutions such as the Museum of Modern Art and, in Britain, the Tate are increasingly developing their holdings in this field, alongside specialist organizations whose focus involves the production or dissemination of moving-image works. Key to these developments has been the rise of artists' distribution agencies, which emerged from the historic legacies of the artist filmmaker cooperatives of the 1960s and 70s, such as both the New York and London-based Filmmakers' Co-ops. From the latter emerged LUX, an agency that not only offers a home to moving-image work by artists but is also a commissioning agency, publishing house, distributor and advisor to the sector. Similar organizations exist around the world, from Electronic Arts Intermix in New York to Vtape in Toronto and Arsenal in Berlin, to name but a few examples. This has been paralleled by the increasing focus on artists' moving-image work at film festivals, from Oberhausen to Rotterdam, Copenhagen and São Paulo, coupled with the work of specialist agencies and bodies such as Film and Video Umbrella, FACT (Foundation for Art and Creative Technology) and Light House Media Centre, to name three institutions based in Britain alone.

This volume brings together a broad constellation of material to form a discussion around artists' moving-image practice. The focus is on visual-arts based moving-image work, a definition that includes experimental film and video, moving-image centred installation and performance, personal documentary and the essay film. The aim here is to survey the formal, theoretical and political strategies that define contemporary practice in a global context. Unlike previous monographs that have sought to tie genealogies of moving-image work to specific geographies, this collection seeks to map out this practice as a rich and dense territory that is global in its breadth and scope. No longer isolated or relegated to medium-specific contexts, artists' moving-image practice has become a universal discipline. Artists who work with the moving image are increasingly nimble in their structure, transporting their work across vast territories instantaneously through formal and informal networks, jettisoning the confines of a single institution to share work with ever more varied audiences and in increasingly diverse contexts.

My approach here has been to trace a condensed genealogy for moving-image practice. Within the space available it is not possible to represent the work of every significant artist, and indeed there are those whose work I deeply admire who are not featured here. Rather, the focus is on key types of practice that exemplify a particular approach to moving-image making, offering different entry points to discussion, and embracing the contradictions that arise out of a medium that is constantly racing against the speed of light – its material form grappling with its own obsolescence.

Apparatus, the first section, looks at the formal possibilities raised by the apparatus of the moving image – not only technological but also social and theoretical – and considers how the machinery of artists' film and video acts as a stepping-stone for such an exploration. Thomas Zummer reaches into the deep history of the projected image to examine how 'the body persists as a common and inextricable component of the apparatus', whenever we 'take up residence within a phantasmatic technology'. Nam June Paik, pioneer of the transformation of the TV set into a counter-cultural medium, reminds us of a wider, ideological sense of apparatus (what the philosopher Michel Foucault terms the *dispositif*) in relation to broadcast television as a structure of power, influence and control. Edith Decker and John Hanhardt describe Paik's subversion and poeticization of television's technology and imagery. Kate Mondloch coins the term 'screen-reliant', as opposed to 'screen-based', to argue that a screen is a performative category in the work of a diverse range of artists of the late 1960s and 70s. Morgan Fisher's statement and *Projection Instructions* from the mid 1970s exemplify a moment of intense self-reflexivity, as film examines its own existence. A decade later Woody Vasulka argues that despite film being superseded by video, and analogue video by the digital, there is an underlying phenomenology that remains constant. Statements by Gary Hill and Hollis Frampton record the possibilities and challenges opened up by the emergence of computer-based visual media in the 1980s, and Tim Griffin assesses the legacy of Gretchen Bender's work during that decade, exploring an embedded position amongst the apparatus and shifting platforms of mass media. In an early instance of the term's use, Félix Guattari airs the notion of 'cracked' media, which 'can blow up like a windshield under the impact of molecular alternative practices'. Sven Lütticken surveys video works by Stan Douglas that reflect on the 'afterlife' of film. And Maxa Zoller proposes – in place of cinema as 'a phallic apparatus of control and dominance' – a 'pregnant apparatus', capable of engendering a distributed, participatory and generative experience. These discussions collectively consider the moving image's phenomenological presence, the ways in which its apparatus is able to create communal, affective spaces where disjointed narratives and scenes are bound together.

Situation looks at issues of site and specificity. Andrew Urowskie, Janine

Marchessault and Susan Lord argue in their respective texts that the 'expanded cinema' of the 1960s and 70s directly challenged the notion of medium-specificity, opening out towards the immersive and interconnected forms of practice explored by artists in the present such as Karen Mirza and Brad Butler, who reflect on what expanded cinema means to them. The work of Judith Barry is discussed by Kate Linker and the artist herself in relation to the ways in which we become constituted as social subjects in specific viewing conditions and environments. The particularities of situation, from trans-cultural transpositions to interstitial spaces and ghostly traces, are explored in projects by, among others, Jananne al-Ani, Francis Alÿs, Olga Chernysheva, Phil Collins, Minerva Cuevas, Omer Fast, Joana Hadjithomas & Khalil Joreige, Susan Hiller and the Otolith Group. A key text here is Ian White's *Kinomuseum*, 'a proposal for considering a particular kind of cinema as a unique kind of museum', which raises further questions around the moving image's territory: what are the confines in which it should live and breathe, or does the moving image always create its own context through the act of its staging?

Embodiment examines how bodies relate to the moving image, and inversely, how the moving image seeks to articulate and visualize that which is bodily. In particular, a number of texts focus on the body as a border or territory, an organizing principle for artists such as Yvonne Rainer, for whom the body becomes a field of resistance which unfolds the potential of the apparatus itself, and VALIE EXPORT, who positions her own body as a directly political antagonist. Dara Birnbaum looks back on two early influences: camera/body/monitor performances of the early 1970s, and a concurrent interest in alternative forms to broadcast television, as contexts for the genesis of her subversive work *Technology/Transformation: Wonder Woman* (1978/79), originally broadcast on cable TV opposite the 'real' *Wonder Woman* on network TV. In works such as *Stinging Kiss* (2000) by Tejal Shah, Bollywood stereotypes are similarly turned on their head as counterblasts to women's continued subordination in the modern Indian metropolis. Other politicized explorations of embodiment are seen in the work of Oreet Ashery, Ali Cherri, Stanya Kahn, Jumana Manna, Rabih Mroué and Lisa Steele. The artists Rob Mullender and Luther Price in different ways relate embodiment to the materiality of the filmic object itself. In 'Performance for the Computer', media artist Jeremy Bailey revisits Rosalind Krauss's 1976 essay 'Video: The Aesthetics of Narcissism' to explore its implications for artistic positions in the changed conditions of digital media.

Materialization focuses on the transition from analogue to digital and more broadly on the ways in which material form can become central to the meaning and effects of artists' work, in practices as diverse as those of Ed Atkins, Black Audio Film Collective, James Coleman, Olafur Eliasson, Harun Farocki, Melanie Gilligan,

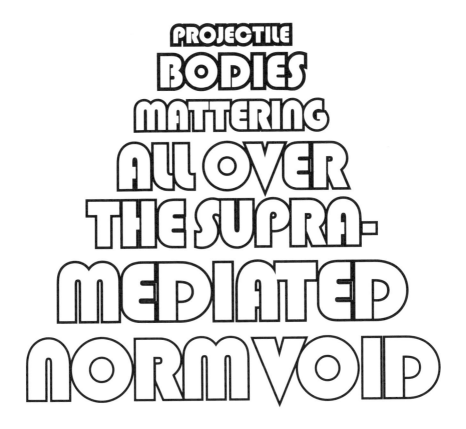

PROJECTILE BODIES MATTERING ALL OVER THE SUPRA-MEDIATED NORMVOID

Ryan Trecartin, from *I-Be Area*, 2007

William Kentridge, Anja Kirschner, George Kuchar, R.V. Ramani, James Richards, Ben Rivers, Trinh T. Minh-ha and Bill Viola. Ed Halter argues that the 'low-res' aesthetic of much contemporary electronic art can be considered as a kind of 'digital materialism', a sensibility theorized by the filmmaker Peter Gidal, in which the material of moving-image technology is made visible within the work itself. Hito Steyerl also considers how different technologies inform the visual aesthetic of moving images. In her influential essay 'In Defence of the Poor Image', Steyerl argues that there is intentionality in the production of the appropriated, low-resolution image: it offers a different kind of visual subjectivity that speaks to a divergent set of viewer experiences, as opposed to the HD glossiness that has come to emblematize so much of current visual culture. Basel Abbas and Ruanne Abou-Rahme round off these provocations with their reappropriation of the manifesto form – simultaneously destructive, subversive, constructive and utopian – in a worldwide call to hack moving images.

Mediation focuses on the ways in which moving-image artworks are mediated, distributed, collected and conserved, and their relation to the worlds of the contemporary media. What are the platforms and forums for artists' film and video, and how has the digital sphere enabled new modes of 'seeing' the moving image in all of its forms? This section includes conversations that take as their starting point the lo-fi online video platform UbuWeb to discuss how such resources and their earlier counterparts have influenced cultures of taste brokering and canon formation. The formative effects of controls on circulation are further contextualized in Erika Balsom's landmark text 'Original Copies: How Film and Video Became Art Objects', which examines the other end of the scale, the emergence of the limited edition filmic object, while Pip Laurenson focuses on the challenges that time-based media works present to practices of conservation centred on the material support. To an artist such as Pipilotti Rist, material conditions take second place to such concerns as the choreography of audience and the invention of new rituals, while Yuri Ancarani elides boundaries between fiction, documentary and 'reality', and Jacolby Satterwhite trawls the unlimited terrain of the digital media environment to forge a perverse and surreal reification of process, 'a dense crystal of information'. J. David Bolter and Richard Grusin identify a 'double logic of "remediation". Our culture wants both to multiply its media and to erase all traces of mediation: it wants to erase its media in the very act of multiplying technologies of mediation.'

Produced with his collaborator Lizzie Fitch, Ryan Trecartin's hyperbolic 'movies', here discussed by Travis Jeppesen, express one of the most embracing engagements with this contemporary media environment among recent artists. In Trecartin's videos, bodies intermingle in a saturated and multilayered universe that incorporates digital debris (of multiple and endless pop-up windows, junk and spam) with the surfeit of visual references that increasingly coat the everyday world. Underpinned by intricate scripts composed of neologisms, his movies collapse and unfold the specificities of multiple media into singular experiences. His world sees technology, and with it, the moving image, as a site of embodiment, as opposed to invention. 'Technology is us', as he has said. It is such affection with and for the moving image and its technologies that this volume seeks to inspire.

1   Raymond Bellour, *Between-the-Images* (1990/1999) (Zurich: JRP/Ringier/Dijon: Les Presses du Réel, 2011) 13.

2   Marshall McLuhan, with Quentin Fiore, *The Medium is the Massage* (1967) (London: Penguin Books, 2008) 26

3   Norman M. Klein, 'Cross-embedded Media: An Introduction', in Andreas Broegger and Omar Kholeif, eds, *Vision, Memory and Media* (Liverpool: Liverpool University Press/Chicago: University of Chicago Press, 2010).

4   Key texts of this period include André Bazin, *What is Cinema?* (1962); Peter Wollen, *Signs and Meaning in the Cinema* (1969); Christian Metz, *Film Language: A Semiotics of the Cinema* (1974); Laura Mulvey, 'Visual Pleasure and Narrative Cinema' (1975) (see bibliography for full details).

5   See Gilles Deleuze, 'The Affection-Image: Face and Close-Up', *Cinema I: The Movement Image* (1983); trans. Hugh Tomlinson and Barbara Habberjam (London: Athlone Press, 1992) 87–95.

6   See, for example, Lev Manovich, *Soft Cinema: Navigating the Database* (Cambridge, Massachusetts: The MIT Press, 2005); Laura U. Marks, *Touch: Sensuous Theory and Multisensory Media* (Minneapolis: University of Minnesota Press, 2002); Jonathan Crary, *24/7: Late Capitalism and the Ends of Sleep* (London and New York: Verso, 2014).

7   For further discussion of these issues see, for example, Stuart Comer, ed., *Film and Video Art* (London: Tate Publishing, 2008); Maeve Connolly, *The Place of Artists' Cinema Space, Site and Screen* (London: Intellect Books, 2009); A.L. Rees, *A History of Experimental Film and Video* (London: Palgrave Macmillan, 2011); Erika Balsom, *Exhibiting Cinema in Contemporary Art (Film Culture in Transition)* (Amsterdam: Amsterdam University Press, 2014).

ANY MEDIUM IN THE FUTURE AUTOMATICALLY CONTAINS THE MEDIA OF THE PAST

Woody Vasulka, In Conversation with Marita Sturken, 1987

APPARATUS

Thomas Zummer
Projection and Dis/embodiment: Genealogies of the Virtual//2001

[...] In as much as it shares certain characteristics with the dream, cinema engages us in the image of the world,[1] and we react almost as if what is represented resides before us. Our hearts may race, our breath becomes rapid and shallow, hair standing on end, uncontrollable spasms of laughter, all in response to the play of shadows and light. Optical devices, says Gaston Bachelard, provide us images to dream with, and cinema's flickering sensibilia constitute perhaps the most replete and consuming instance of an interface for dreaming. Still, we are less unwitting spectators than willing collaborators in this 'artificial dream', and we have retained and refined the capacity to pinch ourselves awake. It is this, our ability to invest in the phantasy of projections – somatically, sensorially, conceptually – in conjunction with our commensurate ability to apprehend and partake in them at the same time as spectacle, that forms the contours of a complex prosthetic relation between sense, memory and technical mediations. Technologies and bodies commingle in this configuration, and there exist substrates, underlying material conditions of reproduction and perception common to all projective phenomena, even to our apprehension of shadows cast on the wall of a cave, even to dreams. Certain of these substrates, in the form of (cinematic) tropes having to do with pretence and recognition, the passage of time, and the presence and absence of phenomena, persist throughout the history of recording media, residing in unconscious memory. They are the active, potential and mutable preconditions of mediated experience, the *habitus* through which we form a primary interface with technological reproduction of the real.

> Our organs are no longer instruments; on the contrary, our instruments are detachable organs. Space is no longer what it was in the *Dioptric*, a network of relations between objects such as would be seen by a witness to my vision or by a geometer looking over it and reconstructing it from outside. It is, rather, a space reckoned starting from me as the zero point or degree zero of spatiality. I do not see it according to its exterior envelope; I live it from the inside; I am immersed in it. After all, the world is around me, not in front of me.
> (Maurice Merleau-Ponty, 'Eye and Mind')[2]

There are certain preconceptions involved in the linking of the body to a register of instrumentation. These are, to use a phenomenological model, the inevitable 'pre-understanding' of the world via the *forms* in which experience is given. The body's senses do not encounter the world except in a culturally prepared subject (ourselves). Sensory phenomena are interpreted by analogy or metaphor in relation to our own somatic memory [...]. Moreover, the body's perception of itself also constitutes a *psychic substrate*, and the unconscious somatic memory that organizes lived experience is, itself, modified by specific technologies. These form still other, *technical substrates* of unconscious memory. Optical devices, for instance, alter the experienced scale of an observer's body, while at the same time changing the apparent *place* of that transformation, affecting our ideas of spatiality and temporality, causing us to perceive things as closer, or larger, or more similar, in relation to our own perceived bodies. Perception, linked to technical instruments, stubbornly apprehends different phenomena according to the most familiar tropes, habitual conventions of pictorial representation, and fundamental intuitions of the body. [...]

The difference between the optics of the eye and of the camera is both marked and subsumed as it is naturalized. 'The camera', Walter Benjamin writes, 'introduces us to unconscious optics as does psychoanalysis to unconscious impulses.'[3] The substrates of unconscious memory, technical or somatic, support an economy of translations between perceptions and instruments, such that 'prosthetic' perceptions occupy the same cognitive space as bodily sensations.

There are memoirs and personal accounts in the development of the electron microscope in the mid twentieth century that sound eerily close to phenomenological descriptions of embodiment. [...] Electron microscopes employ a beam of electrons, operating well below the wavelengths of visible light, to form an image of very small objects. In these devices high-energy electrons associated with considerably shorter wavelengths allow far greater resolution. The transmission electron microscope uses a sharply focused electron beam passing through a metallized specimen onto a fluorescent screen, where a visual image – which can be photographed – is formed. The scanning electron microscope forms a perspectival image, although both magnification and resolution are considerably lower. In this type of instrument, a beam of electrons scans a specimen, and those electrons that are reflected (along with any secondary electrons emitted) are collected. This current is then used to modulate a second electron beam in a television monitor, which scans the screen at the same frequency, thereby building up a picture of the specimen.

Electron microscopists, like the general populace, experienced themselves 'transported by this instrument to an alien landscape',[4] and the habitual conventions of reading 'landscapes' came into play in the representation of these invisible topographies by invoking and communicating common bodily experiences and pictorial conventions. The interface of operator/machine/phenomena is modified – tuned – by both physical limitation and cultural presupposition. The intuitive perception of the resulting micrographs as everyday landscapes is further supported by the fact that in order to be reflective, specimens were coated with a thin layer of metal atoms by spraying them from a low angle. Microscopists use the length of the resulting 'shadow' (formed when a feature has blocked metal deposition onto the surrounding support) to determine the 'height' of that feature, thus casting the electron beam's 'illumination' at 'noon', rather than from the actual direction of metal deposition. In this way the micrograph is constructed in such a familiar manner that it does not intrude on one's intuitive perception of the image as a 'landscape'.[5] In the process of refining our scientific apparatus, the observer's lived experience takes up residence in – is *sutured* into – the machine, such that one 'dwells' in the instrument, in a continuum of decreasing consciousness and increasing familiarity, consequently moving from alterity to embodiment.

Cinema, one might say, is just such a lived technology. In the interface of architecture, technology, perception and habit, we spectators are intimately inscribed into the mediated imaginary, taking up residence – for a moment – within a phantasmatic technology. Here we are an element of the dream, linked to a specular machinery where unconscious behaviour, modifying and modified by the instrument, interactively constructs our experience. In the long history of projective environments – from Ibn al-Haytham to Leonardo da Vinci, Athanasius Kircher to E.G. Robertson, Thomas Edison and the Lumière brothers to today's cineplexes, home entertainment systems and virtual realities – the body persists as a common and inextricable component of the apparatus, and familiar everyday perceptions are linked to a history of cinematic artefacts and behaviours in diverse, complex ways, so much so that even our recognition of their artifice is a culturally mediated form. [...]

1   [footnote 3 in source] See Martin Heidegger, 'The Age of the World Picture' (1938), in *The Question Concerning Technology and Other Essays*, trans. William Lovitt (New York: Harper & Row, 1977).

2   [4] Maurice Merleau-Ponty, 'Eye and Mind' (1961), in Merleau-Ponty, *The Primacy of Perception*, ed. James M. Edie (Chicago: Northwestern University Press, 1964) 178. The *Dioptric* is René Descartes' treatise of 1637 on optics, the senses and related matters, preceded by the *Discourse on Method*.

3   [6] Walter Benjamin, 'The Work of Art in the Age of Mechanical Reproduction' (1936), in Benjamin, *Illuminations*, ed. Hannah Arendt, trans. Harry Zohn (New York: Harcourt, Brace & World, Inc., 1968) 239.

4   [8] Nicolas Rasmussen, *Picture Control: The Electron Microscope and the Transformation of Biology in America, 1940–1960* (Stanford: Stanford University Press, 1997) 232.

5   [9] Ibid.

Thomas Zummer, extracts from 'Projection and Dis/embodiment: Genealogies of the Virtual', in *Into the Light: The Projected Image in American Art 1964–1977*, ed. Chrissie Iles (New York: Whitney Museum of American Art/Harry N. Abrams, 2001).

Jay Leyda
Films Beget Films//1964

When I fixed upon this subject I was somewhat taken aback by the fact that there was no name for it. I wanted to examine the development and problems of the *compilation film* – but what an awkward, incomprehensible and unacceptable term for this form! 'Archive films' – that's too easily confused with the idea of films (of any type) stored in archives. Same fate for 'library films'. 'Stock-shot' films – explicit enough, but how narrow in its associations! Others to whom I've appealed for a neat, clear term have been equally helpless – suggesting even more cumbersome descriptions: for example, 'documentary archive films' or 'chronicle montage films'. Nor does the accepted French term *film de montage* offer us anything but ambiguity. The proper term would have to indicate that the work begins on the cutting table, with already existing film shots. It also has to indicate that the film used originated at some time in the past. The term could also indicate that it is a film of *idea*, for most of the films made in this form are not content to be mere records or documents – and in this factor lies my chief interest in the form, which will have to be referred to in various inconsistent ways. Can you suggest a right term? [...]

Jay Leyda, extract from *Films Beget Films* (London: George Allen & Unwin, 1964) 9.

Nam June Paik
'Pensées' at 59//1991

I told Manfred Eichel of NDR1 that the five principles of the media are

1   Sex
2   Violence
3   Greed
4   Vanity
5   Deception

He said, 'I cannot agree with you more. You must write about it!'

Manfred Eichel has aired 350 cultural TV shows. He knows the practical difficulty of transmitting reasonably important television without unreasonable boredom. He is not like those armchair strategists who just talk about media behind their academic screen. [...]

Nam June Paik, extract from '"Pensées" at 59' (1991), in *Nam June Paik: Video Time – Video Space*, ed. Thomas Kellein, Toni Stooss (New York: Harry N. Abrams, 1993) 17.

Edith Decker
Hardware//1993

While artists have mastered video technology, they've always had to work within the predetermined scope that is offered. Experimental artists like Nam June Paik certainly managed to elicit new functions from the technology that had not been anticipated by designers and manufacturers, but the basic structure of their artistic production was determined by the equipment itself. When I was collecting material for my dissertation on the artist in the early 1980s, I was faced with the question of the categories into which his work should be placed, as I had to follow a certain academically imposed format. After a few attempts to structure the material, it seemed ideal to group Paik's works from the standpoint of their technology. Any particular technique included quite different content elements, and division according to subject matter did not seem possible because of the unusual formal language.

In America, the terms *single channel* and *multichannel* are employed. *Single channel* means a videotape, and *multichannel* as a rule indicates a video installation. But as an installation with an operating video camera is based on quite different technical requirements from an installation with a videotape running in it, I have adopted the familiar terms *closed-circuit installation* and *multi-monitor installation*. A closed-circuit installation records a subject on a closed loop with a camera, and then shows the running footage on monitors or as a projection. A multi-monitor installation shows one or more videotapes. This does not always have to be the case, but it is usual with Paik, and he has worked relatively little with video projectors. The video works with Charlotte Moorman are the principal exceptions to this rule.

Paik lived in Germany as an avant-garde composer between 1956 and 1963, and discovered the affinity between television and electronic music in the early 1960s. In 1962, he started to try out the skills he had learned in the WDR Studio for Electronic Music in Cologne on second-hand black-and-white televisions. Using circuit diagrams and handbooks, he familiarized himself with the inner life of the sets, intending to interfere with the order he found there. After an intervention by Paik, not much remains of the message but the medium. This electronic tinkering is also a destructive Fluxus gesture. Unlike Wolf Vostell, who brought television into artists' studios and exhibition galleries shortly after Paik, he was not concerned with mere interference, but with altering the function of the set. There was no need to learn from Marshall McLuhan; the significance of television was already obvious. When Paik exhibited the first manipulated sets in 1963, the daily news was flickering over seven million screens in West Germany.

Although since then the artist has continued to find new ways to apply existing and rapidly developing television techniques, he must still adhere to preconditions in his use of the technology. Paik has always inclined toward a kind of artistic alternative television that works against 'Big Brother', and this persists right down to his robot families of the 1980s. Only here does the television set experience its apotheosis, in the combination of an 'ancient' exterior and new inner life.

Paik developed his fundamental equipment experimentally in the 1960s, although successive technical developments considerably broadened the presentational range. In the second half of the sixties, after the introduction of the first portable video camera, Paik laid the foundations for his three-dimensional video oeuvre: individually altered single objects, installations with live camera or microphone, and installations with numerous monitors. [...]

Edith Decker, extract from 'Hardware', in *Nam June Paik: Video Time – Video Space*, ed. Thomas Kellein, and Toni Stooss (New York: Harry N. Abrams, 1993) 67 [footnotes not included].

John G. Hanhardt
Non-Fatal Strategies: The Art of Nam June Paik in the Age of Postmodernism//1993

1,000 white pages follow – imagine.
– Nam June Paik (1962)

We are no longer in the drama of alienation, we are in the ecstasy of communication.
– Jean Baudrillard (1983)

In 1982, on the occasion of Nam June Paik's retrospective at the Whitney Museum of American Art, there occurred a public performance event which captured the quality of an artist who has come to symbolize the transformation of video into an artform. The event was a public performance featuring Paik's *Robot K–456* (1964), a human-sized, remote-controlled robot fashioned out of bits and pieces of wire and metal. Lacking the metallic skin of science-fiction robots, this stick-like creature – equipped with giant motorized feet, a tape recorder which originally played John F. Kennedy's 1961 inaugural address, and a digestive tract which defaecated beans on demand – was definitely a handmade object. As it stood on its pedestal in the gallery of the museum, it had the appearance not of a Frankenstein monster waiting to break loose, but of a vulnerable construction made by an artist-scientist working in a studio, not a science lab. In the mid 1960s, the robot performed as a remote-controlled figure in street events and theatre works such as Karlheinz Stockhausen's *Originale*. In 1964, when Paik moved to New York from Japan, he brought the robot, which he had made in Japan in collaboration with the electronics engineer Shuya Abe. Later, *Robot K–456* found its way to Germany, where it became part of a private art collection. By 1982 it had become a historical object, the expression of an extraordinary period in the early 1960s when movements such as Happenings, Fluxus, Minimalism, new dance, avant-garde film and video emerged which transformed our conceptions of the art object.

The performance staged in front of the Whitney Museum brought *Robot K–456* back to life. The performance began with Paik guiding the robot along the sidewalk to the intersection of 75th Street and Madison Avenue. It then proceeded to cross the avenue, where it was struck by an automobile, an accident staged by Paik with the artist Bill Anastasi behind the wheel. When interviewed by the TV news reporters documenting the event, Paik described the accident as the first catastrophe of the 21st century, and added that we were practising how to deal with it. This catastrophe was the sense, created by the impact of new technologies, that things were out of control, that our lives and environment were threatened, as the robot crossing Madison Avenue learned. *Robot K–456*, which, Paik noted in the interview, was twenty years old and had not had its bar mitzvah, was returned to the museum, straightened out, and placed once again on its pedestal. This was an instance of Paik's continuing effort to poeticize technology by refashioning it within an ecology of media into humanly scaled and uniquely expressive forms.

In March 1963, at the Galerie Parnass, Wuppertal, Paik had his first solo exhibition, which included a room of his prepared televisions. When the TV sets were removed from their customary position in the home and scattered around the room, they became objects to be manipulated and transformed by the artist. The consolidation of broadcast television in Europe and the US had determined the content and form of television technology; television had been defined not as a creative tool for the use of the individual, but as a home entertainment appliance. In Paik's hands, the television became the means to produce a new electronic image, which he did by applying magnets to the surface of the TV set and reworking the electronics of its interior. In the spirit of Fluxus, Paik remade the television, exposing its insides, turning it inside out and disrupting its mechanics in order to create an abstract image. It was this potential for abstraction which the industrial codes of manufacturing sought to cover over and fill in with its traditional formats of TV shows and representational, recorded, image-making. [...]

John G. Hanhardt, extract from 'Non-Fatal Strategies: The Art of Nam June Paik in the Age of Postmodernism', in *Nam June Paik: Video Time – Video Space*, ed. Thomas Kellein and Toni Stooss (New York: Harry N. Abrams, 1993) 79.

Kate Mondloch
Interface Matters: Screen-Reliant Installation Art//2010

The brain is the screen – that is to say ourselves.
– Gilles Deleuze (1986)[1]

Art critic and historian Michael Fried's groundbreaking 1967 essay 'Art and Objecthood' is best known as a studied rejection of Minimalism, or, as Fried preferred to call it, 'literalist' art. Fried recognized that this new genre, in as much as it compelled a durational viewing experience akin to theatre, undermined both the medium specificity and the presumed instantaneousness of reception foundational to the Greenbergian/Friedian account of modernism. The impact of Fried's discerning analysis upon contemporary art history and criticism is incontestable. For the purposes of the present study, however, a little remarked upon footnote in this otherwise exhaustively analysed article is especially revelatory. In it, Fried speculates that a close reading of the 'phenomenology of the cinema' would reveal how film manages to escape the degraded relational quality that he believed was endemic to literalist art. 'Exactly how the movies escape theatre is a beautiful question', Fried muses. He goes on to suggest that cinema is not in danger of theatricality because, among other reasons, 'the screen is not experienced as a kind of object existing, so to speak, in a specific relation to us.'[2]

Fried's appreciation of a divide between the cinematic experience and that of minimalist sculpture was soon to be overthrown by the expanded field of art and media practices that emerged in the 1960s and 1970s. In the range of overlapping screen-reliant art practices variously known as structural film, expanded cinema, intermedia environments, moving-image or projected-image installation, and so on, the seemingly discrete boundaries between the cinematic and the sculptural were deliberately and provocatively muddied. Contesting the tenets of formalist modernism, artists as diverse as VALIE EXPORT, Frank Gillette and Ira Schneider, Dan Graham, Joan Jonas, Anthony McCall, Marcel Broodthaers, Bruce Nauman, Peter Campus, Paul Sharits and Michael Snow created evocative sculptures in which cinematic and electronic screens, defying Fried's analysis, are indeed 'experienced as a kind of object existing ... in a specific physical relation to us'. Even before the inception of most film and video installations, then, Fried had instinctively recognized that the screen would be a threat to stable modernist categories should its conventionally overlooked objecthood be exposed (a threat he was keen to avoid). Working in the wake of Minimalism, these artists did just that: they invited viewers to understand the screen – *as well as the site and experience of screen spectatorship* – as material.

Media screens made initial forays into art galleries as early as the late 1950s. Film and video screens served both as constitutive elements of Happenings, performances and expanded cinema events, created by artists such as Carolee Schneemann, Alan Kaprow, John Cage, Robert Whitman and Robert Rauschenberg, and as art materials in their own right, such as the now quaintly anachronistic television sets assembled in Wolf Vostell's early media-critical work and in Nam June Paik's satirical video sculptures. However, the incorporation of mass media screens into art environments or installations in the mid 1960s marked a distinct shift of emphasis. In what I call screen-reliant installations, artists were newly concerned with the viewer-screen interface itself: the multifarious physical and conceptual points at which the observing subject meets the media object. Media objects and their viewing regimes were literally and figuratively put on display in these sculptural and experiential works of art.

I use the term 'screen-reliant' as opposed to 'screen-based' to signal that a screen is a performative category. Almost anything – glass, architecture, three-dimensional objects, and so on – can function as a screen and thus as a connective interface to another (virtual) space. Projected image installations have consistently revealed this ambiguous status – from Robert Whitman's 1964 *Shower*, in which a nude female bather is projected onto a real shower (complete with an actual running shower head), to, more recently, Michal Rover's 2003 *DataZone*, in which diminutive dancing figures are projected inside of what looks like petri dishes mounted on table tops. The screen, then, is a curiously ambivalent object – simultaneously a material entity and a virtual window; it is altogether an object which, when deployed in spatialized sculptural configurations, resists facile categorization.

Although the term 'installation' was not widely used until the late 1970s, the issues associated with the expanded practices now commonly known as installation – considerations such as space, materials, embodiment, duration, site and participation – offer the most relevant criteria for evaluating the variant of post-1960s artistic production. In many ways, Minimalism and its critical legacy set the stage for these developments. Minimalism aspired to overthrow the spatial and temporal idealism associated with modernist sculpture, replacing it with a direct experiential encounter for the spectator in the 'here and now' of the gallery space. By revealing the exhibition space as material, these influential works cleared the way for critical reflection on the physical and ideological constraints of the art gallery by process- and concept-based sculptural practices of the 1960s and 1970s. In these innovative artworks, context and the contingent dynamics of spectatorship emerged as content.

It was in this spirit that artists first created experiential works centred on media screens and sited within the specific institutional context of the visual arts. These hybrid artworks – positioned as they are midway between the cinematic and the sculptural – deliberately engaged the spatial parameters of the gallery, even as they rejected its typical spatial and representational modes. Regardless of the particular approach employed in a given work, these variegated screen-reliant environments are unified by the way in which they foreground the usually overlooked embodied interface between the viewing subject and the technological object. [...]

1 'La cerveau, c'est l'écran. Entretien avec Gilles Deleuze', *Cahiers du Cinéma* (March 1986), trans. Marie Therese Guirgis, in *The Brain is the Screen: Deleuze and the Philosophy of Cinema*, ed. Gregory Flaxman (Minneapolis: University of Minnesota Press, 2000) 366–7.

2 [footnote 1 in source] Michael Fried, 'Art and Objecthood', *Artforum* (Summer 1967) 23, n. 16. [...]

Kate Mondloch, extract from *Screens: Viewing Media Installation Art* (Minneapolis: University of Minnesota Press, 2010) 1–3.

Morgan Fisher
Statement//1975

My films tend to be about the making of films. I didn't programmatically set out to do this, it's just something I can't seem to resist. The more deeply I delve into it, the more inexhaustively rich the subject becomes. the process by which motion pictures are produced is exceedingly complex, and every aspect of it is to me fraught with suggestion, though of a seemingly bathetic sort. So my films incline to the literal and matter-of-fact. In a sense they are educational, in that they explain procedures or processes underlying film production that an audience might not be familiar with. I feel it is important for the viewers to understand how it is that a film comes into being, where it comes from, so to speak, and what it must have undergone (in the material sense) before it appears before their eyes as shadows on the screen. People should know that these phantasms are the upshot of a ponderous and refractory art. If they are not aware of it they are denied the chance to understand film as such.

Actually, it isn't clear to me why some of my films weren't done long ago. For the most part they are obvious ideas. This is a way to say that the films are fundamentally simple, and that the details of their realization are traceable to a single thought. From the beginning there has been a reflexive strain in cinema, but it has always struck me as half-hearted, Dziga Vertov and [his 1941 film] *Hellzapoppin'* notwithstanding. Film should have taken the plunge at the outset and begun by looking at itself, a pursuit as worthy as the treatment of what are ordinarily called subjects. Hence my films represent an effort to catch up, to redress an oversight committed by history.

Morgan Fisher, Untitled statement, first published in the October 1975 calendar for the San Francisco Cinematheque; reprinted in *Morgan Fisher: Writings*, ed. Sabine Folie and Susanne Titz (Cologne: Verlag der Buchhandlung Walther König, 2012) n.p.

Morgan Fisher
Projection Instructions//1976

Text on Screen

Attention projectionist:

This film is a series of instructions addressed to you. The instructions must be followed if the film is to be shown correctly.

Title

PROJECTION INSTRUCTIONS

© 1976 Morgan Fisher

Narration and Text on Screen
[The film consists of the following instructions that appear on the screen one after the other at the same time as the narrator speaks them, but how the projectionist performs the film mediates what we see and hear of the words.]

Turn sound off.

Turn sound on.

Turn lamp off.

Turn lamp on.

Turn volume up.

Frame up.

Turn volume to normal.

Frame in centre.

Turn volume down.

Frame down.

Turn volume to normal.

Frame in centre.

Turn tone to treble.

Throw out of focus.

Turn tone to bass.

Focus normally

Turn tone to normal.

Frame down.
Throw out of focus.

Turn volume up.
Turn tone to bass.

Frame in centre.
Focus normally.

Turn volume down.

Turn tone to treble.

Frame up.
Throw out of focus.

Turn volume to normal.
Turn tone to normal.

Frame in centre.
Focus normally.

Morgan Fisher, narration/script for *Projection Instructions* (1976), 16mm film, black and white, optical sound; duration 4 min. First published in *Morgan Fisher: Writings*, ed. Sabine Folie and Susanne Titz (Cologne: Verlag der Buchhandlung Walther König, 2012) n.p.

Woody Vasulka
In Conversation with Marita Sturken//1987

Woody Vasulka [...] Film came with its utterly unambiguous, culturally broad and intellectually lucid – eventually – concept. So it became obvious that this would be passed on to the general public as a new form of literacy. But this phenomenology that was located in film was specific to film. And that's how it developed culturally also; how its criticism, its language, its intellectual kind of contribution and participation was created. Now with video, suddenly some people would separate these two media. They would say that video belongs to a different cultural environment, and that they can't be talked about using the same language. But in fact I say, sure, the phenomenology that was assigned to film is the same if taken to video, and not only video. You know, when I saw computers, it's basically the same phenomenology. [...] What I'm trying to say is that any medium in the future automatically contains the media of the past, that means video in fact contains the language of ... whatever ... these are terms that are still being debated, but I mean the syntactic devices: fade in, fade out, dissolve [...] and various kinds of interpretation, in the context of the story, how to tell things. It's true that we don't think of [these syntactic devices] as disrelated, because we see them on television and we see them on film. Sometimes we see them on television less than we see them on film because television is designated to a different populus, a much larger populus, and also uses different types of stories. It's as not cultural, to the degree that film is, sort of, avant-garde over narrative exploration. And computers the same; as you know, computers mostly produce scientific or commercial images, but eventually we may count them also into the main cultural stream of expression. [...] The phenomenology – how images are conveyed through this train of frames into our mind – is the same phenomenology.

Marita Sturken [In terms of] how we perceive them or how they're conveyed?

Vasulka They are constructed as framed systems. They deliver phases of movement.

Sturken So when you say phenomenology, you mean as a process that goes through to the actual reception of the viewer?

Vasulka Yes, what I call this axis of perception, which is: when you construct the image, it is the light space, as they call it, which is formed by a pinhole, and it's registered into a frame. So there are these three elements, and when you project them then it's the light that goes to the frame on screen, and it's registered in your visual cortex. All these elements have to be in axis – if they are out of axis in the horizontal and vertical sense the perception of the movement can be ambiguous, it becomes redundant. So film and video, for me, construct the frame. Film constructs the frame sort of physically, and locates the frame mechanically through the sprocket holes, and video or the computer constructs the frame electronically by time and reference. Line drawing and field drawing – it's just different ways of constructing the image. In one case it's the parallel delivery of the whole frame at one time through the opening of the blade in the projector, and in the second, it's a line-by-line construction which is memorized in your visual cortex and held until the next cognitive unit comes and it's compared. But the cinematic interpretation, what's between the first and second phase, the first frame and the second frame, is the extract of that change which some people I guess call the *kine* of movement. And computers have to construct the frame the same way. So we're talking about frames and the delivery of frames, and it seems to be very effective because various magnificent stories have been constructed by this means. What I'm trying to do is take this away from academic confines, because as you know a lot of departments, or tribalists, the film tribe, insist that there is a specificity of images which is much greater than the specificity of the media. I say that the media have their own fluidity and relate to each other phenomenologically. [...]

Woody Vasulka and Marita Sturken, extract from round-table conversation with Steina Vasulka and JoAnn Hanley (24 July 1987), unpublished typescript.

Gary Hill
Inter-view//1993

[...] *Within contemporary art, what would you say is the primary difference between video and other mediums, particularly in the context of conceptual art and related practices?*

Time, this is what is central to video; it is not seeing, as its etymological roots imply. Video's intrinsic principle is feedback. So it is not linear time but a movement that is bound up in thinking – a topology of time that is accessible. This experience of time exists within a specific electronic parameter that to the eye is a rectangular screen, but which is very distant from a cybernetic process that includes oneself. I think this paradox of being intimate with time and estranged from it is what brought me to speech, and specifically speech rather than some form of written text on the screen. Vocalization was a way physically to mark the time with the body through utterance – the speaking voice acting as a kind of motor generating images. This really puts one inside the time of speaking. Every syllable is tied to an image; suddenly words seem quite spatial, and the viewer becomes conscious of a single word's time. [...]

Most of your work deals with the interrelationship of words and images – confrontations between them. Would you say this is more of a European concern than an American one, let's say in the tradition of semiology?

Certainly with a number of my works from the early 1980s – *Primarily Speaking* (1981–83), *Around & About* (1980), *War Zone* (1980) – it would be hard to deny the relationship to semiology, but this was never a focal point. The works are not grounded in theory in that way; I'm rather distrustful of polemics and prone to look for inconsistencies – breakdowns. My ideas seem to shift, turn, invert, contradict, rather than develop, refine and serialize. Of course, working in this way I come face to face with particular writers, or artists, who are identified with certain theories. The significant difference is that my preoccupation with language began with very sculptural notions, coming out of sound, the body, utterance and speaking. Furthermore, this took place within the discourse of electronic media: when you work in real time the mediation of signs is very different from a reading/writing context. If one is going to talk about my work in a deconstruction context I think it is worth keeping in mind that Derrida, from whom the origin of this notion comes, is said to be primarily a reader. I am primarily an image maker. Video embodies a reflexive space of difference, through the simultaneous production of presence and distance. I think it has a visceral reality more encompassing than writing, and still allows for mediation without falling prey to the image. And yet, although my art is based on images, I am very much involved in the undermining of those images through language. [...]

You've worked with both single-channel tapes and installations for quite some time. Conceptually, what do you see as the difference in terms of time, the use of scale, and methodology?

Making tape, and likewise viewing tape, has similarities to reading and writing. Videotape lives in linear time; it's always an assemblage – one image/sound after another (one single pixel after another) – it writes left to right. Although the non-linear nature of memory can be played with extensively through editing, a single-channel work is not *in the world* the way installation and sculpture are. The moving image in a box cannot have the same physical relationship with the viewer. There's a definite trade-off. With installation there's an inevitable theatricality, which I try to minimize. I want the viewer incorporated into the work; to be self-conscious about his or her sense of place within the conceptual strategy of the specific piece. The experience of time is displaced by the physical experience to a much greater degree. Hopefully, the viewer is viscerally confronted with things, images and ideas.

I think the most difficult aspect of using video in an installation is decentralizing the focus on the television object itself, and its never-ending image. How does one get away from that everyday seduction of the continuous flow of images couched as information. I tried to do this in different ways. For example, in *Beacon (two versions of the imaginary)* (1990), the television object disappears completely and is seen as the dual beacon of a lighthouse. Light as source and image as source become interchangeable. Not only has the 'TV' been physically removed from its frame of reference, but the object producing the image is a metaphor turned in on itself, conversing with its own image. [...]

Gary Hill, extracts from 'Inter-view', text assembled and reworked by the artist from previous interviews, in *Gary Hill* (Paris: Centre Pompidou/Amsterdam: Stedelijk Museum, 1993) 13–16.

Hollis Frampton
Proposal: Hardware and Software for Computer-Processed-and-Generated Video//1982

History of the Project

During recent years, as costs for goods and services in many of the media-related technologies (e.g. film) have increased steadily, the cost of video has fallen dramatically, and the computer has become available at the personal level. It is literally true that more computational power is available today, for a few thousand dollars, than was imaginable on the multi-million dollar mainframe computers of twenty years ago.

It has been true for some time that established video artists in mid career may afford, with some sacrifice, to own the tools of their craft; younger artists have been able to share these means through a developing network of local non-profit facilities. This availability of tools has encouraged the growth of a new artform in a way comparable to the rapid development of independent film after the advent and acceptance of a relatively cheap 16mm film technology, which afforded wide distribution without seriously diminishing technical quality.

In the meantime, there has been great eagerness on the part of artists to explore the new possibilities for image generation and processing made available by the computer. In the past, this enthusiasm was thwarted by the scarcity and expense of computer time, by the problems that anyone has in communicating with others highly trained in a foreign discipline, and by a fundamental alienation from the extreme generality of computation. It has never before been possible for an artist to explore the uses of the computer in art with the intimacy and flexibility that the painter or writer takes for granted and finds the necessary condition of creative work.

However, most existing computer programming languages were designed, from economic necessity, to accommodate the scientific and business communities: the result has been a computing environment uncongenial to users in other fields. And the additional hardware required for video image generation, except for devices of very limited capability, is still too expensive for individuals to afford.

Since 1977 I have worked, both alone and with a small group of students in workshops at SUNY/Buffalo, to formulate the hardware and software requirements for a hospitable computing environment for the arts, emphasizing the notion of the computer as a personal creative tool. In practice, this experimentation has entailed the writing and testing of hundreds of programs, and the design and building of dozens of hardware devices, during an estimated interval of 20,000 hours. The conceptual portion of this work is now complete. It has produced two results.

The first is a design for a hardware device, called a frame buffer, that may be interfaced to virtually any mini-computer or micro-computer. The device treats a portion of computer memory as an image, and outputs as NTSC standard RGB colour video a picture composed of 256 by 256 elements, each of which may be any 256 out of about 16.8 million possible colours. Up to four images are available within the device itself at any given time: further images may be stored on, and retrieved from, magnetic media such as tape or floppy disk. The contents of a frame may be generated directly by the host computer or loaded from a video camera. Embellishments within the buffer permit complex manipulations of picture information in real time, but the design, while versatile, is essentially conservative. This portion of the project exists, at the moment, as completed schematic and timing diagrams and parts specifications. I would emphasize that the prototype device can be completely constructed for less than $5,000 in materials, and that additional units should cost less than $3,000.

The second result is the conceptual design of a software system for using the hardware to create and modify images. This design specifies a programming language containing more than 160 commands, and 19 additional software subsystems for performing special tasks such as building character type fonts, sequencing the output of images to a video monitor, redefining the set of colours in use, and so forth. The language is highly interactive, permitting a user to work with images after very brief instruction and without previous programming experience, but it is of sufficient richness to afford scope to experienced programmers as well as experienced artists. I have brought to bear, in the design of this software, 25 years of experience as a working visual artist and six years as a programmer and user of programs. I will write the programs as in-kind matching for funds. This will probably take about 2,000 hours and produce 15,000 lines of program code.

Work of the Project
The work of the project will consist in (1) construction of the frame buffer by Robert Coggeshall, and (2) implementation of the software by myself.

Results of the Project
1. Complete documentation for the frame buffer, including schematic and timing diagrams, bill of materials, theory of operation, construction and troubleshooting information, and specification of interface to software.

2. A high level interpretive language and subsystems, in both human and

computer-readable form, together with its formal specification, user manual, implementation manual, and hardware test and alignment programs. The software will operate on the Zilog 280 and/or the DEC L51-11 microcomputer(s).

3. Demonstration and tutorial video cassettes of the system in operation.

4. A descriptive and critical report of the project.

All these materials will be placed in the public domain. Using them, any person with reasonable electronic skills should be able to build the hardware and bring up the software in about 80 hours. [...]

Hollis Frampton, extract from 'Proposal: Hardware and Software for Computer-Processed-and-Generated Video', undated proposal (1982) submitted to the Media Arts Program of the National Endowment for the Arts; in *On the Camera Arts and Consecutive Matters: The Writings of Hollis Frampton*, ed. Bruce Jenkins (Cambridge, Massachusetts: The MIT Press, 2009) 269–71.

Kim Gordon
Performing/Guzzling//2009

Looking out into the audience light comes from the back of the projector at the back of the hall. It makes the back of peoples' heads look illuminated, like saints. The projector changes and some of the faces disappear into the dark. The ones further back I can't see at all. Toward the front of the hall half cheeks appear dappled with swirling colours from the light show. I'm trying not to look directly at anyone in the front so the spell of concentration won't be broken. Instead they appear as a collective mood. Suddenly something whirs by my head and smashes onto the stage. It's a cassette. I'm spinning around in a circle trying not to get dizzy but liking the dizziness of the blurry images. It looks like a flicker camera in 360 degrees. I wish I had a camera to record what it looks like.

Kim Gordon, extract from *Performing/Guzzling*, artist's book (New York: Rizzoli, 2009) n.p.

Tim Griffin
On Multiple Screens//2013

When one surmises the legacy of Gretchen Bender today, two statements by the artist leap out from an interview conducted on the occasion of her 1991 survey at the Everson Museum of Art in upstate New York. The first is a somewhat counter-intuitive assertion regarding Bender's tactical relationship to the mass media and its increasingly variegated platforms throughout culture. 'I ... believe', she says,

> that an acceleration into, rather than a resistance to, our multilayered visual environment will reveal structures or open windows to the development of a critical consciousness we can't yet perceive as useful from within our immediate vantage point.[1]

In other words, only a kind of mimicry of contemporary media platforms – an implementation of their fundamental modality (if not a literal infiltration of their systems) with respect to the speed and distribution of imagery and textual information – will give rise to analytical perspectives on present society and its technologies. Indeed, and more provocatively, only through such conjoining will the very *possibility* for this vantage arise. For Bender's argument is entirely conditional, pertaining to the 'development' not only of a critical model germane to contemporary media but also of a consciousness whose fundamental orientation and purpose is not yet legible to us, let alone articulated and deployed. In fact, while Bender elsewhere indicates that artists who are especially attuned to conditions of the present are apt to make 'new technologies look like old art' – implying that a modernist notion of criticality in art is sustainable in the face of new media and technologies – here she suggests that both the material and intellectual shape of art is immediately subject to permutation.[2] Bender's is an art, in so many words, steeped in the process of adapting. It seems not incongruous that she would wryly deploy clips of *Videodrome* (David Cronenberg, 1983) in her work.

A second statement by the artist ostensibly describes the physical apparatus necessary to support such mimicry, providing a rationale for her scaffolds of television monitors and screen projections in works like *Dumping Core* (1984) or *Total Recall* (1987):

> When you look at one screen, there's one source coming at you which presumes the authority of its viewpoint. Yet, if you have several TVs going at once, you can

see the structure and watch it with more critical consciousness. So, instead of a single political message getting through, you watch multiple screens revealing complexity, contradiction and manipulation of political viewpoints.[3]

On the one hand, Bender's observation here is noteworthy just for being sculptural in character. Through sheer multiplication and a subsequent decentralization of perspective, the everyday choreography of images on television – and, more important, of their framing and encasing by computer-generated interstitials – becomes more apparent, and even concrete. In a word, this choreography is made dimensional in actual space, and in correspondence with the special effects featured on screen. What was once a continuous and uninterrupted stream for viewers becomes spatial – a clear construction – with animations such as the gleaming of a US marine's sword effectively teased out of their ordinarily fleeting place in editing sequences as subliminal fetish. (Notably, Bender herself also repeatedly speaks of an alternative sense of the 'present' operating in her work, whereby the atemporal images on screen – figures of the endless exchangeability of commodities posited without origin or end in a ceaseless flow of televisual passages – are given roots again in our finite material world.)[4] As important, however, is how the artist's statement also suggests a perpetual repositioning of the viewer, who is prompted to navigate and shuttle among perspectives. As one of Bender's early champions, Jonathan Crary, described it, works such as *Total Recall* made 'eyes move continually from one screen to another, never resting, never becoming hypnotized'.[5]

Significant for our understanding of Bender's work today, however, is what Crary argued in 1984, four years before he wrote on *Total Recall*, in a review of Bender's exhibition of photographs, silkscreens and video silkscreened objects at Nature Morte Gallery in New York: that images themselves were being mobilized by the artist to sidestep the appropriative techniques of the day by underscoring how 'an object inheres in an infinite network of processing, multiplication and circulation undisturbed by the loss of singularity'.[6] In this respect, Bender offers a string precedent for many artists' anticipatory postures today, which posit the continual motion of texts and images through different contexts as *fait accompli*. As Crary concluded his review, 'The role she assumes is not one who makes, quotes or binds together images, but one who regulates flows and channels currents on a homogeneous surface of pure data'.[7] So it is that Crary's phrasing resonates strongly with observations put forward by contemporary artists such as Seth Price, to cite just one example: 'With more and more media readily available through this unruly archive [of the internet], the task becomes one of packaging, producing, reframing and distributing; a mode of production analagous not to the creation of material goods, but to the creation of social contexts, using existing material.'[8]

If Bender is teasing the role of special effects and interstitials on television to the surface in her work, it is only by adopting their contextual operations herself – as so many artists currently do as a matter of course.

In fact, it is essential to acknowledge an interstitial cultural period lying between these two artistic moments. Already, within ten years of Bender's Everson Museum survey, precisely the deconstructive perspective and consciousness Crary applauded was being engaged by online media. Consider just one observation, by the chief creative officer of the interactive-media design house Razorfish, a leader in the field during the late 1990s, citing the overriding importance of corporations' ability to present interfaces that could accommodate poles of attention, both concentrated and abstract, or 'Mindful': 'When we move through on-screen experiences, Mindfulness is the pure noticing factor. It sees everything and does not categorize. The attention flows, shifting across the changing screen.'[9] In this regard, one might reasonably ask to what extent Bender's situating of the medium of television anticipates digital media and, more specifically, its two-way street between user and content provider, whereby any act of de- and recontextualization of imagery by itself does not necessarily manifest any critical manoeuvre at all.

Yet today it is most tempting to suggest that precisely the elemental matter of context – or of platform – is the most provocative thing about Bender's work. For example, when *Total Recall* was first installed at The Kitchen in 1987, her televisions likely seemed incongruous with their surroundings; the temporality of their visuals was not bound to the theatre and its 'lights up, lights down' conventions; and, moreover, the conditions of television viewing were rendered collective and public, as opposed to solitary and private. But this kind of incongruity is by now conditional within culture, with such qualities anything but mutually exclusive. So it is by showing the seams, and the potential difference, among contexts (placing them in dialogue) that Bender foregrounds her apparatus, the distribution system, whether it is for images, ideas or experience. And having to negotiate among these perpetually changing platforms in order to arrive at a language that might meaningfully encompass them is the basic challenge presented by her art. Or, more succinctly put, it is the very notion of a platform that Bender forces us to consider anew.

1   Peter Doroshenko, 'Interview with Gretchen Bender', in *Gretchen Bender: Work 1981–1991* (Syracuse, New York: Everson Museum of Art, 1991) 4.

2   Gretchen Bender, 'The Perversion of the Visual', in *Damaged Goods: Desire and the Economy of the Object*, ed. Brian Wallis (New York: New Museum of Contemporary Art, 1986) 9.

3   Peter Doroshenko, op. cit., 5

4   Gretchen Bender, op. cit., 9.

5   Jonathan Crary, 'Gretchen Bender: Total Recall', in *Gretchen Bender: Total Recall* (Houston: Contemporary Arts Museum) n.p.

6   Jonathan Crary, 'Gretchen Bender at Nature Morte', *Art in America* (April 1984) 190.

7   Ibid.

8   Peter Seidler, 'Mindfulness and Concentration', *ArtByte* (April/May 1999) 25.

Tim Griffin, 'On Multiple Screens', in *Gretchen Bender: Tracking the Thrill* (New York: The Kitchen, 2013) 28–9.

Félix Guattari
Towards a Post-Media Era//1990

The junction of television, telematics and informatics is taking place before our eyes, and will be completed within the decade to come.

The digitization of the television image will soon reach the point where the television screen is at the same time that of the computer and the telematic receiver. Practices that are separated today will find their articulation. And what are passive attitudes today may perhaps begin to evolve. Cabling and the satellite will allow us to zap through 50 channels, while telematics will give us access to countless image databases and cognitive data. The element of suggestion, even hypnotism, in the present relation to television will vanish. From that moment on, we can hope for a transformation of mass-media power that will overcome contemporary subjectivity, and for the beginning of a post-media era of collective-individual reappropriation and an interactive use of machines of information, communication, intelligence, art and culture.

Through this transformation the classical triangulation – the expressive chain (*chaînon expressif*), the object of reference (*l'objet référé*) and the meaning (*signification*) – will be reshaped. For instance, the electronic photo is no longer the expression of a univocal referent but the production of a reality among others. The television news was already composed of several heterogeneous elements: the figurability of the sequence, the modelling of subjectivity according to prevailing patterns, normalizing political pressure, the concern to keep singularizing ruptures to a minimum. At present such production of immaterial reality takes precedence in all fields, ahead of the production of physical connections and services.

Should one be nostalgic about 'the good old days' when things were as they were, regardless of their mode of representation? But did these 'good old days' ever exist anywhere other than in the scientific and positivist imaginary? Already, during the Palaeolithic age – with its own myths and rituals – expressive mediation had distanced itself from 'reality'. In any case, all prior formations of power and their particular ways of shaping the world have been deterritorialized. Money, identity, social control fall under the aegis of the smart card. Far from being a return to earth, the events in Iraq made us lift off into an almost delirious universe of mass-media subjectivity. New technologies foster efficiency and madness in the same flow. The growing power of software engineering does not necessarily lead to the power of Big Brother. In fact it is way more cracked than it seems. It can blow up like a windshield under the impact of molecular alternative practices.

Félix Guattari, extract from 'Towards a Post-Media Era' (1990); first published in *Chimères*, no. 28 (Spring/Summer 1996); trans. Alya Sebti and Clemens Apprich, in *Provocative Alloys: A Post-Media Anthology*, ed. Clemens Apprich, et al. (London: Mute/PML Books, 2013) 27.

Sven Lütticken
Media Memories//2005

The film installations produced by Stan Douglas from the late 1980s – *Overture* (1986), to the present, *Inconsolable Memories* (2005) – are part of the wider reconsideration of cinema in recent art. Often the medium used by artists such as Douglas Gordon or Pierre Huyghe is in fact video: film has an afterlife, a *Nachleben*, as video art.[1] Is it significant that, while works such as *Nu•tka* (1996) or *Suspiria* (2003) are video, Douglas also often opts for actual celluloid. Now that film projection in movie theatres is being replaced by digital projection, Douglas's choice for film in a work such as *Inconsolable Memories* begins to have a defiantly anachronistic streak. However, Douglas does not attempt to return to some kind of 'pure' cinema, to some state of grace before the fall of digitization, or before video.

    Overture combines footage shot from a train in British Columbia by the Edison Company in 1899 and 1901, with a soundtrack containing quotations from Proust's *À la Recherche du temps perdu* that evoke the state of semi-consciousness when waking up. As in most of his work, Douglas is acting as an allegorical historian, combining various sources in unexpected and – in a literal sense – questionable ways, rather than someone who seeks purity in some idealized past. There certainly is an exhilarating quality to the images: the camera, mounted on the front of the train, produces images that were at the time unprecedented: a movement-image that changes the conditions and possibilities of representation. As a celebration of a new-found mobility of visual representation, these images are still compelling. However, Douglas combines them with spoken words lifted from Proust to create a new sound-image montage, a work whose components change each other. In the 1930s, critics such as Rudolf Arnheim looked back on silent films as a lost paradise, before the talkies exchanged 'the visually fruitful image of man in action' for 'the sterile [one] of the man who talks'.[2] Douglas turns silent film footage into a 'talkie' of sorts, but we do not see the speaker – like filmmakers such as Godard, Douglas creates a *son/image* beyond both silent and conventional sound film.

In its return to early cinema, *Overture* could be compared to some of Marcel Broodthaers' filmic works – for all the difference between the elegant rigour of Douglas's work and Broodthaers' flirtation with slapstick and vaudeville. As Rosalind Krauss has argued, Broodthaers used elements from early cinema to effect a return to the 'promesse de bonheur' of early film, against dominant Hollywood practices.[3] Krauss uses Broodthaers as a pawn in her attempt to oppose 'the international fashion of installation and intermedia work, in which art essentially finds itself complicit with a globalization of the image in the service of capital.'[4] Marcel Broodthaers is often presented as one of the progenitors of an art which triumphantly declares that 'we now inhabit a post-medium age', but for Krauss he was one who realized that the collapse of modernist notions of medium-specificity required the reinvention of the media, a new notion of the medium based on 'differential specificity'.[5] Whereas modernists such as Greenberg identified the medium with the material support (the canvas in the case of painting), Krauss proposes to regard the medium as a layering of conventions on a material support. It is never identical with its support; this is its differential specificity.

For Krauss, one of the traumatic events that shattered the modernist dream and created the need to redefine the medium was the arrival of video in the 1960s, specifically the PortaPak equipment. Television and video are 'Hydra-headed, existing in endlessly diverse forms, spaces and temporalities for which no single instance seems to provide a formal unity for the whole'.[6] Conceptual and video artists often saw in video an opportunity to leave behind gallery and museum as media for the presentation – and commodification – of contemporary art; like the artist's book, videos could be produced in comparatively high quantities for relatively low prices. With the arrival of cable, it also seemed feasible to use local cable channels to make a different kind of TV, one not dominated by corporate interests. Artists also tried to insert their works in mainstream television; Chris

Burden purchased commercial spots during the mid 1970s in order to air short video pieces. Douglas's *Television Spots* (1987–88) and *Monodramas* (1991) were also broadcast between commercials, creating confusion among viewers who wondered what these short, non-dramatic situations, with their meaningless dialogues, were intended to sell. During the 1980s, many artists abandoned their often fruitless attempts to work for television, leading to a triumph of video installation in art institutions; rather than being transmitted in Hydra-headed ways, video now became something to be installed in art institutions. Douglas too increasingly focused on works for gallery spaces, but without abandoning TV altogether; what changed was his approach to television. [...]

The essays in which Krauss attempts to 'redefine the medium' are beset by tensions and contradictions; while her definition of media as 'self-differing' is based on the poststructuralist notion that an apparently pure interiority is always pervaded by an outside (the self-identical is always the self-different), Krauss, in the end, wants to define the limits of a valid artistic use of media or 'mediums'. In order to achieve this, she privileges reflection on a medium's 'own' history rather than the use of elements from other media. Although she discusses works of art such as Broodthaers' film *A Voyage on the North Sea* (1974) – with its shots of a painting – she does not want to draw the inevitable conclusion that the conventions associated with one medium can be layered on the other, and that specificity has itself become a topos *within* generic art practice.[7] I would argue that Douglas's art shows that Krauss's opposition between, on the one hand, specificity (which creates plurality) and, on the other hand, 'the deadening embrace of the general' is a false one. The readymade signifies the transition from specific to general or generic; it is not the result of the mastery of any medium but the result of a choice, a minimal act.[8] The act itself became the second 'post-medium' of generic art: events, happenings and performances used the body as a performative readymade. The readymade can also take the form of the appropriation of photographic or filmic images, and in a less literal sense it can lead to the re-use of all kinds of conventions associated with various media as sets of readymade conventions and references. Generic art is a generality haunted by media and their afterlives.

While the writer Bruce Stirling has initiated a 'Dead Media Project' to take stock of media – devices for data storage – that have become anachronisms, Douglas's art constitutes a kind of 'Undead Media Project'.[9] If the museum is, in Thomas Elsaesser's words, both a 'site of distance and reflection' and a 'storage space of obsolete media technologies', Douglas proceeds to use these obsolete media as *media of reflection*.[10] If the use of readymade footage in *Overture* is relatively exceptional in his overall work, Douglas nonetheless constantly appropriates elements from the archive of undead media. These elements possess meanings that can be questioned, manipulated, recharged; obsolete media are undead precisely as *signifying practices*. Whereas Krauss remains enmeshed in a neo-formalist media fetishism that seeks to impose limits on artistic practice, Douglas uses generic visual art as a medium for an archaeology of modernity that offers anachronistic clues for reading and challenging the present. [...]

1   Aby Warburg used the term *Nachleben* to refer to the use of antique motifs in post-antique art. Although Warburg's use of *Nachleben* was inspired by E.B. Tylor's notion of 'survival', it could also be translated back into English as 'afterlife'. See Georges Didi-Huberman, *L'Image survivante: Histoire de l'art et temps des fantômes selon Aby Warburg* (Paris: Éditions de Minuit, 2002) 51–2.

2   Rudolf Arnheim, 'A New *Laocoön*: Artistic Composites and the Talking Film', *Film as Art* (London: Faber & Faber, 1958) 188.

3   Rosalind Krauss, *A Voyage on the North Sea: Art in the Age of the Post-Medium Condition* (London: Thames & Hudson, 1999) 42–5.

4   Ibid., 56.

5   Ibid., 54.

6   Ibid., 31.

7   [footnote 8 in source] See also Rosalind Krauss, 'Reinventing the Medium', *Critical Enquiry* (Winter 1999) 289–305.

8   [9] On the readymade as the most characteristic manifestation (though not the 'cause') of the generic condition of art, see Thierry de Duve, *Kant after Duchamp* (Cambridge, Massachusetts: The MIT Press, 1996).

9   [10] See www.deadmedia.org

10   [11]Thomas Elsaesser, 'Harun Farocki: Filmmaker, Artist, Media Theorist', in Elsaesser, ed., *Harun Farocki: Working the Sight-Lines* (Amsterdam: Amsterdam University Press, 2004) 25.

Sven Lütticken, extracts from 'Media Memories', in *Stan Douglas: Inconsolable Memories* (Vancouver: University of British Columbia Press, 2005) 124–6.

Maxa Zoller
The Pregnant Apparatus//2014

[...] How can we even begin to envisage a utopia if we allow alienation to dominate our perspective on society?

One could invoke the argument that the alienated, divided modern subject preserves its egocentric position through disengagement with the other. Seeking refuge in apparatuses of repression, the alienated subject goes to the cinema, where she can passively consume her projections of desire – this at least is the way cinema was theorized in the postwar school of critical thinking, in particular the so-called 'apparatus theory'. Inspired by the psychoanalyst Christian Metz and the philosopher Louis Althusser, French theorist Jean-Louis Baudry developed a theory of the 'cinematic apparatus' in the late 1960s, drawing an analogy between the technical conditions of cinema, such as the placement of the audience in relation to the screen and the projector, and Marxist relations between dominant values, governance and power.[1] He considered the cinematic apparatus primarily as an instrument of oppressive ideology, a means of manipulating, pacifying and indoctrinating the audience. While the apparatus theory was important in the context of postwar consumerism and the cold war, it is time to rethink its validity in the context of a digitalized and profoundly transforming global world. What kind of apparatus of thought could help us imagine a better world? How can we reimagine cinema as a space of organic procreation rather than an industrial, alienated and alienating production? How can we construct a relational space in which the boundary between me and you is thin and dynamic? What if the split never happened and the world is in fact a womb unfolding outwardly?[2]

In his short essay 'What is an Apparatus?', Giorgio Agamben traces back the 'apparatus' via Althusser and Michel Foucault to Hegel's notion of *positivity* and to the Greek term *oikonomia*, meaning the administration of the *oikos* (home), or more generally 'management'. This refers to the divine economy developed in the second century, the *oikonomia*, the administration of God's life. *Oikonomia* became thereafter an apparatus through which 'the Trinitarian dogma and the idea of a divine providential governance of the world were introduced into the Christian faith'.[3] Another important, less theorized, *oikos* is the Virgin Mary's body, and specifically her womb. In Jan Van Eyck's painting *Madonna in the Church* of 1425, the larger than life body of the Virgin Mary represents the cathedral in which she is standing; the spirit (God) is materialized as flesh (Christ) in her '*oikos*' (womb).

So what if cinema is not a phallic apparatus of control and dominance, but a pregnant one? What would a pregnant apparatus look like? A procreative social space shared by the self and the other, a womb-like dispositive of continuous productive plenitude (lack is beautiful!)? a dark space where televisual communication is replaced by placental proximity, where information is passed through non-verbal umbilical tubes? There is not much visibility in the thick space of the pregnant apparatus; it is not meant for the theatre of the eye. Can we envision an image whose impact is similar to the phenomenological effects of sound, an image radiating light waves from body to body, like a womb unfolding to the outside?

As playful or crazy as the idea of a pregnant apparatus might sound, it is based on forty years of feminist theories of embodied vision and haptic cinema formulated by thinkers such as Constance Penley, Jacqueline Rose, Hélène Cixous, Vivian Sobchack, Jennifer M. Barker, Laura U. Marks, to mention just a few. Without going into the details of these schools of thought it is interesting to mention that the phenomenological turn in cinema studies and a renewed interest in affect theory in the last decade are indicative of major shifts in the way in which cinema is discussed, analysed and taught.

Cinema can be a phenomenological, communal, affective, active, generative experience. With political upheaval reconfiguring the social and vice versa, the image of the pregnant apparatus could help us to imagine a new utopia, rather than avoiding utopia altogether.

1   [footnote 3 in source] See *The Cinematic Apparatus*, ed. Teresa de Lauretis and Stephen Heath (London: Macmillan, 1980).

2   [4] The idea of an unfolding womb has been greatly inspired by Heidi Tikka's experimental film *On the Threshold of Liberty* (1992).

3   [5] Giorgio Agamben, 'What is an Apparatus' (2006), in *What is an Apparatus? And Other Essays* (Stanford: Stanford University Press, 2009) 10.

Maxa Zoller, extracts from *The Pregnant Apparatus* (Halle, Germany: Werkleitz Media Art Festival, 2014) n.p. Zoller's programme for the Werkleitz festival in 2013 was titled 'The people want the downfall of the image' and included the films *Kinshasa 2.0* (2008) by Teboho Edkins; *Hold Your Ground* (2012) by Karen Mirza and Brad Butler; *Technoviking Archive* (2012) by Matthias Fritsch; *Walk (Square)* (2011) by Melanie Manchot, and *Line Describing a Cone* (1973) by Anthony McCall.

THE
BEAUTY
OF *NON-PLACES*
IS THAT YOU
ARE ASKED
TO STOP DEAD
IN THE SPACE
WITHIN
THE FILM,
AND THE AMBIGUITY
OF WHETHER
YOU'RE IN
THE FILM OR NOT
IS RIGHT
THERE

Karen Mirza, 'On Expanded Cinema', 2008

SITUATION

Andrew J. Urowskie
The Homelessness of the Moving Image//2014

In her *Passages in Modern Sculpture* (1977), Rosalind Krauss famously described the emergence of modernist sculpture in terms of a new condition of homelessness, as the traditional monumental vocation of site marking gave way before the newly peripatetic condition of objecthood. Cinema, while never originally site-specific in the same way, was nevertheless culturally bound to the cinematic theatre as its proper exhibitionary site. A whole complex of social, cultural and economic conventions would adhere to this particular model of exhibition. The postwar expanded cinema divorced the idea of cinema from the historical contingency of this exhibitionary model, creating a new and provocative condition of homelessness for the moving image within the institutions and discourses of contemporary art. [...]

Krauss's succinct yet ambitious genealogy of our contemporary 'post-medium condition' [in *A Voyage on the North Sea* (1999)], claims that the 'constitutive heterogeneity' of video marked the definitive collapse of the modernist conception of medium specificity as an ontological investigation. No doubt, video's constitutive heterogeneity played an important role in this historical process. Yet [...] it was the heterogeneity of *cinema* – its complex of mechanical, chemical, optical, cognitive, affective and mnemonic processes – that the artists and theorists of the mid 1960s expanded cinema had already sought to reveal. Krauss chooses to begin her story at this later point because the structural film of the late 1960s and early 1970s was often understood within Clement Greenberg's high modernist conception of medium-specificity, and by overlooking the expanded cinema, she is able to construct an orderly progression whereby the postmodern heterogeneity of video comes to replace the modernist specificity of film. It allows her to leave these discrete historical categories intact. Yet, as Krauss herself makes clear, the structural film intentionally de-emphasized film's differential condition so as to help it accede to the coveted stature of modern art: 'Structuralist film's self-definition, as I have said, was modernist', Krauss writes; 'the impulse was to try to sublate the internal differences within the filmic apparatus into a single, indivisible, experiential unit that would serve as an ontological metaphor, a figure – like the 45-minute zoom – for the essence of the whole.'[1] Yet the proliferation of these 'internal differences' in the widespread adoption of video over the next decade would foreground what had already been inherent in film – its fundamental instability as a medium and the challenge its constitutive heterogeneity held for the modernist conception of medium-specificity as such.

I risk belabouring Krauss's account because the rhetorical construction of the moving image at this early moment – when its history and theory were only just beginning to be institutionalized within academic research and pedagogy – would frame much of the subsequent discourse around the place of the moving image within contemporary art. The heterogeneous, situationally oriented model of expanded cinema that emerged in the early to mid 1960s was not without its theorists, but it would prove too diffuse and inchoate to upset the dominant high modernist paradigm established by Greenberg. Within the academy, medium-specificity dictated that a body of practice called experimental film be made the exclusive province of a new discipline of film studies – partitioning off an aesthetic and conceptual domain whose practitioners had rarely understood themselves as far removed from the other arts. It dictated an autonomous study of the history, theory and practice of film, rather than pursuit of its intersections with adjacent domains such as photography, video or performance. […]

[T]he idea of expanded cinema that emerged in the 1960s was not a straightforward repudiation of medium: its artists and critics were almost single-mindedly concerned with the specific ways in which cinema functioned to destabilize existing art institutions and practices. It was rather that the cinema *had no specificity* in Greenberg's strict ontological sense. The material of projection was multiple – consisting of the celluloid strip, projector and screen, to say nothing of the original camera and processing. Varying across space and time, the celluloid frame indexed a reality both past and distant, while its projection constituted an event both present and local. The complexity of the cinematic *dispositif* included not simply the material conditions of production, but also the psychological conditions of spectatorship: conditions both innate in human biology and born of the disciplinary codes of spectatorship formed over a half century of industrial exhibition. […]

Much of the historical and conceptual significance of the expanded cinema arises from its rejection of the legitimizing models of both the European art film and the avant-garde structural film – both attempts to stabilize a singular conception of cinema as a proper modern art. The failure of the historical expanded cinema to establish itself within postwar discourses of film studies or art history should thus in no way be understood as a simple historical oversight or accidental case of benign neglect. Its omission was rather structurally requisite, in so far as it constituted a direct challenge to medium-specificity and even disciplinary specificity as a regulatory ideal. The discursive and institutional *promiscuity* of the expanded cinema – its interstitial location between physical, institutional or discursive sites – would necessarily relegate it to a netherworld between art history and film studies, in so far as those disciplines remained grounded in this ideal. Despite photography's challenge to the romantic conceptions of authorship and originality, D.N. Rodowick speculates that film was the first artform fully to confound Gotthold Lessing's division of the spatial and temporal arts, and thus 'to challenge fundamentally the concepts on which the idea of the aesthetic was founded.'[2] [...]

1   [footnote 2 in source] Rosalind Krauss, *A Voyage on the North Sea: Art in the Age of the Post-Medium Condition* (London: Thames & Hudson, 1999) 30.

2   [5] D.N. Rodowick, *Reading the Figural, or Philosophy after the New Media* (Durham, North Carolina: Duke University Press, 2001).

Andrew V. Uroskie, extracts from *Between the Black Box and the White Cube: Expanded Cinema and Postwar Art* (Chicago: University of Chicago Press, 2014) 233–5.

Janine Marchessault and Susan Lord
Fluid Screens, Expanded Cinema//2008

[...] *Fluid Screens, Expanded Cinema* begins with the phenomenon Gene Youngblood described three decades ago as 'expanded cinema', that is, an explosion of the frame outward towards immersive, interactive and interconnected forms of culture.[1] [...] In his essay 'Cinema and the Code' (2003), Youngblood defines cinema in the following way:

> The subject of 'digital imaging', we agree, exists in the context of both video and the computer (different only in the source of the image and in the possibility of real time operation) and covers the generic areas of image processing, image synthesis, and writing or organizing digital code in a procedural or linguistic manner. But in every case where we refer to the phenomenology of the moving image, we call it cinema. For us, it is important to separate cinema from its medium, just as we separate music from particular instruments. Cinema is the art of organizing a stream of audiovisual events in time. It is an event-stream, like music. There are at least four media through which we can practise cinema – film, video, holography and structured digital code – just as there are many instruments through which we can practise music.[2]

Through his intellectual collaboration with artists Peter Weibel and Steina and Woody Vasulka, Youngblood comes to a consideration that distinguishes between different media of cinema and a unified view of the multiplicity of image culture. We find these distinctions useful particularly as they encourage the cross-media and intermedial analysis that we believe is imperative in the present context of hypermediation.

Youngblood's groundbreaking book *Expanded Cinema* (1970) offers us three particular avenues from which to approach the immersive, interactive and interconnected field of digital screen culture: synaesthesia, intermediality and the global public. The intense utopianism of Youngblood's era is embedded in every page of his book – from the idea of the collective ownership of the earth and the cosmic consciousness of its citizens to the idea that science teaches ethics, to the final chapter's assertion that the 'open empire' balancing nature and technology is all but upon us. He begins the book with the explanation that expansion refers not to 'computer films, video phosphors, atomic light or spherical projections', but to consciousness. […]

Using the experiments of the expanded cinema artists of the 1960s and 1970s as a pivotal point in the archaeology of digital media culture, we would be remiss not to mention Walter Benjamin's and Siegfried Kracauer's early engagements [in the 1920s and 1930s] with cinema as sensorium, as architecture, as street, and as a concretion of the flow of everyday life. […]

Benjamin [discusses the] idea of the phantasmagoria and its reorganization of the sensorium, and Kracauer, the idea of the mass ornament as an immersive experience of modernity's technologies and spectacles. […] [They] also provide media theorists with a grammar for thinking about convergence as a principle of fascism. […] Their writings help to articulate the potentialities of another form and context of the moving image, which the institutional mode of representation displaces – the heterogeneity of temporal and spatial elements within which the moving image appeared coeval with the sociocultural potentiality of a previously unthinkable experience of democracy. With the emergence of the institutional mode of representation, the heterogeneity of contextually derived experience is abstracted into film form. […]

1   [footnote 8 in source] Gene Youngblood, *Expanded Cinema* (New York: Dutton, 1970).
2   [9] Gene Youngblood, 'Cinema and the Code', in *Future Cinema: The Cinematic Imaginary after Film*, ed. Jeffrey Shaw and Peter Weibel (Cambridge, Massachusetts; The MIT Press, 2003) 156–61.

Janine Marchessault and Susan Lord, extracts from editors' introduction, *Fluid Screens, Expanded Cinema* (Toronto: University of Toronto Press, 2008) 5–10.

Susan Hiller
Slow Motion: In Conversation with Andrew Renton//1991

Andrew Renton In a well-known work like *Belshazzar's Feast* (1983–84), it's clear that, as a critic has recently written, your work creates its own special participation mystique, a situation where perhaps the unconscious of the viewer is brought to the surface, due to the way you've made the piece.[1] As a video installation it exists in a number of versions, as a camp fire, a very British sitting room, etc., but in all cases its focus is the videotape itself. What do you think happens when one sits and watches it?

Susan Hiller *Belshazzar's Feast* is a conscious attempt on my part to create a situation of reverie for the viewer. But like all my work it didn't start off like that; what happened was I came across some newspaper articles about people who saw ghost images on their television set after close-down. There was a spate of these articles, and I collected them and decided to make a work which dealt with something that has been said many times (it was said first by Marshall McLuhan), that the television set now exists in everybody's front room as the fire used to, where you had this moving image all the time. It was the focus; people could sit around the fire and look into it and see pictures, tell stories, regenerate imaginative, creative thinking on the basis of this eidetic imagery. Television is exactly the same thing. I'm convinced that one of the sources of pleasure in television viewing is not to do with the programme, it's actually to do with that moving thing. We go back to the cave and the fire, it was important for our species. I think people are using the television set for something quite creative and subversive and original, and these newspaper articles were really about that; that's why I used the reference to Belshazzar's Feast, a story from the Bible about how one would interpret a mysterious apparition.

What happened to the people in the newspaper articles was made peculiar by the cultural interpretation and by the denial of the unconscious and the denial of what's actually going on when they looked at their television and saw ghosts. All the interpretations which they got were either, 'It's a flying saucer beaming messages', or 'It's a hoax'; it was always empirical, they always wanted to explain these things by saying there's something outside you that's making a picture on your television set. At no point did anyone say, 'Oh, isn't that interesting, the moving imagery has triggered off your imagination, in connection with certain anxieties you may have, and you have seen a picture that has spoken to you and prophesied the doom of the planet, as in the Bible.' No one said that. There was this total denial. I wanted to recreate that situation, to make it possible for everybody, including myself, to have that sort of visionary experience. I made a video which consisted of a fire, and the fire is slowed down – people see things in the flames – and the soundtrack consists of a reading of newspaper articles. I read them in a whisper, as though this were a dreadful secret that I'm sharing with everybody. There is also some improvised singing that I consider analogous to the kind of automatic writing that I do, which creates a sort of uncanny atmosphere. When it was shown on Channel 4, they told me that aside from the flying saucer contingent who were very enthusiastic, they also had numbers of other letters. I was immensely moved by the response of people who said, 'I turned on the television and there was this strange programme, and I didn't think I'd like it, but I watched it and I thought it was wonderful; I saw all sorts of things and had all sorts of feelings; my eyes felt different.' [...]

1   See Barbara Einzig, 'Within and Against: Susan Hiller's Non-objective Reality', *Arts Magazine*, vol. 66, no. 2 (October 1991) 60.

Susan Hiller and Andrew Renton, extract from edited transcript of conversation at the Institute of Contemporary Arts, London, 31 October 1991 (ICA, 1995); reprinted in *Thinking about Art: Conversations with Susan Hiller*, ed. Barbara Einzig (Manchester: Manchester University Press, 1996) 198–9.

Kate Linker
Cinema and Space(s) in the Art of Judith Barry//2009

For Gilles Deleuze, Michel Foucault did not write a history of 'subjects' so much as a history of the processes of 'subjectivation'.[1] Foucault, he observed, saw the relations of power implicit in discursive practices and institutions as operating through simultaneously concrete and abstract 'machines' – respectively, visible forms and invisible forces. Thus the panopticon in *Discipline and Punish* was at once a tangible architecture ('an optical or luminous arrangement') and an abstract diagram that 'impose[d] a particular conduct on a ... human multiplicity'.[2] A visible form was the expression of informal forces that both caused and exceeded it. Deleuze noted that the forces in Foucault's diagrams mapped out different possibilities of interaction; they were 'virtual, potential, unstable, vanishing and molecular', as well as 'strategic' and 'multipunctual'. In Deleuze's reading these diffuse functions established the social field, constituting a kind of 'human technology'. They operated as an immanent cause, directing the assemblages or mechanisms that executed their relations and producing effects that extended throughout society. Deleuze concluded by observing that in Foucault's work, 'machines are social before being technical'.

This duality of forms and formation provides an entry to the art of Judith Barry, who has investigated the way in which visual technologies both produce the social realm and diagram the modes of subjectivity by which we inhabit it. [...]

Barry's work is informed by the Foucauldian concept of film as an *apparatus*, a spatial and social instrument that constructs or produces its subjects. More generally, however, her art confirms a shift of the 1970s away from the analysis of films as discrete objects or 'texts' to an attention to the different signifying practices that produce meaning in and through a given work. This semiotic approach, which roughly corresponds to poststructuralism, addresses the constitution of human subjects in specific viewing contexts and the social situations that allow or impede different discursive formations. A key topic in poststructuralist analysis was the association of subject construction with the 'machine' of cinema: the *camera obscura*, itself built around the geometric system of classical perspective, with parallel planes arranged so as to converge optically in space. As numerous writers have observed, the authority of perspective rests on the viewing point from which the rays of light originate, one that mirrors the vanishing point located on the other side of the plane or screen. In film, the spectator fills in or assumes this position, formerly occupied by the camera. As Mary Ann Doane has observed, the coincidence of viewing and vanishing points 'stabilize[s] the representational logic [of the image], producing its readability, which is coincident with the notions of unity, coherency, and mastery'.[3] The perspective system thus constructs a 'punctiform' subject, located outside the represented scene, that is complicit with an ideological view of the self.[4]

Perspective's construction of a transcendental subject – the 'mastering' subject of consciousness – is responsible for its longstanding hold over Western representation. But its ocular regime, which privileges vision over other senses, also establishes a detached and disembodied subject, one whose unity through time and in space masks the division or disunity inherent in the body. As Barry has noted in her essay collection *Public Fantasy*, perspective displaces disparate perceptions and conflictual emotions 'onto a kind of mechanics',[5] providing 'a way to order the world in relation to the observer'.[6] The multiplicity of senses – touch, smell and hearing among them – and the irrevocable truth of 'other' impressions cede to the unifying authority of a singular viewpoint.

Public Fantasy elucidates key themes in Barry's oeuvre, offering a verbal gloss on her visual arts practice: works like *Casual Shopper* (1981) and *First and Third* (1987), for example, are discussed in chapters addressing consumption, desire and spectatorship. A central theme is the development of forms of spectatorship out of the methodology of perspective, a methodology that has increasingly defined social life as well as determining individual viewpoints. A result of this transformation was a focus on the image as individually perceived but collectively experienced. Because architecture transcribes social relations into tangible forms, architectural history provides a concrete record of this change in the collective imaginary. Barry notes, for example, that the conventional theatre, with a stage and an auditorium incorporating spectator seating, is a sixteenth-century invention that coincided with the development of perspective.[7] With its sequence of changing scenes, the Renaissance stage offered a window onto a represented world in much the same way as the simultaneously emerging science of pictorial representation. Vitruvius, Palladio, Serlio and other architects conceived of theatre as a world space, a *theatrum mundi* in which the new urban life might be represented. Much as in later theatres for collective experience such as the cinema, each scene was individually accessible to multiple viewers through an optical construction that converged on the discrete 'point' of the percipient. As a human technology, perspective thus constructed an isomorphism between 'eye' and 'I', permitting the observer to be installed in a position of supremacy as master of the visual field.

Barry has compared the construction of this oculocentric technology with the shift from the haphazard, unstructured medieval street to the modern boulevard, whose perspectival construction 'impos[ed] order from a fixed plan, demonstrating the illusion of harmony' and providing the itinerant viewer with an ever-emerging vista.[8] During the expansion of consumer capitalism in the nineteenth century, the public dimension of spectatorship's private experience became embodied in the shopping arcade. As a realm of spectacle dedicated to visual delectation as well as display, the arcade found its emblematic subject in the Baudelairean *flâneur* and its function in the practice of voyeurism. Strolling through a city now dominated by the commodity, experiencing the characteristic pleasure-in-vision of bourgeois capitalism, this new subject-flaneur submitted to what Marcel Duchamp would later describe as 'the interrogation of shop windows'.[9] The art historian Norman Bryson has remarked that the viewer/voyeur made use of perspective's 'personal' address, by which 'the image recognizes (more accurately constructs) the viewer as a unitary subject, master of the prospect, unique possessor of the scene'.[10] Hence the illusion of completion through consumption became the aim and practice of the disembodied subject. With the development of mass culture and the expansion of consumer society, the promised satisfaction of the image-world installed in the subject an endless, insatiable desire for images that Barry has called 'vampyric'. Presenting what Johanna Drucker has called a historical analogue to Walter Benjamin's 'paradigmatic analysis of space as cultural formation', Barry's videotape *Casual Shopper* (1980–81) maps the transformation of the arcade into a contemporary equivalent, the shopping mall.[11] But she has also traced the rise of other spaces under the scopic regime of the disembodied eye, focusing on the museum (which developed in the nineteenth century to answer demands for pleasure and ocular 'possession') and the universal exhibition, a testimony to late nineteenth-century colonialist power. In each case, architecture provided a coordinated public response to the demands of the period's immanent ideology, offering 'one controlling image serving many people'.[12] [...]

1   Gilles Deleuze, *Foucault*, trans. Sean Hand (Minneapolis: University of Minnesota Press, 1988) 116.

2   Quotations of Deleuze used in this paragraph come from ibid., 33–40.

3   Mary Ann Doane, 'Remembering Women: Psychical and Historical Constructions in Film Theory', in E. Ann Kaplan, ed., *Psychoanalysis and Cinema* (London and New York: Routledge, 1990) 51.

4   The term 'punctiform' is the psychoanalyst Jacques Lacan's. For a discussion of Lacanian concepts in film theory, see, among others, my 'Engaging Perspectives: Film, Feminism, Psychoanalysis and the Problem of Vision', in Russell Ferguson, ed., *Art and Film Since 1945: Hall of Mirrors* (Los Angeles: The Museum of Contemporary Art/New York: The Monacelli Press, 1996) 216–43.

5   Judith Barry, *Public Fantasy: An Anthology of Critical Essays, Fictions and Project Descriptions*, ed. Iwona Blazwick (London: Institute of Contemporary Arts, 1991) 23.

6   Ibid., 114.

7   Ibid., 21.

8   Ibid., 23.

9   Marcel Duchamp, in *Salt Seller: The Writings of Marcel Duchamp*, ed. Michel Sanouillet and Elmer Peterson (New York: Oxford University Press, 1973) 74.

10   Norman Bryson, *Tradition and Desire: From David to Delacroix* (Cambridge: Cambridge University Press, 1984) 77.

11   Johanna Drucker, 'Spectacle and Subjectivity: The Work of Judith Barry', in Barry, *Public Fantasy*, op. cit., 9.

12   Barry, 'Wilful Amnesia', in *Public Fantasy*, op. cit., 77.

Kate Linker, extract from 'Cinema and Space(s) in the Art of Judith Barry', in *Judith Barry: Body without Limits* (Salamanca: Domus Artium, 2009) 178–80.

Judith Barry and Ken Saylor
(Home)icide – House of the Present//1993

Cyber-Subjects

There is no 'there', no time anywhere, and no real anymore … what to do? The eighties legacy has left us with no sense of place, as all spaces, in an attempt to cover for one another, seek to repeat the boring sameness of their utter muteness. Perhaps this is a screen for those older spatial paradigms that lent the machine its form – a mechanical system of moving, seeable parts – and an attempt to create those 'naked spaces' where what is really 'in there' – the transfer of information as it speeds through the city – will finally show itself. The question becomes how to give form to what is often invisible?

Michel Foucault's analysis of the asylum, the prison, the factory, the school and the home most aptly described the ways in which discourses of subjectivity are articulated through the built environment and inscribed within architecture, forcing specific relations of power, gender, and ultimately social norms, in which conformity is the only choice. This is also the legacy of Le Corbusier. And even now as the password replaces the watchword and the code substitutes for the norm, the spatial paradigms that might effect these representations refuse to take shape outside of fictions, across boundaries, geographies, or among people.

The machine age gave birth to the cinema, which allowed for believable simulations of spatial paradigms by tying a coherent sense of space to a coherent sense of time, mimicking how reality was perceived. It might be argued that television has produced the visual paradigm of the 'space of flows', allowing the 'zapping' viewer to experience the discontinuity of daily life by cruising through the channels, juxtaposing seemingly incoherent bits of information, and recombining them into new configurations, whose ability to phase us is dependent on our willingness to surrender to an illogical order which is predictable only in its randomness.

The computer and its invisible nets allow for a transformation of information, and we as users can constantly travel its streams, escaping within this unrepresented, and hence 'pure' machine the contamination of disciplinary forces comprised of real bodies who must yield to the spectre of its power. Yet we know the fallacy of this pureness merely articulates older class relations, as it measures keystrokes for the computer worker while partially liberating the managerial class and rendering useless what remains of the working class who are not computer literate. If writing is the model for communicating with the algorithms that are the computer, is there a way in which literature can give a shape to the multiplicity of flows set in motion by information technologies?

How to shape these invisible nows, how to transform these random bits of information into knowledge, how to describe the series of relations that these spaces provoke? Postmodernism in art, not architecture, provided for a way of representing the breakdown of 'master-narratives' by showing how 'subject-positions' were constructed across a heterogenous field of inquiry. Not one 'I', but many, not one 'history', but many. This is precisely the type of analysis that we are proposing to apply to Le Corbusier's 'modular man', and by implication the space of architecture.

In order to place the viewer in the position of the producer, rather than the passive consumer of these discourses, we are liberating various built-in architectural devices and appliances by anthropomorphically mating them with 'modular man'. 'Morphing', as it is known in the computer world, is a way of literally transforming one object into another. Popularized by such films as *Terminator 2* and numerous television commercials, it is the most apt metaphor for the idea of Liquid Space, as the resulting objects are less important than the act of transformation itself. What is made visible are the previously invisible networks and lines cohering into spaces that can be seen to render disparate objects across time and space, uniting them in time and space rather than collapsing one into the other (depending on whether you prefer Paul Virilio or Leo Marx).

This paradigm allows for a kind of cyber-subjectivity, as it provides for the 'morphing' of any object, plant, human, animal or machine, escaping the boundaries of its former function as it potentially becomes something else. As Donna Harraway suggests, this kind of cyborg places in question older notions of humanness, and potentially provides a radical yet specific reworking of precisely what these hybrids can do, possibly suggesting a new form of cognitive mapping, and generating other, less humanly oriented spatial paradigms. [...]

Judith Barry and Ken Saylor, extract from '(Home)icide – House of the Present', in *Unité Project* [published to accompany a site-specific project at Le Corbusier's Unité d'habitation, Firminy, France] (Firminy, 1993) n.p.

Steven Bode
From Video Art to Artists' Video//1995

There are years whose hotline to the Zeitgeist turns out to be nothing of the kind. There are others that go on to acquire a significance that never fully registered at the time. At least that's how I feel about 1995. The mid point of a volatile decade which video entered hitched to the star of technology and ended, slightly self-consciously, in the art world's air-kissing embrace, 1995 was a genuine turning-point, whose influence continues to reverberate.

It's easy to forget the level of hype that had gathered around new forms of digital and computer technology at the beginning of the 1990s. One of the main talking points, and by far the worst offender, was virtual reality: a kind of clunky, Chad Valley parallel universe that one 'entered' with the help of a visor and a data glove. Even though, by 1995, wearing a VR helmet in public would have been almost as embarrassing as sporting a mullet, a number of dreams and assumptions still persisted, like a ghostly after-image. At international electronic arts festivals like Ars Electronica (although less so in more sceptical Britain), it was remarkable how many apparently intelligent people were placing their faith in technology as a fully-blown cultural saviour (if not now, then in its next upgrade, shipping very soon). Even Stelarc, the long-suffering, self-flagellating prophet of the techno-art circuit, was trading in the meat hooks on which he would regularly impale his body during his semi-legendary 'suspension performances' for a new breed of implants and prosthetics, to better transform himself into that quintessential mid-nineties fetish, the cyborg.

This face-off between the virtual and the visceral was a recurring feature of 1995. At a time when much of the work and almost all of the hype that was generated around the impact of new technology appeared to involve a fantasy of escaping from the body, it was interesting to see the resurgence of a low-tech, often performative aesthetic that mined the body as a source of material. There probably weren't that many people during 1995 who had reason to compare the impossibly fluid, shape-shifting morphs of the French computer artist Bériou with a piece like Mona Hatoum's *Corps Étranger* (1994), an eerie, endoscopic voyage through the inside of the artist's body. To me, however, they were two sides of the same coin. For much of the time, though, works from these different points of origin stayed either side of a rigidly enforced dividing line. On the one hand, you had a number of art-world approved (mostly conceptual) artists, whose work embodied fashionable themes like 'intersubjectivity' and 'abjection'. On the other, you had the new media crew, with their expensive PowerBooks and their indefatigably utopian activist agenda. Each seemed to inhabit completely different orbits, strangely uninterested in what the other was doing.

As the cybernauts set sail on their shiny, computer-generated sea, a parallel generation of young British artists was plunging head first into 'shark-infested waters'. As was often the case, Damien Hirst had given the lead, as artist and as agent provocateur, as enfant terrible and as entrepreneur. Hirst's coronation (at the second time of asking) in the 1995 Turner Prize confirmed the arrival of a phenomenon that commentators, sensing its media-friendly appeal to the demotic, were quick to label Brit Art. Work by a number of Hirst's contemporaries was profiled extensively in the British Art Show 4, which opened in Manchester in the autumn of 1995. Precocious twenty-something artists like Gillian Wearing, Georgina Starr, Douglas Gordon, Sam Taylor-Wood, Steve McQueen and Jane and Louise Wilson (who had started working increasingly, though not always exclusively, in film and video) figured prominently in the line-up, with work that exuded a new fascination with popular culture and a penchant for everyday subjects and materials.

After Hirst's success in the 1995 Turner Prize, three of those artists (Gordon, Wearing and McQueen) would go on to win the award in the space of the next four years, confirming the so-called YBAs as major players in the contemporary art scene, and securing video's place in the commercial and cultural mainstream. It was significant, perhaps, that neither Wearing nor Gordon (nor many of their contemporaries) ever referred to themselves as 'video artists' (it was always quite sobering to discover how little some of them knew, or cared, about video art history). Yet, in its own way, it was equally telling that a new Arts Council book, A Directory of Film and Video Artists, compiled by David Curtis during 1995 and published in 1996, while fastidiously detailed and scholarly in its history, neglected to mention any of these newer arrivals (with the exception of Tacita Dean) – which was probably rather confusing for those growing numbers of people who had started being switched onto video by the work of Wearing, Gordon, et al. As if to help us all through this impasse, 1995 marked the time when critics began discarding the appellation 'video art' in favour of a broader definition of 'artists' video' – a switch in semantics that, pointedly if slightly belatedly, helped to emphasize the position of the artist over the role of the technology. [...]

It was intriguing that this explosion of interest in the internet should coincide with the centenary of the cinema, an event that precipitated a number of major international shows that set out to explore the historical and contemporary relationship between art and film. Britain, of course, had to wait until the following year for its landmark art-and-cinema exhibition ... and then, as is often the way of things, two of them came along at once. The sprawling, hubristic 'Spellbound', at the Hayward Gallery, was definitely not worth the wait, although it did play host to the first London staging of Douglas Gordon's *24 Hour Psycho*, premiered at Tramway in Glasgow two years previously, and one of the most celebrated conceptual video works of the mid 1990s. 'Scream and Scream Again', at the Museum of Modern Art in Oxford, was, as its title implied, a satisfying B-Movie second-feature, full of spiky, 'noirish' film works by artists like Isaac Julien, Sadie Benning and Douglas Gordon, again. [...]

At the end of the year, Film and Video Umbrella joined forces with Moviola (now FACT) and Tramway, Glasgow, to curate and produce an exhibition called 'Instant'. Taking its title from the Lottery scratch-card phenomenon, and showcasing a number of low-tech conceptual/performance works – by artists like Jane and Louise Wilson, Wood and Harrison, and Roderick Buchanan, within an interactive touch-screen interface that took on the virtual appearance of a scratch-card – it seemed to capture something of the pleasures and contradictions of 1995.

Steven Bode, extracts from 'From Video Art to Artists' Video', in *FACTORS* (Liverpool: Video Positive Festival, 1995) n.p.

Steve McQueen
In Conversation with Adrian Searle//2013

Adrian Searle I guess *Exodus* (1992/97) came out of being open enough to recognize what's there in front of you.

Steve McQueen That's a beautiful thing, the openness to recognize what's there. That's why the audience has to be with you and open themselves up when they're looking. That's what you have to trust. The work can be so fragile because you're reliant on the viewer so much, and if viewers don't want to see it they won't, but if they do they will.

Searle You're learning not just to be an artist and how to be open to things. You're also learning to be a spectator.

McQueen [...] *Exodus* was only the second thing I shot. I was in [East London's] Brick Lane market and I suddenly saw these palm trees walking towards me. I got out my camera and started shooting. There were these two old fellows with their pork-pie hats almost ceremonially walking along, one behind the other, carrying palm trees. I got the impression that they were in a relationship, that they were a couple. Then they crossed the road, got on a bus and disappeared, and that was it. I filmed it but I didn't know what it was, and I put it away for three years. Having the sensitivity to recognize what it is comes through training. I'm very grateful to art school for giving me the time to actually think, to process things myself. Because I don't have a regime. I don't have a studio. I don't have a planned way of working. What art school gave me was the space. [...]

Searle In *Five Easy Pieces* it's quite hard to work out at first viewing what exactly is going on, what you're looking at. And it's a bit like a Rodchenko, with these hoops revolving, and the overhead view of a man's body. And in *Bear* similarly intriguing, enigmatic things happen. You make viewers work to discover what it is they're looking at.

McQueen The imagery is a seduction. But at the same time there's space: there has to be a situation that the viewer has to work out. It's about investigating the construct. I remember an article in the American press which said that *Five Easy Pieces* was hard to understand. It was. Damn right, I thought, *I'm* not easy to understand. [...]

Searle You used to refer to your films as sculpture. Do you still?

McQueen In some ways I do. It's a different experience to that of cinema or watching your TV at home. When you're in a museum or institution, you're looking at the piece in a different environment. Your headset is switched on in a different way. You can't go to the fridge for a snack or munch popcorn like you can in a theatre. [...]

Searle You like the idea of beginning and end, and people coming in and sticking with it.

McQueen Sometimes and sometimes not. Sometimes it's been a continuous projection. Other times I want people to come in at the beginning and leave at the end. [...]

Steve McQueen and Adrian Searle, extracts from interview, in *Steve McQueen: Works* (Basel: Schaulager, 2013) 192–200.

Karen Mirza and Brad Butler
On Expanded Cinema//2008

Karen Mirza For me, expanded cinema is the spatial aspect of the moving image. I'm interested in the relationship between time, tense and duration. I want to incorporate a past within the present moment – that kind of complex relationship with time that is within either conceptual or formal subject matter. Then there is the physical expansion, in that it expands outside of just one screen, taking on the specificity of its context, whether a neutral space, an underground car park, an auditorium, or a museum or gallery. The work becomes a reading of the work itself. It's not simply a form of display. The spatial or architectural element is an integral part of the meaning that the work explores. It expands in relationship to a temporal, or filmic, cinematic moment.

Brad Butler Expanded cinema can also really problematize spectatorship. We did a project called *Instructions for Films*, based on the Yoko Ono piece, and one could argue it's expanded cinema even though it's in publication form, because it's about the idea of what cinema is. It's useful to keep it as open as possible, rather than try to force through a definition, because I feel that as soon as we reduce it down to a single term we create certain creative limitations.

Mirza I feel that my strongest connection to the avant-garde is through expanded cinema, because it explores and allows different kinds of performative action, or ways of engaging with the body. Within the 'cinematic', single-screen format of cinema you have only one, relatively fixed, ocular experience. But you can also involve the maker's body in relationship to the work, or you have pieces that are critically immersive, rather than immersive in the sense that narrative cinema works as a window on the world, taking you away from yourself. I'm drawn to critical immersion, where you're inside the cinematic moment, rather than standing outside looking in, or using it as a portal, as a window. My interest has always been in work that doesn't situate itself neatly into the cinema or the theatrical space or the auditorium. It is removed from the cinematic context, still in dialogue in some way with cinema, but interrogating the exhibition space.

Butler Expanded cinema is also exciting because its parameters are still moving, and I'm interested in working out contemporary uses of this fluid language. I'm also really interested in picking up trajectories of thought. I study what happened in the past, to work out where ideas were channelled, and why. And then I try to think very deeply about how I would want to engage with these ideas. A tension for me is trying to separate expanded cinema from what it 'does', to think about what it 'is'. To look beyond the product, to embody the *thinking*, to amalgamate the process. I like the idea that it is a way of thinking that questions where cinema begins and ends. [...]

Mirza I think these issues are in [our work] *The Glass Stare* (2006). It's a three-screen installation with two back-projected film loops on two separate screens, and a third screen in front of them showing a composite image made up of the reflected light from the two back projections. It functions in the installation just as the optic system does in our heads, in the sense of projected and reflected light. In the two back-projection loops, one positive and one negative, images of a figure facing the camera are upside-down, but they are the right way round on the third screen. It's almost an undoing of photography, of the photographic moments of fixing or embalming a moment in time. My interest in this got me excited about the dematerialized art object. And that's why expanded cinema is still in that awkward place, and causes the same headache for museums, trusts, foundations, collectors. It's a very ephemeral practice.

Butler I think I'm not so interested in what it is. I'm interested in how our knowledge of it is imbued with meaning. Some things in expanded cinema are happening outside language because they're almost sensorial impacts. They're not something we can just transfer into words in that way.

Mirza In the 1990s videos were being shown on loops in galleries, without any relationship to the viewer. So if it was a narrative piece and you came in halfway through, you missed half of the content, but it didn't matter. When we made *Non Places* (1999), we wanted it to be non-linear and linear at the same time. Also, it was made for a public space, not the auditorium. It was made to be projected back into the space represented in the middle of the film, the Marble Arch underpass, and for that reason it was projected onto the wall. People were arriving from different points, from up above, from different tunnels, and there was a kind of conflated sense of what was live and what was recorded – and it was stopping people in a space, arresting them to engage with or recount their own memories, and so it was an agent in transforming the space. It inverted the screen, inverted the stage, so this kind of everyday moment became quite a theatrical space, but in its banality.

Butler That's why it was screened in the middle of the spaces where it was shot. But the cinematic experience in the cinema does that to you too, because inherent in the construction of film is that the actual experience in space is transferred into the cinematic experience of being in the auditorium. At the very end, picture and sound are – phhppt! – just ripped away from you, and you realize where you've been. It's a mental space – experiencing film. It's a journey from one point to another, but it's the journey that's crucial. You fall into it as you would fall into a non-place, you're focused on where you're going rather than where you are. But in the expanded cinema you're actually asked to stop. I think the beauty of *Non-Places* is that you are asked to stop dead in the space within the film, and the ambiguity of whether you're in the film or not is right there. [...]

Karen Mirza and Brad Butler, extracts from dialogue 'On Expanded Cinema' (London, 2008), in *Expanded Cinema: Art, Performance, Film* (London: Tate Publishing, 2010) 255–8.

Mark Godfrey
Making History: Omer Fast//2006

Ten years after its release the Israeli-born, American-educated and Berlin-based artist Omer Fast travelled to Krakow to research the aftermath of Stephen Spielberg's *Schindler's List* (1993) and found a burgeoning tourist industry devoted to the film. As well as doing tours of Auschwitz, guides were driving mainly American visitors to the still intact concentration camp sets. Fast recorded some of these tours and conducted interviews with Poles who, ten years earlier, had played extras in the film. Some described the ways in which potential 'Jewish' and 'Polish' characters were divided during the auditions, while older extras mingled their memories of the 1940s with their recollections of the early 1990s. All of them, however, recalled the events of 1993, describing their motivations and experiences in acting out scenes in reconstructed camps and gas chambers.

Fast's footage addressed the Hollywoodization of the Holocaust, scrutinizing Spielberg's magnum opus by deploying tactics associated with filmmaker Claude Lanzmann, who had refused to use archival footage or to re-create scenes of the Holocaust when making his nine-and-a-half-hour documentary *Shoah* (1985); instead Lanzmann forged his encounter with history from interviews with Jewish survivors and Poles who had lived near the camps. The critical bent of Fast's project was in no way tempered by his acknowledgement that the extras' experience was real and deserving of serious attention; the artist allowed them to articulate the difficulties of reconstructing such a traumatic event in Polish history. Editing the footage for his two-screen installation *Spielberg's List* (2003), Fast made a crucial intervention. Working with a Polish translator, he was made aware of the contingencies of translation in the interviews he had conducted. Reflecting on this, he decided to play identical footage on each screen but to subtitle it with slightly different texts, one referring to the actual events of the 1940s and the other to the film. During some footage of the tour, for instance, one screen is subtitled with the words 'And the building opposite – there was one of the gates', while on the other we read 'And the building opposite – there was one of the takes'. Fast even employed this device when speakers are English, but when they are Polish it is often impossible to tell which period the speaker is referring to.

The subtitles further compounded the confusion of history and its representation, but it's interesting to note how the strategy operated for the viewer in the screening environment. With two screens illuminating fast-moving complex material, it was at first difficult to understand what was going on. At first, all that could be sensed was a flickering difference on the peripheries of the two screens, the contrast between the subtitles registering more in terms of divergent shapes than alternative translations. Only later, with repetition, could the viewer divine the tactic at work. Fast's device emphasized our incapacity to fully apprehend a work at the first encounter, while encouraging us to pay attention to the fickleness of subtitles – an aspect of the video image we might usually take for granted – and to choose between the two meanings.

Spielberg's List indicates the complexity of Fast's project, aiming to address both the information film and TV provides us with, and the manner in which it is delivered. By attending to aspects of the image such as the subtitle and the soundtrack, he sheds light on the subtle ways in which meanings are disseminated. Sometimes he has used tactics of insertion as well as interruption. In 2001 he hired copies of *The Terminator* (1984) from New York video outlets and, during some of the most brutal and silent scenes in the film, overdubbed sections of dialogue that he had taped, in which adults describe violent memories from their childhood. The videos were returned to the rental shops to await the next unsuspecting customers, whose Schwarzneggerian fantasies would be interrupted by a sour dose of the real. If his strategies here owed much to Cildo Meireles [*Insertions in Ideological Circuits*, 1970–75], elsewhere, in a mammoth act of manipulation, Fast updated Richard Serra's savage articulation of TV's commercialism, *Television Delivers People* (1973). Through 2001 Fast recorded hundreds of hours of CNN presenters speaking directly to camera. He fed the footage into a computer and cut it up into words and syllables. From this database he constructed an 18-minute monologue, *CNN Concatenated* (2002), which is delivered by individual news presenters, in a fast, jolting fashion, word by word. Just as Serra's rolling titles spoke directly to their readers ('You are delivered to the advertiser, who is the customer'), so Fast's presenters address their viewer – 'Look, I know that you're scared ...' – indirectly admitting the manner in which news programmes foster and feed off the neuroses of their audiences. As well as being incisive, the work is also very funny: the slick and slimy anchors are made to utter sentiments quite beyond their sensibilities but appear absolutely unruffled, their manicures and fake tans always immaculate.

Fast's most recent project is *Godville* (2004–5), made at the Living History Museum of Colonial Williamsburg in Virginia, where visitors can talk to various staff members who are dressed up as eighteenth-century characters representing different facets of colonial American life. Fast interviewed and filmed the costumed staff in, but also out of character, speaking about their motivations for working and living at the museum. If such places can sometimes encourage what Fast called a 'pornography of the past', he disrupted the illusion by confronting the characters as 21st-century individuals. As might be expected, various other forms of disruption take place in the work. Fast chopped up the interviews and strung words back together again, making it difficult to know whether the speaker is talking in or out of character; after a while it is impossible to gauge whether the monologues resemble the actual recorded interviews at all. While such confusion is in some ways appropriate to the temporal confusion of the interviewees and museum visitors, what's exemplary about Fast's approach is that the final product does not gel into some spectacular reconfigured whole (think of Candice Breitz's recent use of splicing). His Brechtian interruptions genuinely interfere with the coherence of the subject matter, providing space for critical thought.

The installation requirements of *Godville* enact another cut: the work comprises two films projected onto either side of the same floating screen, as in Michael Snow's *Two Sides to Every Story* (1974). On one side we watch the chopped-up interviews; on the other Fast plays footage of the museum and of its employees' houses. At times it is hard to tell the genuine colonial buildings from the 21st-century dwellings, such is the actors' taste for period kitsch. The footage segues into shots of the recent construction of faux eighteenth-century houses, a passage that recalls a kind of updated *Homes for America* (1966) in which Dan Graham's 1960s' minimalist forms make way for 21st-century traditionalism. While economically representing the human and architectural aspects of Colonial Williamsburg, the two films as much complement as interrupt one another. Watching either screen, viewers can feel distracted, realizing they are missing the footage playing on the reverse.

Godville ends on one side with a medley of images of Southern churches, while on the other an actor is made by Fast's edit to intone countless sayings about what God means to him. Fast seems to view the increasing religiosity of the South as an end result of the nostalgia often perpetuated by institutions such as Colonial Williamsburg, but his research indicated that the Living History Museum was not a monolithic entity. Indeed he discovered that there have been times when the museum has put history to work in an almost Benjaminian manner – as, for instance, when an estate auction was re-enacted one day and visitors to the tourist attraction encountered the sale of families of slaves. While conducting his interviews, Fast also discovered that some of the actors were inflecting their performances to reflect their criticism of the current American administration. Playing colonial British subjects questioning their allegiance to the crown, they hoped that inquisitive viewers might draw parallels with the present situation of American citizens. Knowing that the employees had a range of political affiliations that weren't circumscribed by the museum's overarching ideology, Fast decided to complicate matters further. Some way through their fractured monologues, the interviewees begin to speak back to the camera, accusing Fast of manipulating their words. They complain that he is turning them into stereotypes and ask him what all his editing and studio trickery can possibly achieve.

Of course, we cannot know whether or not the employees did address Fast like this, but by twisting their words in this way he articulates within the project the most severe criticism *Godville* could possibly attract. Every bit as much as he questions the spectacular ways in which history is presented in the culture industry at the moment, he scrutinizes the facilities of his practice and the ethics of his own art's criticality.

Mark Godfrey, 'Making History: Omer Fast', *frieze*, no. 97 (March 2006). (www.frieze.com)

Francis Alÿs
Walking the Line: In Conversation with
Anna Dezeuze//2009

Anna Dezeuze [...] Can a witness be a force for change?

Francis Alÿs There are different levels. There is a kind of consciousness-raising, which is the first stage – to awaken a reaction which might help improve the reading of the situation. [...] I think the artist can intervene by provoking a situation in which you suddenly step out of everyday life and start looking at things again from a different perspective – even if it is just for an instant. That may be the artist's privilege, and that's where one's field of intervention differs from that of a NGO or a local journalist.

Dezeuze This kind of poetic rupture is of course at the heart of your 2004 work, *Sometimes doing something poetic leads to something political and sometimes something political leads to something poetic*, also known as 'The Green Line'.[1]

Alÿs Yes, particularly here, the action had to be borderline ridiculous for people to start talking beyond stereotypical discourses on the left or right, whether Palestinian or Israeli. It was about recreating spontaneity in a situation which is not spontaneous, so weighed-down by its own inertia, its 'impasse'.

Dezeuze Is this why you chose to make the piece on your own, rather than make a collective work like *When Faith Moves Mountains* in Lima in 2002 or *Bridge/ Puente* in Key West–La Havana in 2006?

Alÿs I didn't consider the option of doing a collective piece, maybe because someone had to take on the responsibility in order to provoke a shift, and in this specific case this responsibility had to fall on one individual rather than on a collective body. But it was the collective action of *When Faith Moves Mountains* that raised the question of the extent to which one can play between the poetical and the political, and which triggered the piece in Jerusalem. There were specific reasons why I chose Jerusalem as the site for that project. It wasn't a commission, it was a project that I sought out, and I think I chose Jerusalem because it was – in terms of an intervention within a conflict situation – the one that was the most archetypal, the most historically representative of a conflict situation that was …

Dezeuze Extreme?

Alÿs It's extreme because – to use a cliché – Jerusalem is the cradle of western civilization, and that's a large part of the reason why it has such international resonance. But it is a minor conflict. I'm afraid to say this, but as important as it may be – and of course any human life that is lost is the most important thing in the world – if you look at the numbers, I would say that since the beginning of this year [2008] there must have been around a maximum of 100 victims or so, whereas the narcotics conflict in Mexico has so far claimed the shocking figure of almost 3,000 victims. Does the British press talk much about this internal gang war? I doubt it. In terms of casualties only, the Palestinian-Israeli conflict is a minor conflict, yet it is a millennial conflict, and perhaps one of the most representative today of the clash between two cultural models. It has incredible international resonance, although in comparison with many conflicts taking place on the planet today, it is a small conflict. It's this paradox that I found interesting.

Dezeuze It's a conflict that's very violent at the level of discourse, too.

Alÿs I was criticized for interviewing mostly left-wing people, whether on the Palestinian or Israeli side. The reality was that because of my personal sympathies, my contacts naturally happened to be left wing, so it was very difficult to approach right-wing people who would agree to talk. We tried to approach the Rabbi of Jerusalem, but we got nowhere. The closest we got in terms of centre-right was Shimon Peres – we had three meetings scheduled with Peres, which were all cancelled at the last moment. The action itself was a pretext for the commentary. In a way there were fifteen potential actions, and I chose the most obvious, the most immediate one, in order to provoke a reaction. My intention was not to intervene within the space of a conflict situation, but to generate, through this act, a commentary about that situation, the opposite, if you like, of what I do here in Mexico, where a given situation exists, and I try to – I was going to say 'exploit it' – to transcend it, to translate it. In the case of Jerusalem, I first had to interact with the situation in order to trigger the discourse, whereas here it is the existing situation that triggers the discourse.

Dezeuze And in terms of your practical experience, did you have problems intervening within the city – at the checkpoints perhaps?

Alÿs Very little. In fact, one of the interviewed people – Rima Hamami – said when she saw the film: 'You are a real sneaker, you walk fast, like a Palestinian in the crowd.'

Dezeuze But another of your interviewees, Eyal Weizman, criticizes this ease. He says it's not easy for a Palestinian to walk around.

Alÿs The action was made easier by the fact that a lot of people did not identify the route, or the action, and that has something to do with the issue of memory, the fact that history is forgotten more quickly than we think. And I certainly played on the tactical margin described by Meron Benvenisti when he recounts how Moshe Dayan drew the original green line with a green wax crayon and the 3–4 millimetre line on the 1:20,000 scale map represented, on the ground, a 60–80 metre wide strip of land equivalent to a whole city block. This allowed me to avoid the checkpoints in advance by walking along the other side of the block, while remaining within the width of the green line.

Dezeuze So you were able to avoid checkpoints. But there is one at the end of the film.

Alÿs Yes, it was the exit, it was inevitable – it's the only road in that place.

Dezeuze But if you'd been Palestinian you may not have been allowed to pass.

Alÿs That's true. Maybe it's something similar to what happened with my revolver work, *Re-enactments* (2000), in which I walked down the street with a gun until the Mexico City police stopped me. Perhaps because of its ridiculous or absurd quality, an artistic action becomes excusable, and sometimes it can make its way through unlikely situations because it simply cannot be taken seriously. Humour – or a humorous dimension – often allows you to bypass situations that would not otherwise have been allowed to happen if I had taken, for instance, a militant attitude. […]

1   [In 1995 Alÿs had performed a walk in São Paulo which traced a line using a leaking can of blue paint. In 2004 he re-enacted this work in Jerusalem, this time using green paint to trace the 'green line' of demarcation. The filmed documentation (17.34 min.) was presented shortly afterwards to a number of people whom Alÿs asked to react to the action and the circumstances in which it was performed.]

Francis Alÿs and Anna Dezeuze, extract from 'Walking the Line: Francis Alÿs interviewed by Anna Dezeuze', *Art Monthly*, no. 323 (February 2009) 1–4.

Robert Bird
Mundane Virtuosity: Olga Chernysheva's Work on Video//2014

The protesters file by, their obscure cause betrayed by their disheartened posture. The loneliness of the march is disrupted only by small groups deep in conversation, indifferent to the occasion that has gathered them. There is nothing of visual interest here: a wintry street; drearily clothed pensioners; a Russian-made police car; Marlboro logos on street kiosks. In search of a subject, the camera zooms out, then zeroes in on a woman clad in fur at the left margin of the scene. The demonstration and its minor subplots become a vague backdrop for the profoundly private, even lonely self-absorption of our heroine, proud in her anachronistic elegance, transfixed by the contents of her handbag. She fixes a brooch on her neck and gathers a pile of coins, perhaps the proceeds from selling the newspaper she carries multiple copies of, named after a battle cry of the Soviet Army in World War II: *Za rodinu! Za Stalina! (For the Motherland! For Stalin!)* We make out a laminated portrait of the great man himself that she has temporarily put down as she sorts out her other belongings. It's a veritable juggling act. A character comes into focus: she has been driven to idealize the past by her poverty, though her impoverishment might equally be seen as a refuge from the present. Her character in turn clarifies the event from which she has defected momentarily: these are the outcasts of the new Russia, rallying around the ideology they associate with better days. Our heroine is ready to re-join the demonstration, but the communism she advocates is clearly a private affair, between her and her Stalin.

In her published commentary to the two-and-a-half-minute video *Surok* (*Marmot*, 1999), Olga Chernysheva tells that she was surprised to encounter this protest march on Tverskaia Street in central Moscow — even if it was 7 November, the day the Soviets had traditionally celebrated the Bolshevik Revolution:

> A few people were already filming the demonstration with their video cameras and I did not feel any urgent need to switch mine on. Everything was happening according to the customary scheme. Someone was demonstrating, someone recording it. Everyone was occupied. I was not needed. I did not yet feel any nostalgia for the colour red.
>
> I looked again and suddenly saw something that caught my eye; something strangely touching, that disrupted the general rhythm. A woman became separated from the demonstrators' ranks. She stopped at the edge of a pedestrian crossing and began to fidget, making some small movements. There was a sense that the force of collectivism that brings these people out onto the street is not totally powerful.[1]

Like many of Chernysheva's subjects, the primary figure in *Marmot* struggles to emerge from workaday post-Soviet life. She becomes individuated from the disjointed collective, less the protagonist of an unfolding drama than a practitioner of some private art, and this awakens an equally focused response from Chernysheva's voyeuristic camera. The sympathy between subject and camera trains a new lens on the crowd and its cause:

> [The force of collectivism] tries to encompass and absorb the entire person, but at the same time it absorbs the person's uncertainty. And this uncertainty, and the rummaging around that characterizes individual, private life – these familiar

vibrations – enchanted me. I began to film this disruption, which so shifted the tone of the event.

   I immediately felt to what degree this demonstration consists of just such lost women and men. And to what degree this woman is made of the demonstration and of the attempt to be together with everyone, of a possibility that until recently had been a duty.[2]

The oscillations of the woman's inscrutable soul disrupt the collective slumber and reanimate long-dead social rituals. The moment of shared virtuosity redeems the possibility of ideology.

Superficially *Marmot* fits into the mainstream of contemporary Russian art, which, as Boris Groys and Petre Petrov have recently discussed, commodifies communist ideology and post-communist despair, making them available for consumption and even enjoyment.[3] In the West artists package dissent and put it on sale as artwork; yet even commodified dissent remains potentially productive of social change. Of what social use is the packaged abjection of post-Soviet art that we recognize, for instance, in Boris Mikhailov's lurid portraits of the underclasses in post-Soviet territories? *Chernukha*, as this dismal art is known in Russia – literally, 'black stuff' – is imbued with a negativity that, though socially and politically justifiable, serves mainly as an outlet for the artist's aggression. This latent violence is realized quite literally in the video documentation of the performances of the Moscow Actionists during the 1990s, primarily Oleg Kulik and Aleksandr Brener. In his infamous performance *Beshenyi pes, ili Poslednee tabu, okhraniaemoe odinokim Tserberom* (*Mad Dog, or the Final Taboo Guarded by Lonely Cerberus*, 1994), Kulik ran around a Moscow street on all fours, barking, jumping and even biting passers-by, while Brener held him on a leash and yelled 'stupid [tupoe] art for stupid people in a stupid country'. Originally provoked by the senile self-satisfaction of the USSR in the 1970s and 1980s, under Leonid Brezhnev and his successors, *chernukha* persists today as a counterbalance to the belligerent, glossy nationalism of Vladimir Putin's Russia. A recent example is Sergei Loznitsa's feature film *Schast'e moe* (*My Joy*, 2010), in which a man's journey across Russia spirals down into the history of state-sponsored violence, all the way back to World War II. Loznitsa's film has parlayed anti-nationalist sentiment into success at international film festivals, but it ultimately descends into mere diatribe: the protagonist exacts vengeance on the policemen who sent him on his odyssey – killing three innocent victims to boot – before walking out into the night. Chernysheva's deep sympathy for her subjects disrupts this ruling dichotomy of nationalism and abjection. But does her deployment of this sympathy possess a positive social force, or does it lapse into sentimental nostalgia?

At first we might take the title *Marmot* to refer to our heroine's fur collar and hat, relics of Soviet comfort, but then the street noise subsides and is replaced by Beethoven's song 'Marmotte' (op. 52, no. 7, c. 1790–92), performed in a domestic setting replete with the squawk of a caged bird. The song, based on a text by Goethe, narrates the vicissitudes of an itinerant performer from Savoy with a trained marmot, ending with a request for alms. Commonly used as a practice piece, 'Marmotte' is well known in Russia as a children's song in the Soviet-era translation of poet Sergei Spassky. The beggarly and bedraggled figure is also familiar in Russia from Antoine Watteau's painting *Savoyard avec marmotte* (*Savoyard with a Marmot*, 1716), held in the Hermitage Museum in Saint Petersburg and widely reproduced. Chernysheva's film does not ask us to take account of the deep history of its central image, or to read its main character's plight as an allegory for some public trauma. It asks nothing more than that we join the protagonist in her obscure ministrations, perhaps as a pedagogical or therapeutic exercise, like the piano lesson on the soundtrack. Chernysheva's film *Samostoiatel'nye zaniatiia* (*Seven Exercises*, 2004) is based wholly on such a therapeutic conceit: seven enigmatic sequences of images are set to a soundtrack of home piano lessons. Repetition is a mode not only of coping with trauma, not only of developing skills for negotiating the world in a practical sense, but also of rehearsing an explanatory account capable of reordering social relations.

In post-Soviet Russia, repetition is inextricably linked to nostalgia, which is signified in *Marmot* by Stalin and Soviet print culture. The main character of Chernysheva's later film *Neizvestnye. Chast' 2* (*Anonymous. Part 2*, 2004) displays a quite different token of nostalgia: a bottle of vodka, with which he wrestles for an improbably long time in a verdant wood, rapt in Edenic abjection. As in *Marmot*, the camera stays patiently trained upon its central subject in one long take, allowing the protagonist to claim the public space as a sovereign realm. The soundtrack of Zen meditation music emphasises the asceticism of his devout piety, as well as the piety of the camera's restraint. The almost religious cult of Soviet alcoholism, familiar through such novels as *Venedikt Erofeev's Moskva–Petushki* (*Moscow to the End of the Line*, 1969–70), has come under intense pressure under the new Russian capitalism: not only has the drink become expensive and its hours of sale restricted, but time, in general, has become money. Busy passers-by cast our hero glances more of curiosity than of disdain, recognizing him as an emissary – albeit a deeply flawed one – from a lost world they might also wish to keep hold of, if only they had the time, if only they were freer. They have places to go; he can simply be himself. One senses Chernysheva's desire to share in his tawdry paradise and reclaim time as free potentiality.

When the camera zooms out at the end of the film, in a parting gesture typical of Chernysheva's work on video, the wood is revealed to be a mere copse behind a suburban train platform. The pastoral image of a man and his bottle becomes embedded in a broader social panorama, and one fears Chernysheva is lapsing into ideological cliché: the locomotive of modernity shunting Russian inertia into the wake of its forward progress. But her protagonist resists being confined within his social situation and its contradictions; he is rather located alongside, nearby and apart. Chernysheva's hand-held but steady camera also stands apart, respecting both its subject's sovereignty and his desire for community.

In Chernysheva's videos, public space forms a background that ripples and folds up into a fabric of intimacies; each of the separate, introverted figures shapes our sense of the larger event taking place outside of the frame. In the seven-minute video *Marsh* (*March*, 2005) we know not what or who is being celebrated in the solemn public ritual; possibly the participants are not even certain what has gathered them together. The young cadets stand in bored attention, fighting off distractions, while teenage girls with pom-poms dance in a row behind them, roughly coordinated and all under the watchful but detached eyes of adult officers. The lack of any evident audience makes it seem more a rehearsal than a performance. It is a space of intense self-absorption on the part of the cheerleaders (an exotic sight in Russia) and sexual awakening on the part of the younger cadets. The pointed camera angles drip with irony, but it is directed less against the participants than against the system that has brought them into such an awkward juxtaposition. Chernysheva does not pin her subjects to their social roles; instead she patiently documents and magnifies their efforts to liberate themselves within them. […]

1   Olga Chernysheva, 'Marmot', in Antonio Geusa, ed., *History of Russian Video Art*, vol. 1 (Moscow: Moscow Museum of Modern Art, 2007) 172. Translation adjusted for emphasis.

2   Ibid.

3   See 'The Temporalities of Soviet and Postcommunist Visual Culture: Boris Groys and Petre Petrov in Conversation' (with Robert Bailey and Cristina Albu), *Contemporaneity: Historical Presence in Visual Culture*, no. 1 (2011) 58.

Robert Bird, extract from 'Mundane Virtuosity: Olga Chernysheva's Work on Video', *Afterall*, no. 35 (Spring 2014) 107–9.

Claire Bishop and Francesco Manacorda
The Producer as Artist//2005

The more the assignment is emptied of what could normatively be considered to be compelling social subject matter, the more visible it is simply as the instance of a structure, an order.
– Jeff Wall

In one of his most provocative and overquoted essays on the relationship between art and politics, Walter Benjamin argues that 'a work which exhibits the right tendency must, of necessity, show every other quality as well', implying that if the artist adopts a desirable political stance, this will always be reflected in the form of the work of art.[1] He then goes on to complicate this assertion by claiming that it is not the artist's *attitude* towards topical subject matter that counts, but the artist's *position* within the relations of production of his or her times. To be politically progressive, a work's aesthetic tendency must be embedded in the process of its fabrication in such a way as to establish new paradigmatic relations of production. Within the field of visual arts, there has recently been a growth in documentary-style work that aspires to be committed through its depiction of politically-charged peoples, places and events. This tendency seeks to give visibility to neglected subjects by the transparent formats of photography or video as documents that may permit access to alternative narratives about reality. It might therefore be worth considering Benjamin's notion of 'tendency' in 'The Author as Producer' in order to assess the position within this trend of an artist like Phil Collins who seems consciously to adopt a politically-incorrect or frivolous attitude towards his subject matter.

At the same time as this surge of documentary-style film, photography and video in contemporary art in the last fifteen years, another approach to social engagement emerged: an art preoccupied with interactivity through which the audience was given a limited power of decision within a scheme predetermined by the artist. The unspoken consensus was that giving the viewer a collaborative role in the making or completion of the work of art served as a model of social behaviour: art would be a free space of experimentation permitting the invention of new ways of living in and interacting with the real world. In response to this, a type of art criticism has arisen that judges practices to be successful if they embody an egalitarian and progressive paradigm of interpersonal relations. By contrast, the art of Phil Collins could never serve as a model of social behaviour.[2] The actions that he documents take place in strictly staged environments into which people are channelled, unwittingly believing that they are fulfilling their own fantasies: singing along to the Smiths (*the world won't listen*, 2004–5), removing their clothes in a five-star hotel (*real society*, 2002), giving up their rolls of 35mm film for the artist to present as his own work (*free fotolab*, 2005). As such, the art of Phil Collins – particularly his recent ambitious projects in San Sebastián, Ramallah and Bogotá – provides an ethical and gestural positioning that differentiates it from the political aspirations of many contemporary 'micro-utopian' works.

The clearest example of Collins' approach can be seen in *they shoot horses* (2004), which emerged from a residency at the Al-Ma'amal Foundation for Contemporary Art in Jerusalem. The artist's proposal was to hold a disco-dancing marathon for a small number of teenagers in Ramallah, a marathon that would be eight hours in duration, and which he would record on video. Thirty Palestinian teenagers were invited to come to an audition; ten were chosen; nine turned up to be filmed. They were paid a daily wage per hour (with a bonus if they lasted all day) to dance in front of a bright pink wall to a relentless compilation of pop hits from the past three decades. What the viewer sees is a real-time unedited projection of this event. The pink is garish, the music is contagious, the teenagers are mesmerizing, sexy, hilarious. But as the hours wear on, they begin to fade. The fantasy world of pop music contrasts with the disenchantment generated by repetition and physical exhaustion.

Considering that the living conditions of these teenagers are the subject matter of daily coverage in the newspapers, Collins' decision to avoid reference to the political situation that dominates their lives seems perverse. Watching the adolescents be subjected to the saccharine dance marathon, in front of a wall bearing a 'usual suspects' line in bright orange, cannot help but invoke the spectre of their day-to-day endurance of unresolved non-citizenship. Collins thus twists a formula familiar from the work of Santiago Sierra and Vanessa Beecroft: if the participants in the latters' performances are paid to be a representative of a particular social group (workers, blacks, prostitutes, beauties, etc.), then Collins pays his participants to try and free them from their primary identity as political subjects. Instead, his participants become generic globalized teenagers, shaking their hips to Bananarama, twisting on their Nikes to Britney Spears, punching the air to Olivia Newton-John. The implicit politics of this identity switch arises in the puzzled questions that emerge while watching the video: how come Palestinians know Beyoncé? How come those girls dance like in an MTV video? How come they're wearing US trainers? By voiding the work of direct political narrative, Collins' video demonstrates how swiftly this space is filled by fantasies generated by the media and its selective production and dissemination of images from the Middle East.

This perverse de-amplification of politically charged subjects and situations is a strategy that has become a hallmark of Collins' work: direct allusions to a conflict are silenced in favour of presenting images of those who live in and endure these zones (as for example in the photographic series *beautiful boys of belfast*, 2000, or *young serbs*, 2001). The amateurism of his images enacts a further formal reduction of aestheticized reportage, such as that of Sebastião Salgado, and thereby unpicks the discourse of committed photography. As such, Collins' work positions itself on the cusp of the two traditions of conceptual photography of the 1960s and 70s as delineated by Jeff Wall: the recording of events and performances staged for the camera, and a critique of photojournalism's authentic relationship to reality.[3] While much of Collins' work destabilizes the photo-documentary validity of pictures, he nevertheless makes every effort to achieve the highest degree of authenticity in the pro-filmic while injecting it with something slightly ludicrous (not unlike Nauman's *Failing to Levitate in the Studio* (1966), or Robert Barry's photographs of gas returning to the atmosphere, 1969).

The staging is not concealed but is an essential protagonist within the set, such as the 'tropical' and 'alpine' backdrops in *the world won't listen*, the dancers' ability to see themselves in a monitor in *they shoot horses*, and the artist's hand that keeps refilling the mug of whisky in *hero* (2002). Collins contrives to produce the ideal setting for all the participants involved to reveal themselves with the highest degree of vulnerability. In this context, photography and video are not ends in themselves, but the necessary pretext for an event to occur at all: the camera is a trigger, a facilitator for interaction, a protagonist whose presence is one of the main subjects of the picture.

This is perhaps why Collins' photographs and videos often generate a sense of frustration in the viewer, since he seems deliberately to disregard the formal quality of the visual product. The artist appears not to be interested in producing visually seductive images. Although the photographs share much of the subject matter we associate with Nan Goldin or Wolfgang Tillmans (portraits, landscapes, a spot of reportage, friends in the shower), they have none of the former's grungy atmosphere, nor the latter's effortless poise. Collins' photographs differ from both in seeming amateurishly casual; as in a family snapshot, any fleeting effects of light, glimpses of character, or compositional satisfaction appear serendipitous rather than premeditated. One way to address this frustration is to recall that Collins' videos and photographs are not autonomous entities, but the residual traces of a larger aesthetic and conceptual scheme. His interests and interventions lie with the set of relations that occur *before* the moment in which the camera is at work, as if the specificity of his art consisted in the relationship that he constructs in order to shoot, rather than in the product with which the viewer is presented.

More than in the creation of photographs or videos, then, Collins' art could be said to lie primarily in his approach to *production*. The task of a producer is normally subordinated to the result: his/her job is to work towards the achievement of the highest standards in the final creation of film, play, TV programme, etc. By contrast, Collins subordinates the outcome of his activity to the inappropriate manipulation of the means that allow him to produce them. Small interventions in the apparatus that generates the work become the medium through which to trace his artistic intentions: the announcement for the casting, the process of selecting individuals to be involved in the projects, the way in which they are treated, the construction of the set, the relationship between photographer, camera and subject. Before the picture is taken there is thus a positioning within the production process that revolutionizes the way in which the means and subjects are conventionally used in the social and political situation that Collins has selected. These decisions are as much the artwork as the pictures and videos that ensue, which ultimately are metonymies for the production as a whole.

Yet there is an important component missing in this account of Collins' work. The artist does not simply de-amplify or redirect emphasis away from the obvious foci of a politically charged locale, but consciously mismatches the situation with an inappropriate – and often frivolous – production strategy. One of the achievements of the first mode of photo-conceptualism, as outlined by Wall, is the reduction of subject matter to a degree zero: in the work of Douglas Huebler, for example, the artist parodies the techniques of reportage and photojournalism while training his camera on minimally eventful occurrences, according to an abstract and predetermined set of rules, as if instructed by an eccentric news editor. For *Duration Piece No. 5, New York* (1969), Huebler took ten photographs, 'each documenting the location in Central Park where an individually distinguishable bird call was heard. Each photograph was made with the camera pointed in the direction of the sound.' The resulting images impersonate the style of a reporter in the midst of a war zone, but the pictures are triggered by the banal sweetness of birdsong rather than the sound of gunfire.

Collins' work twists and reverses Huebler's structure: unlike the latter, his subjects (and therefore subject matter) are worthy of reportage but the procedures he imports, in terms of style and production, are entirely at odds with the potential gravity of what is exposed to the camera. […]

1   Walter Benjamin, 'The Author as Producer', in *Understanding Brecht* (London: New Left Books, 1973) 86.

2   For example, Collins has slapped critics, gallerists and curators around the face before photographing them, in his ongoing project *you'll never work in this town again* (2004–5) and has asked youngsters to undress in a public space in *beautiful boys of belfast* (2000).

3   Jeff Wall, 'Marks of Indifference: Aspects of Photography in, or as, Conceptual art', in Anne Goldstein and Ann Rorimer, eds, *Reconsidering the Object of Art: 1965–75* (Cambridge, Massachusetts: The MIT Press, 1995) 253: 'This introversion, or subjectivization, of reportage was manifested in two important directions. First, it brought photography into a new relationship with the problematics of the staged, or posed, picture, through new concepts of performance. Second, the inscription of photography into a nexus of experimental practices led to a direct but distantiated and parodic relationship with the art-concept of photojournalism. Although the work of many artists could be discussed in this context, for the sake of brevity I will discuss the photographic work of Richard Long and Bruce Nauman as representative of the first issue, that of Dan Graham, Douglas Huebler and Robert Smithson of the second.'

4   Extract from the artist's statement that forms part of the work.

Claire Bishop and Francesco Manacorda, extract from 'The Producer as Artist', in *Phil Collins: yeah … you, baby you*, ed. Sinisa Mitrovic (Milton Keynes: Milton Keynes Gallery/Shady Lane Publications, 2005) 24–7.

Jean Fisher
Minerva Cuevas and the Art of Para-sitic Intervention//2011

[…] Minerva Cuevas launched Mejor Vida Corp (Better Life Corporation) in 1998, designing a logo of clasped hands; a slogan ('for a human interface') and an international activist website (irational.org); and renting an office in Mexico City's iconic skyscraper, the Torre Latinoamericana. MVC's aim was to subvert the conventions of corporate trading, and by extension art as commodity form, by providing free services, products and publicity campaigns. These gestures of hospitality have included sweeping the Mexico City Metro, distributing free lottery tickets, handing out free travel tickets among rush-hour queues, issuing student identity cards for free museum entry or for discounted goods and the production of barcodes and stickers to reduce the price of supermarket produce. Alongside philanthropic interventions in the spaces of daily life, MVC has produced street and gallery versions of publicity campaigns that manipulate well-known corporate logos in juxtaposition with graphics or statements that expose the corrupt underside of company operations or the illusions projected by advertising. […]

One might say that MVC's counterfeit corporation parasitizes the parasitic counterfeiters – the corporate peddlers of unrealizable dreams and fake utopias of equality that mask the real inequities and iniquities of the capitalist system. [...]

Cuevas' form of social activism is clearly distinct from oppositional political art activism. 'Oppositionality' is typically the 're-actionary' partner in a binary system in which the language of power remains the privileged term. Thus, oppositional critique risks being absorbed into the very system it seeks to challenge, in so far as it helps to redefine the boundaries of the system itself, leaving infrastructure and power relations intact. Moreover, the subject cannot stand wholly outside of the dominant reality that formed him or her. Therefore, he or she either refuses to participate in its forms of exchange – along the lines of Herman Melville's character Bartleby, who responds to every request with the words 'I would prefer not to' (a disengagement or *suspension* of communication, in so far as there is no possible answer to this statement); or, in an equal refusal of hegemonic truth claims, he or she hijacks the system's channels of communication and diverts them to other pathways. Cuevas' interventions take no 'position' as such; rather, they operate through more subtle diversionary tactics, trespassing onto the territory of the other whilst camouflaged in the insignia of its own livery.

Clearly, MVC's primary targets are the communications media and information networks through which power exercises and sustains itself, and in which we are all implicated as consumers. According to Michel de Certeau, however, we do not need to regard this situation as wholly disempowering, but rather as a ground from which other relations between self and world can be forged. De Certeau is concerned not with representational structures as such, but with how consumers use them in everyday life. Arguing that consumerism may not be as passive as is commonly thought, he suggests that consumers opportunistically select mediated codes and reuse them for their own purposes, often subverting those intended by producers. That is, consumption is also a form of *production*. Creative reinvention and re-empowerment through subterfuge are tactics of survival by the weak and oppressed, and familiar from the narratives of dispossessed peoples under colonial rule: the colonized were unable overtly to oppose the language of colonial authority, but they could subtly insinuate its codes to disclose the inconsistencies and fallacies behind its projected certainties. De Certeau calls such subterfuges 'camouflaged transgressions', through which, as in Cuevas' work, 'to acknowledge the authority of rules is the exact opposite of applying them'.[1]

MVC's 'camouflaged transgressions' are operations that also engage what de Certeau calls a 'subterranean economy': parallel networks of social relations – barter, hospitality, the exchange of non-remunerative services and so forth – that are regarded by capitalist technocracy as worthless, discarded or useless exchanges that cannot (yet) be reduced to its law, but whose role 'is decisive for the survival of groups or individuals'.[2] As de Certeau points out, central to the relay of communication in such social networks are itinerant intermediaries, or *shifters*, with the capacity to put goods and discourses into circulation: 'they select, diffuse and dynamize information; they make it desirable and assimilable, and are the active agents of its appropriation and its transformation'.[3] In this sense, MVC's tactics are similar to those of the shifter, who disarticulates the language of power towards collective change.

Cuevas' tactics recall a further model that we might describe – following Michel Serres – as a 'parasitic economy':[4] MVC is neither inside nor outside the dominant system of exchange but *para-sitic* to it. Serres notes that what is important in communication is not only the points of emission and reception, but also the pathways that link (or bypass) them. The two points must be both 'same' and 'different', where difference lies in *perspective*. It is this difference operating in the transmission pathway that creates 'noise' or interference in the message depending on where one is standing, and without which there would be nothing to communicate. Serres names this mediation the logic of the parasite. For instance, in the relation between the host and the parasite, the latter exchanges a meal for nothing (like the 'translator', another parasite, who intervenes and exchanges a primary text for another text), but this eccentric presence irrevocably transfigures the situation. Without the parasite there would be no relation, no transformation: the creation and communication of a new perception can only take place through the interference of vectors of change, similar to de Certeau's shifters. This parasitic economy is essentially intersubjective, but is not one of equal exchange, in so far as exchange implies stability and equilibrium, whereas the movement here is towards a rupture in the law of exchange that exposes the concealed imbalance in the system. MVC's interventions are likewise directed towards change conceived in this way – the precipitation of disequilibrium – an interruption or swerve in the messages relayed by corporate capitalism.

Cuevas' parasitic economy takes on various aspects in her major multifaceted installations, *La venganza del elefante* (*The Revenge of the Elephant*) and *Phenomena* (both 2007), which primarily play with the potential isomorphism between our representations of human social relations and human relations to the natural world. [...]

The hostage of the body to the operations of social power becomes [particularly] explicit in *Phenomena*, which brought together a number of individual works and installations that feature contemporary video projection alongside antique or obsolete scientific magnifying and projection devices (microscopes and magic lanterns) adapted with fibre-optic technology. During the nineteenth and early twentieth centuries, these devices were the tools of empirical science's methods of observation, collection, taxonomy and demonstration, as well as being phantasmagoric, pre-animation forms of mass entertainment, as the term 'magic lantern' indicates. From a scientific perspective they were intended to render the invisible visible and legible by artificially enhancing the forensic gaze of an observer in a position that was supposedly detached from that of the observed, but Cuevas' juxtaposition of often bizarre imagery exposes the ambivalence in this distinction.

Similarly, the collection of objects and images that constitute *Social Entomology* (2007) makes direct reference to scientific method: a hexagonal table displaying, amongst other items, brass magnifying instruments; old wooden slide trays; books on histology and nature (often how to kill it); microscope slides and insect specimens; and references to social bees and cricket songs, in which, together with the microscope projections, external parasites like fleas, bedbugs and ticks figure prominently. The best one can say about these creatures is that they do not discriminate according to class, gender or race. At the same time, a text accompanying the installation reminds us of the common analogy empirical science made – also drawing on observations of insect colonies – between the human body as an organism of separate cells and the social body as organism. Any distinction between the human and 'nature' becomes further blurred in the magic lantern projections *Ape with Jacket* (2007), which depicts a chimpanzee wearing a blazer and sitting in a tree like an errant schoolboy, and *Like me* (2007), in which a zoo keeper holds a baby chimpanzee in a paternal grasp. If these two works comically point to the way we anthropomorphize nature – or, rather, reduce it to our own measure – the set of videos *Dreamlike I, II* and *III* (2007), shown simultaneously on three monitors, opens a disturbing window onto how, by contrast, the human becomes the object of scientific scrutiny. The three projections show film footage, perhaps dating from the 1950s, recording behavioural studies on motor functions in naked human infants whilst they are crawling, swimming and climbing. The babies are induced to move with the lure of a toy on a string (thereby fulfilling the purpose of the study), which, in the clinical context of the scene, seems less a game than torture.

The technology of Cuevas' devices predates the emergence of the 'society of the spectacle' (though they are consistent with what Michel Foucault, in his discussion of the panopticon, described as the 'society of surveillance'): they still linked vision to the position of a human observer in the perceptible world, to 'phenomena' that were apprehended by sight and touch, unlike the digitalized media of contemporary 'spectacularized' life, capable of producing a fictitious pictorialism independent of reference to an observer's body. This is not to say that there was ever an 'innocent' eye to which the world was rendered transparent. As Jonathan Crary has shown, changing technologies of vision, techniques of the observer and visual representations are all bound to larger assemblages of social forces and fields of knowledge and practice: 'The same knowledge that allowed the increasing rationalization and control of the human subject in terms of new institutional and economic requirements was also a condition for new experiments in visual representation.'[5] But although Cuevas' devices belong to an era in which there was still a referential relationship between the body and the perceptible world, it was also the modernizing era that released the forces from which spectacularized life was to emerge.

Foucault spoke at length of how, in the eighteenth and nineteenth centuries, modernity's uprooting of the masses from rural life to urban manufacturing centres drove the need for control and the invention of disciplinary techniques that would ensure the smooth circulation of goods, money and services. In turn, the management of populations through rationalization and standardization depended on the accumulation of knowledge of human behaviour across the spectrum of bodily functions and social relations, whereby the subject as such became *visible*, but to a now disembodied observer. As Edward Said once said, the human being became a *specimen*. Nowhere is this more acutely demonstrated than in colonialism and slavery, the exogenous twins of Western modernity – in fact, its motor. The bodies of the colonized and enslaved were not only the objects of economic exchange, but also subjected to forensic, panoptical scrutiny by all manner of measuring and recording devices engaged by the agents of the newly instituted human sciences and their colonial authorities. [...]

As we move into the twentieth century, photography and cinema join money as homologous forms of social power; as Crary states, 'they are equally totalizing systems for binding and unifying all subjects within a single global network of valuation and desire [in which] the social world is represented and constituted exclusively as signs'.[6] Despite its later date, the film footage projected in Cuevas' 16mm film installation *I have never been a believer* (2007) is consistent with the technological and ideological turn that produced the 'society of the spectacle', which Crary dates from the 1920s, concurrent with the technological and institutional origins of television, the beginning of synchronized sound in movies and the use of mass-media techniques by the Nazi party in Germany.[7] The latter, of course, was symptomatic of the way cinema could manipulate and unify desire and identification in quasi-religious terms. Cuevas' projection shows Fidel Castro giving a public speech in the rain, and counter-shots of close-ups of an attentive (white male) crowd that recall the cinematic techniques of the Russian Constructivists, which also influenced post- revolutionary Cuban cinema. The fragment of footage therefore has the feel of a propaganda film, not unlike that of the Nazis, in which, through mass media manipulation, the political leader becomes a semi-divine figure to which the social body is encouraged to cohere (much like worker bees around their queen). And yet, is that one fellow in the crowd attending more to his hair than to Castro? [...]

The affect of any artistic practice depends on how it draws the viewer into its field of action and possible meanings. As Jacques Rancière says, 'artistic practices are "ways of doing and making" that intervene in the general distribution of ways of doing and making as well as in the relationships they maintain to modes of being and forms of visibility'.[8] Minerva Cuevas' para-sitic interventions are analogous to the performance of what indigenous North Americans call 'coyote giving': a theft by trickery of someone's property from which the thief does not necessarily benefit, but by violating the circuit of exchange the old order is undermined and a new communication is made available for the transformation of collective understanding. Such 'camouflaged transgressions' may not produce political emancipation, but they represent a modest quantum of agency, little psychic freedoms from the traumatic effects of daily life, the circulation of subterranean economies vital for cultural survival and, perhaps, a latent source of insurrection.

1   [footnote 6 in source] Michel de Certeau, *The Practice of Everyday Life*, trans. Steven F. Randall (Berkeley and Los Angeles: University of California Press, 1984) 54–5.

2   [7] Michel de Certeau, *The Capture of Speech and Other Political Writings*, trans. Tom Conley (Minneapolis: University of Minnesota Press, 1997) 93.

3   [8] Ibid., 97.

4   [9] Michel Serres, *Hermes: Literature, Science, Philosophy*, ed. Josué V. Hari and David F. Bell (Baltimore: Johns Hopkins University Press, 1982) xxv–vi and 66–7.

5   [11] Jonathan Crary, *Techniques of the Observer: On Vision and Modernity in the Nineteenth Century* (Cambridge, Massachusetts: The MIT Press, 1992) 9.

6   [12] Ibid., 13.

7   [13] Ibid., 18, note 26.

8   [15] Jacques Rancière, *The Politics of Aesthetics*, trans. Gabriel Rockhill (London and New York: Continuum, 2004) 13.

Jean Fisher, extracts from 'Minerva Cuevas and the Art of Para-sitic Intervention', *Afterall*, no. 27 (Summer 2011).

Ian White
Kinomuseum//2008

The extraordinary fact is that we live in a world in which virtually anything may be exhibited *in* a museum, and in which virtually anything can be made to function *as* a museum …
– Donald Preziosi and Claire Farago, 'What Are Museums *For*?' (2004)

Through reproductive technology postmodernist art dispenses with the aura. The fiction of the creating subject gives way to the frank confiscation, quotation, excerptation, accumulation and repetition of already existing images. Notions of originality, authenticity and presence, essential to the ordered discourse of the museum, are undermined.
– Douglas Crimp, 'On the Museum's Ruins' (1980)

Kinomuseum is a project that occurs at the intersection of these two statements, between the museum's seemingly unlimited ability to reproduce itself and the threat that reproduction poses to the art museum's primary function as the keeper of unique objects. Ultimately, *Kinomuseum* is a proposal for considering a particular kind of cinema as a unique kind of museum: one where 'originality, authenticity and presence' are not undermined by reproduction, but where reproduction either turns these qualities into a new set of questions for the museum, almost physically disrupting it, or, perversely, where film and video as potentially infinitely reproducible objects make these same terms manifest in moving images considered as works of art. It leads to a differentiated cinema, a museum based on the principles of impermanence, immediacy, the temporal and the temporary, manifested in the minds of an audience who experience it in the space and time of the auditorium that is the museum's permutating exhibition hall, and who are its active, defining agent. […]

Preziosi and Farago describe the museum as a construct, re-presenting things in order to make sense of them. And it is this – to reiterate – the removal of a thing from one place and its re-situation in another place, which forms a continuous thread through the various cultural readings of the museum. It is the pivot upon which turns Adorno's essay 'Valéry Proust Museum', as it compares the two French poets' positions, and links institutional responsibility to personal experience and pleasure. The culturally conservative Valéry experiences almost an act of violence in the curatorial frame of the Louvre: 'Neither a hedonistic nor a rationalistic civilization could have constructed a house of such disparities.'[1] On the other hand,

Adorno quotes Proust: 'the masterpiece observed during dinner no longer produces in us the exhilarating happiness that can be had only in a museum ...'[2] [...]

Generically, an undifferentiated cinema, defined by its industrial model that is both symbolized by and dependent upon the theatrical auditorium, functions in a strikingly different way from the art museum's collection of objects (the art museum which Daniel Sherman suggests Adorno regarded as 'the most elaborately articulated instance of decontextualization as a strategy of power').[3] The principle of distribution, dependent on film as an infinitely reproducible medium, is to show the same work to the maximum number of people, the maximum number of times. Cinema audiences exert a collective ownership over the work which each member pays a small amount of money to watch, and the same work might be watched simultaneously in different cities and different countries. This is a comprehensive and continuous *re*contextualization by a market, upon which we might argue the form – and meaning – of this work is contingent. The art museum, by contrast, collects and preserves unique objects, at great expense, and their exhibition is strictly controlled. Anyone wanting to see an exhibit must travel to the one location in which it is on display. The fixed start times and fixed seating of the auditorium are different from the perambulatory space of the gallery. [...]

Specific examples aside, we don't have to look very far at the world around us to discover the boundaries between the disciplines of the cinema and the museum starting to erode. The art museum has had to incorporate (industrial) cinema into its strategies of display. Contemporary artists such as Daria Martin or Nick Relph and Oliver Payne show their work in the museum *in the manner of* the cinema: single channel works shown in dark rooms, with some fixed seating and sometimes fixed start times. But these films and videos also enter into the museum collection – following the principle of unique objects – by virtue of being editioned, and they are controlled rather than distributed. As with Rauschenberg's montages (contrary to the revolutionary status that Crimp affords them in 'On the Museum's Ruins'), their acquisition does not provoke an actual collapse of the museum even though it might suggest a conceptual one. [...]

The insistence on a work's status as a unique (or almost unique) art object is a recent validation that the museum and the artist have deployed to legitimize the acquisition of some film and video. It is not the only model. At the Centre Pompidou, for example, industrial cinema (feature films) and artists' films – both potentially infinitely reproducible, the former definitely uneditioned – are contained within a film collection, the acquisition process for which is the same as for the museum's other departments. The appearance of the cinema auditorium itself – today as often curated as programmed – as a common feature of the modern art museum is not unrelated to another alternative, a founding problem if you like: the Film Library established by the Museum of Modern Art, New York, in 1935.

In many respects, Haidee Wasson's book *Museum Movies: The Museum of Modern Art and the Birth of Art Cinema* (2005), which articulates the institution of the film library, was one of the starting points for *Kinomuseum* as a project, and partly why my archival research began with major American museums, the precedents and contexts that the Film Library was established amongst. Wasson describes how this unique collection not only instituted cinema through its catholic remit, collecting Hollywood feature films as well as artists' film, but also extended museological practices to radically affect the film industry, introducing a system of dating and attributing authorship to films for the first time and, by introducing the principal of conservation, establishing the new economy of repertory cinema. Prints previously regarded as depleted of any value after the film had been released once were instead kept to be shown again.

The MoMA Film Library and its 'exhibition' in the museum's cinema also had an important social influence. Audiences used to verbally and physically expressing themselves as they watched popular feature films were expected to behave differently in the Museum of Modern Art's own auditorium, to the extent that Iris Barry, the Film Library's champion and first curator, 'had a slide projector permanently installed in the museum's auditorium, equipped with a slide that read: "If the disturbance in the auditorium does not cease, the showing of this film will be discontinued."' Wasson situates the Film Library as one among a number of tactics employed by MoMA as a critical mediation and implicit extension of itself. Touring film programmes served ideally to 'civilize' provincial Americans, as well as to entertain and inform. The unique status of film as an auxiliary to the museum('s collection) that could be safely distributed (i.e. was replaceable, reproducible), and as an educational tool loaded with institutional authority, turns cinema into a vital annex for the museum's social (and political) agenda. In representing the museum that Preziosi and Farago describe as already being a representation itself, the Film Library – cinema – *becomes* the museum. [...]

1   [footnote 7 in source] Theodor W. Adorno, 'Valéry Proust Museum', *Prisms*, trans. Samuel and Shierry Weber (Cambridge, Massachusetts: The MIT Press, 1967) 176–7.

2   [8] Ibid., 179.

3   [14] Daniel J. Sherman, 'Quatremère/Benjamin/Marx: Art Museums, Aura and Commodity Fetishism', in *Museum Culture: Histories, Discourses, Spectacles* (London: Routledge, 1994) 138.

Ian White, extracts from 'Kinomuseum', in *Kinomuseum: Towards an Artists' Cinema*, ed. Mike Sperlinger and Ian White (Cologne: Verlag der Buchhandlung Walther König, 2008) 13–24. *Kinomuseum* was originally a programme of screenings and discussions, curated by Ian White for the Oberhausen International Short Film Festival in 2007.

H.G. Masters
Disembodied Perspective: Jananne al-Ani//2012

Immersing yourself in Jananne al-Ani's 15-minute film *Shadow Sites I* (2010), you feel like a soaring predator. Beneath you there is a dry river bed, a few scrubs in the sandy soil and a lone tree. A path leads through rows of crops resembling thin green scratches on the landscape. The stone walls of an old settlement divide what were once rooms. The land becomes patterns, formations – information – but exactly what it is revealing, you do not know. What are those mounds that come after the ruins? A long-disused fort? An ancient settlement in the lone and level sands? As you become mesmerized by this voyage, the land becomes alien and abstract, a place seemingly without people, but marked by civilizations, old and new. Slowly you feel less and less like a corporeal being, and closer to the disembodied eye of the camera.

Halfway through the film, the sound of an airplane's propeller kicks in, which jolts you out of deep absorption. As you soar over a large excavation site – perhaps an extinct mine – you begin to feel as if you are on a reconnaissance mission. You find yourself looking for clues, trying to make sense of the structures. A network of roads around plots of land could be a housing development in the making. Rows of sheds are surrounded by thousands of sheep. Around 12 minutes into the film, you come upon the circular green patterns identifiable as an industrial farm, a welcome burst of colour in the muted landscape.

Formally beautiful and subtly sinister in equal measure, al-Ani's *Shadow Sites I* reveals how seeing the landscape from above creates a feeling of physical disembodiment, and how accustomed we are to viewing the earth and sky from a fixed position on the ground. It quickly becomes apparent how this unique vantage point gives access to places and information one is not afforded by travelling along the ground, and how we intuitively associate aerial images with those places that are otherwise off-limits – whether it is the Iranian nuclear facilities at Natanz and Qom, or the Baba Amr neighbourhood of Homs, to take two locations whose aerial depictions have been frequently in the news this year. These pictures, captured by remotely operated cameras, represent the visualization of the continuing mechanization and virtualization of espionage, warfare and the media coverage of foreign affairs. They are the pictures that in turn shape the political and ethical dialogue about conflicts.

In mid January, al-Ani was in Istanbul where *Shadow Sites* was being screened at the research centre SALT in conjunction with an exhibition about Ottoman-era archaeological practices. At an evening lecture, she described the process of shooting the film over the course often days in southern Jordan, near the borders with both Saudi Arabia and Israel, from a small airport in the Wadi Rum area. Al-Ani explained how she and her crew attached a camera to a strut on the wing of a small plane, and how recording in Super-16mm film meant she could only film for up to eight minutes before the pilot had to land to change the roll.

She referred to French cultural theorist Paul Virilio's writings on military technology and film, particularly his book *The Aesthetics of Disappearance* (1980), and Virilio's interest in Edward Steichen's World War I reconnaissance photographs of the trenches on the Western Front taken from the air – several examples of which she showed. Virilio summarizes Steichen's ventures as a project that 'blends motor, eye and weapon', and quotes artist and writer Allan Sekula's essay 'The Instrumental Image: Steichen at War' (originally published in Artforum in December 1975), in which Sekula writes: 'The meaning of the aerial photo, its reading, depends on all that can be drawn from the rationalized act of interpretation as a source of military intelligence … few pictures, except possibly in the medical field, are as "free", seemingly, from a meaning higher than that of their usage.' For al-Ani, Steichen's photographs had something like the opposite effect: 'I was struck by how this scene of carnage and horror could be transformed through the distancing of the photographer, of the camera, into something really beautiful.'

Al-Ani has uncovered other uses for aerial photography, albeit ones still connected to the history of warfare. 'Shadow sites', she explained, is a term that comes from aerial archaeology, referring to locations that are revealed from the air only very early in the morning or late in the evening, when the shadows are longest. This practice dates back to the First and Second World Wars, when pilots who were flying sorties from the United Kingdom to continental Europe discovered archaeological sites on the ground that no one had ever seen before. After World War II, archaeologists and universities enlisted a number of these pilots and planes to begin surveying the newly found locations. Al-Ani said she was surprised that, 'out of conflict could come a revelation, or something redeeming, maybe'.

The film, along with its companion works – *Shadow Sites II* (2011), made from still aerial images of the same sites, and *Excavators* (2010), a short video of ants building a nest – are part of a larger ongoing project begun in 2008, 'The Aesthetics of Disappearance: A Land without People'. Each piece shares, in the artist's words, 'an extreme vertical perspective that doesn't allow you to see anything expansive of the landscape'. While the title comes from Virilio's text, and particularly references his notion of what al-Ani glosses as the 'trickery and magic of cinema', it also refers to how, from certain perspectives – physical or ideological – the body disappears into the landscape. She notes that the phrase 'a land without people' comes from a very famous and controversial comment that is attributed to early Zionists in Palestine, 'the idea that Palestine is a land without people, for a people without a land. So it's also this idea of the poetics of the place. The way in which a place is occupied but the people who are occupying it are in the way'. [...]

H.G. Masters, extract from 'Disembodied Perspective: Jananne Al-Ani', *Art Asia Pacific*, no. 78 (May/June 2012) 36–7.

Jean-Michel Frodon
From Films to Cinema: Entering the Life of Traces//2013

[T]he huge 'work in progress' represented by the artistic activities of Joana Hadjithomas and Khalil Joreige, which deserve to be considered as a whole, not only continually challenges distinctions between visual arts, video and cinema, feature film and documentary, but above all only develops by being constantly reshaped by these distinctions. [...] For their oeuvre is mobilized by a question that is likewise central to the cinematographic process, the question of traces. [...] While the question of traces – the imprints left by a being, an event, an emotion, or an idea – is logically a preoccupation for many creative artists, it is a particular concern of theirs to display the way in which traces survive, *as traces.*

In a departure from what normally occurs, they perceive traces not as vestiges of what has been, but as existing in their own right: living beings that evolve. So their works construct the conditions that make it possible to perceive this: the life of traces, the dynamics that transform them, and in transforming them affect human beings, individual and collective relationships, and representations.

It is not that the past 'does not pass', in the sense that it remains present, like a stone in a shoe. It passes, and even never finishes passing, going deeper, being transformed, metabolizing what surrounds it. Traces are not inert, they live off their strange life, like parasitic organisms, not necessarily harmful, moreover, but inhabited by modes of development that are peculiar to them, and interact with that of living creatures; of all living creatures, those who have known what they are traces of, and the others, those who were not there, those who had not been born. It is in this respect that the work of these two Lebanese artists, so powerfully rooted in a time and a place, let us say the contemporary Middle East, is addressed to everyone, everywhere.

Now, cinema is the supreme art of the trace. It is the practice that records the existence of what has been in four dimensions – the temporal dimension (absent from the still photograph) obviously being at least as important as the spatial. But cinema naturally tends to freeze a certain state of the traces it records, and of course always composes – by framing, editing, etc. It seems that the sensitivity and artistic intelligence of Hadjithomas and Joreige have lain in accepting, then prompting, the way in which the dynamics of reality could, on the contrary, come back right inside their practice as filmmakers. In this, they have been faithful to this living relationship to traces that is active in all their work. [...]

Looking at their films, it is clear that they have not always been aware of the extent to which the cinematographic gesture and practice challenged the spirit of their undertaking as artists. Film after film, reality took care to remind them of it. It must be said that reality incessantly reminds us all, but few of us hear or understand. [...]

In *A Perfect Day* (2005), the photograph of a [real] man (actually a fleeting image), the uncle of an assistant, who had died some time previously, had been used in the newspapers to represent the fictional character who had disappeared. Suddenly, that man's second wife asked for an explanation, rejecting this exploitation of her husband. A threat of seizure, a lawsuit, ruin for the film, its authors, its producers, its distributors: an abrupt twist of reality and the law. Of course they had taken precautions, believed they were respecting the rules, but reality, and a woman's grief, wanted more.

Then it did not happen. Something else happened, something very beautiful and very human. It was the joint invention, by the artists and the woman, henceforth called Aïda, of a way to move beyond those oppositions, with intelligence and respect. That story is told in another work, *Aïda, Save Me!* (2009). In concrete terms, it was about a public lecture where the two filmmakers recounted what had happened.

And what happened, what they did, but also caused to be done, made possible, was cinema in the purest meaning of the term. Cinema is obviously not the video recording of their lecture, it is the joint 'production' of the work by Joana, Khalil and Aïda: a collective gesture accomplished that makes it possible to move beyond the law, beyond the antagonism between reality and fiction, to elaborate a different state of problematizing our relationship to the world, to the living and the dead, the past and the present, to loved ones and human beings, whoever they may be.

And it is enriched by this already long experience that runs through all their work, but which has taken on a kind of theatrical form in the adventure of the photograph that comes back, that Hadjithomas and Joreige were able to devise the great cinematographic machination that *I Want to See* (2008) represents. [...]

Seeing and not seeing. All those things combine to make cinema, i.e. manufacture step by step, shot by shot, minute after minute and frame after frame, an organization of knowledge and ignorance, phantasms and facts, visible and invisible: with elegance, affection and humour, they engender the conditions for a different perception, a different understanding.

Jean-Michel Frodon, extracts from 'From Films to Cinema: Entering the Life of Traces', in *Joana Hadjithomas and Khalil Joreige*, ed. Clément Dirie and Michele Theriault (Zurich: JRP/Ringier, 2013) 58–64.

Shanay Jhaveri
Shared Senses of Inquietude: *Communists Like Us*//2011

In 1989, after witnessing the final coming undone, within seeming moments, of the collapsed Soviet Union, and the fall of the Berlin Wall, the Indian government, once a key figure in the Non-Aligned Movement, swiftly realigned itself in a newly unipolar world. A realignment that unbolted a padlocked Indian market. […] Ushered in was an economic totalitarianism that over two decades has initiated a maelstrom of transformations, injustices that are nakedly on display in a fraught and divided present-day India.

The Otolith Group completed *Otolith I* in 2003, at an instant in which the USA, with the support of Britain and the rest of the Coalition of the Willing, was embarking on the invasion and occupation of Iraq. The political depression that Anjalika Sagar and Kodwo Eshun combated during the failure of the anti-war demonstrations of those times informed their decision to locate their film in the perspective of the future. […] Proposing temporal disturbances, the folding of past, present and future onto and into one another by mixing features from heterogeneous sources is an approach employed by the group to 'challenge the current unfolding globalization, particularly its outcome, presumed to be a result of historical inevitability'.[1]

Their work *Communists Like Us* (2006/2010), exists in multiple modalities, as a performance, a double-channel and single-channel projection, and a sound assemblage. It is composed of a series of captivating archival photographs, recording journeys made by Indian stateswomen during the mid 1950s and early 1960s to the USSR and Mao's China. Delegations of Indian, Soviet and Chinese feminists are beheld intermingling, arm in arm, shoulder to shoulder, visiting museums, factories, schools, nurseries and laboratories, participating in conferences, meetings, plenary sessions and discussions. The photographs, found in Sagar's family home in Mumbai, belonged to her grandmother, the former President of the National Federation of Indian Women.

English subtitles from Jean-Luc Godard's *La Chinoise* (1967), mostly known for its presaging of May 1968, are added to the recto and verso of these images. It is the transcription of a sixteen-minute exchange set on a train between the indexical figure of activist and philosopher Francis Jeanson and the fictional character of Véronique, his Maoist student, played by Anne Wiasemzky. Insurrection is debated, Véronique advocates terror to shut down the universities, and Francis attempts to discourage her provocations. This melding of images and text produces astonishing conjunctions, some planned, others intuitive, all supplemented with a soundtrack assembled from two sequences in two parts. The first half is driving, surging, almost heroic, courtesy of Cornelius Cardew and the Scratch Orchestra, then it switches over to the tense, brittle and taut mood of Ennio Morricone. It is a dramatic shift, felt palpably in both the performance and the single-channel version of the piece. Both composers shared attachments to Maoism at points in their careers, affording the group the licence to incorporate these compositions. Drawing together these components, territories and histories overlap, intertwine and converge, but still maintain parallel autonomies. A contrapuntal conversation is begun between photography, subtitle and music, and discrepant engagements with divergent Maoisms are brought into dialogue with one another.

Intended originally as notes towards *Otolith II* (2007), the only part of *Communists Like Us* that survives into the epic structure of that work is a photographic arrangement from the delegation archive. The presence of these images across different projects in variable tenors expresses the group's expansive and multi-platformed practice. Their foregrounding and backgrounding at alternate frequencies accommodates active spectators willing to re-view works and to carry the memory and usage of factors in one method and play the memory of that methodology off its usage and positioning in another. Alternatively, the associations remain latent, as allusions yet to be discovered. An iteration of *Communists Like Us*, at its most disembodied, devised especially for the group's solo exhibition 'A Lure a Part Allure Apart' at Betonsalon in Paris, proposed precisely such a calling forwards and backwards in its dynamics of prolepsis and retrospection. At the core of that showing was the Otolith Trilogy, which was projected according to a set schedule, shown either on the 30-minute or the 60-minute mark, thereby generating intervals of eight and twelve minutes that provided the opportunity for developing new assemblages. These new reworkings enact a second (subliminal) exhibition inside the first exhibition that delivers the viewer a space for the stimulation of anticipation and acquaintance.

Of the three assemblages, the first, which revisited *Communists Like Us*, was scheduled to appear after the projection of *Otolith I*. It was comprised of a sound montage isolated from *Otolith II* that compares young workers making wallets with the on-set activity of an advertisement for financial services, shot in Film City, Mumbai, overlaid over seven and a half minutes of subtitles from *La Chinoise* that served as the dialogue from *Communists Like Us*. There are no images, only the subtitles, which are presented both in English and French. Véronique is in red and Francis is in blue; the dialogue is positioned not at the bottom of the screen, but slightly higher than the standard height for subtitles, going backwards and forwards at the same time as two conversations in Hindi can be heard. After the assemblage plays itself out, *Otolith II* will screen, and the conversations will replay themselves, embedded within the film, inviting the viewer to reconnect the audio with its accompanying images. *Communists Like Us* will nonetheless retain a phantasmic presence, something to be found out.

Communists Like Us was first performed in 2006 at Utrecht's Huis aan de Werf, with Sagar and Eshun seated centre-stage, slides of the delegation photographs projected onto two screens above them with the English subtitles culled from *La Chinoise*, while a third screen revealed details from the pages of *Chinese Propaganda Posters* edited by Anchee Min, Duo Duo and Stefan R. Landsberger (Taschen, 2003), slowly turned by both performers. Eleven minutes into the performance, the duo would pause Paragraph 2 of the CD of *The Great Learning* by the Scratch Orchestra, lift *Chinese Propaganda Posters* off the lid of the record player, remove the lid and place the needle on the vinyl record of Morricone's soundtrack for *Il gatto a nove code*, all of which was visible on the overhead screen. After the performance, the duo would explain the constituent elements of the performance for the audience. This act of explication diminished with successive presentations. By its last enactment, in 2010, at Homeworks V in Beirut, no contextual framework was offered after the performance. Evolving from a performance accompanied by a painstaking elucidation to a deliberately decontextualized event, the delay between the encounter with the work and its retroactive assimilation forced an appreciation of the inherent disjunctions contained within the work, while aggravating continual yearnings for the archeological certitudes of archival specificity.

When it was installed as a double channel projection at MACBA, Barcelona, in 2011, confronting the 'wrong' asymmetries of the work was inescapable. The projected photographs were an assortment of portrait and landscape formats, fronts and backs. Consequentially, a slippage between the recto and verso of these photographs was observed in the movement between the back of each front and the front of each back. There were no visual implications of neatness or inherited design sensibilities that prioritized the ordered, mirrored and harmonious. A graphic balance would have invoked an equilibrium, which in actuality was wholly falsifying. It would smooth over the important asymmetries of the pictured communist friendships. Symmetry would function as a kind of aspiration towards a rhetoric of harmony. The awkward irregularities insisted upon by the double projection attested more faithfully to the complexities of what was being attempted by these affiliations. An error lay in the assumption that a double projection denoted a symmetrical projection; this assumption equated the simultaneity of projection with the symmetry of format; equally there was no reason to infer that successive images should mirror the form of the preceding or subsequent image.

The explicative mode of address used to situate earlier performances could have implied a kind of expertise, a possession of the materials used by the performers, which is in fact not the case. The gradual subtraction of the pedagogical impulse of the work as it travelled from 2006 to 2010 suggests that Sagar and Eshun too are attempting to return to the position of being viewers amongst viewers, constantly configuring and building relations to the images, sounds and text in differing ways. Sagar's retrieval of this family archive does not suggest a predisposed condition to appreciate them. There is no pre-existing relation, by way of the biographical or genealogical, that dispels the enigma of the project; there still is a gap, an emphatic distance that separates the Otolith Group from the images. So instead of closing the discontinuity in the name of biography or history or geography or aesthetics, conditions are generated and iterated in which this distance can be dramatized and shared with viewers.

Every modality of *Communists Like Us* is invested in raising an awareness of the labour involved in constructing such links. It is an aesthetic of revision, an aesthetic of discrepancy in which the artifice, the postproduction, the synthetic nature of growing connections rather than continuities, is never hidden. As such, it advances a mindfulness towards how archives are received, utilized and appraised in *Communists Like Us*. There is the temptation to interpret the work literally, from the front, as a series of delegation archives. To perceive the work as an archive of Indian feminist delegations and Soviet delegations is only a first reading; on the reverse of most of the photographs are myriad notations and stamps. They name the photographers intermittently; details about the agencies that actually produced the photographs remain scant. These marks become missing signs that could lead to another kind of investigation and understanding of the archive. To inquire into the actual federations themselves, into the organizations that constituted the Federation of Indian Women, the women in these photographs, and correspondingly to investigate the realities of the agencies whose photographers were commissioned to wander behind these women, constitutes a double, if not triple, history of Soviet agency photography, Chinese agency photography and Indian feminist federations; these trajectories of inquiry have, in all probability, not yet been situated in conversation with each other; such a task remains to be carried out.

Approaching the work from the perspective of a possible future undertaking […] serves a broader project of revisiting and rethinking the disremembered histories of India and the international. Doing critical work in this area, Devika Singh points to 'the Cold War context' as an often 'neglected dimension of the history of art in India' that acts to place the 'history of group exhibitions of Indian artists at the centre of international cultural policies'.[2] In light of this observation, *Communists Like Us* can be understood as a unique and seminal work in its exposition of the visual cultures of India's bygone commitments to the Non-Aligned Movement, socialist collectivism, and postcolonial and feminist agendas. Its triumphs lie in the way it makes a space for and summons the memories of pivotal yet overlooked figures such as the communist M.N. Roy. Crucially, it exceeds India and its particular histories. In its reimagining and redreaming of socialist aspirations, it should be coupled with affective works searching out the remnants of the peoples and places of past ideologies, movements and politics, such as Robert Kramer's *Milestones* (1975), Wang Bing's *Fengming: A Chinese Memoir* (2007), Apichatpong Weerasethakul's *Primitive Project* (2009), and Phil Collins' *Marxism Today* (2010).

1   See T.J. Demos, 'Sabotaging he Future: The Essay Films of the Otolith Group', in The Otolith Group and Will Holder, eds, *A Long Time Between Suns* (Berlin and New York: Sternberg Press, 2009) 57.

2   [footnote 6 in source] Devika Singh, 'Contextualiser l'art contemporain indien: une histoire des expositions de groupe de 1968 à nos jours', in *Paris-Delhi-Bombay* (Paris: Centre Pompidou, 2011) 90; and 'Writing the History of Indian Art from a Global Perspective: The 1960s–70s', paper presented at Musee d'Art Contemporain, Lyon, 19 May 2011.

Shanay Jhaveri, extracts from 'Shared Senses of Inquietude: *Communists Like Us*' (2011), in *The Otolith Group: Thoughtform* (Milan: Mousse Publishing, 2011) 54–70.

I could capture

WONDER WOMAN

and disassemble the 'her'
from a seamless flow...
Before the onset of
home video recorders,
that type of imagery
was only coming
one way at you

Dara Birnbaum, 'Cable TV's Failed Utopian Vision', 2002

EMBODIMENT

Marcia Tucker
PheNAUMANology//1970

[...] Bruce Nauman carefully constructs his pieces to create a specific physical situation. Although he is no longer interested in ways of making art nor in the 'interpretation' of a made object, he feels it is still important that a piece be neither over- nor under-refined. In this way focus can be directed to the experience and our response to it, rather than to the object itself. [...] He has utilized progressively intricate 'extensions' of the human body, the same extensions that man has evolved in order to live, to communicate and to adapt to his environment. They range from writing which extends language and the telephone which extends the voice, to complicated mechanisms like the computer, allowing memory and calculation far beyond the capacity of any human source. [...]

Our bodies are necessary to the experience of any phenomenon. It is characteristic of Nauman's work that he has always used his own body and its activities as both subject and object of his pieces. He has made casts from it (*From Hand to Mouth, Neon Templates of the Left Half of My Body Taken at Ten-Inch Intervals*, etc.) and manipulated it (in earlier performances using his body in relation to a T-bar or neon tube, as well as in holograms). He has made video tapes of his own activities (*Bouncing Balls in the Studio*) and films of parts of his body being acted upon; *Bouncing Balls* and *Black Balls* are slow-motion films of Nauman's testicles moving and being painted black. He has questioned, in various pieces, his behaviour as an artist and his attitudes toward himself as such. He has contorted his body and face to the limits of physical action as well as representation. By making audiotapes of himself clapping, breathing, whispering and playing the violin, he has also explored a range of noises made and perceived by his own body.

This concern with physical self is not simple artistic egocentrism, but use of the body to transform intimate subjectivity into objective demonstration. Man is the perceiver and the perceived, he acts and is acted upon, he is the sensor and the sensed. His behaviour constitutes a dialectical interchange with the world he occupies. Merleau-Ponty, in *The Structure of Behaviour*, stresses that man is, in fact, his body, despite the essential ambiguity of its being at once lived from the inside and observed from the outside. Nauman has used himself in this way as a prototypical subject for the pieces. These works are meant, essentially, to be encountered privately by one person at a time. Where earlier the artist was the subject and object of recorded situations, now it is the spectator who becomes both the actor and observer of his own activity.

Ordinarily we are unable to experience both things simultaneously – at least, not without a mirror and an extraordinary degree of self-consciousness. At the Nicholas Wilder Gallery in Los Angeles Nauman set up a series of wallboard panels running parallel along the length of the gallery. Cameras and videotape monitors were set up in such a way that a person walking the length of one corridor and turning into the next would see himself on a monitor only as he turned the corner. The space set up is longer and narrower than most spaces we find or make for ourselves. The corridors therefore occupy an ambiguous and uncomfortable realm between too much space, which creates feelings of isolation and disorientation, and too little space, which causes cramping and tension. In this case, both are experienced simultaneously. At the same time, the image on the screen further disorients the viewer because he sees himself at a distance, from below and behind. He is prevented from being intimate with himself because he is not even allowed to meet his image head-on. Ordinary experience of the space between man and his image is the frontal 12 to 18 inch space we normally allow when looking into a mirror.

Like most of his work, this situation does not deal with a concept of space, but with the sensation of it. Its effect goes beyond that of a purely physiological reaction to become a highly charged emotional experience. It is similar in feeling to the impact of seeing but not immediately recognizing yourself in the reflective surface of a store window as you pass it.

Other pieces deal more specifically with the physiological and emotional effects of time. Even according to the most stringent scientific analyses of time, pure (or absolute) time cannot be measured, because every lapse of time must be connected with some process in order to be perceived. We define time, therefore, according to our experience of it. When looking at a static object, the phenomenon of time, of *how* we perceive something, can be separated from what we are looking at, which does not change. In Nauman's slow-motion films, he uses uncut footage, taken from an unchanging vantage point. In them, a repeated simple change occurs in the object itself, while the way we perceive it does not change. *Bouncing in the Corner, Bouncing Balls* and similar films confound our experience of time by a transference of the functions usually assigned to objects and phenomena. [...]

Marcia Tucker, extracts from 'PheNAUMANology', *Artforum*, no. 9 (December 1970) 38–40; reprinted in *Bruce Nauman*, ed. Christine van Assche (London: Hayward Gallery, 1998) 82–4.

Andrew Grossman
Finger Envy//2012

[...] Much in VALIE EXPORT's work evinces themes familiar from sixties-era Actionism: the body as a sensory canvas; the body as, alternately, mediator, inhibitor, and conduit of reality; the artist's ritual self-mutilations as an inverted projection of an insufficiently mutilated reality or objectivity; and the supplanting of traditionally framed or commodified art with living performances in ambiguously bounded public spheres. Yet the primitive (rather than neoprimitive) actions of Otto Muehl, inspired by Wilhelm Reich at his most irrational, have at their core a metaphysical rhetoric. When Muehl makes love to the goose he slays in the action *O Sensibility* (1970), he imagines himself engaged in primaeval trance and high spirits, enacting both a mock-pagan sacrilege and a mock eternal return, in which the object of ceremonial slaughter stands in for every ardent organism and every inconsequential death. Muehl's physiological offence, emboldened by ego and a little humour, quickly turns into a philosophy. EXPORT's feminism, on the other hand, dispenses with such metaphysical pretence – though not the humour – and instead positions the female body as an expressly political actor and antagonist, rebelling against the tepid objectifications of commercial art and the male egoisms of her contemporaries.

In her early public actions, EXPORT typically deploys her body as a feministic weapon and mobilizes her unabashed nudity as an organic assault, not as passive pornography. In the 1969 action *Action Pants: Genital Panic* (*Aktionshose: Genitalpanik*), perhaps her most discussed, simplest action, EXPORT descended in open-crotched pants upon unwitting members of a theatre and taunted them with her unmediated clitoris (an action that seems rather less shocking today). The omnidirectional assault on the audience becomes turned inward in the 1971 action *Eros/ion*, in which EXPORT rolls 'naked on a plate of glass, and then on a paper screen',[1] such that her broken skin no longer becomes a unitary, unresisting surface onto which consumerist Austria can impose its homogenizing projections. The 'cuts and tears in the projection surface' (that is, her skin) then taint the paper screen on which she subsequently rolls, revealing traces of the bleeding humanity that projected surfaces – by extension, the cinema – conspire to absorb, bury, or camouflage. *Eros/ion*'s punning link between the erotic and the decadent becomes a sardonic inversion of the Wagnerian *Liebestod*: rather than harbouring a romantic tragedy in which love passively surrenders to death, EXPORT's antagonistic body undergoes a bloody rebirth, her mutilation inhibiting the screen's attempt to dominate the body and recentring a commodified humanity whose 'eros' struggles to leave its sanguine imprint.

While self-inflicted wounds stain the limp paper screen of *Eros/ion*, EXPORT's *Tapp- und Tastkino* (*Tap and Touch Cinema*, 1968) more playfully addresses the ways in which frames – aesthetic and ideological – ensconce and reflect the particularly feminine body. Of this, one of her earliest public provocations, EXPORT says, 'I wore a cardboard box with openings over my naked breasts. The visitors stuck their hands in there. I said: 'This box is the movie theatre ... my body is the screen.'[2] As the autonomous body now frames the theatre, rather than the theatre enveloping anonymous spectators, EXPORT undoes the traditional bounds in which erotics and catharses allegedly transpire. The work of transformation is no longer given over to the master *auteur*; actor and audience become co-conspirators in an organic cinema – what EXPORT called 'expanded cinema' – whose ephemeral frames know neither fixity nor exclusion. 'There was a time when the artist mobilized all his defects to produce a work which concealed himself', says E.M. Cioran, in a characteristically bitter denunciation of the Western tradition of the novel.[3] For the Actionist, the antiquarian age of the novel is justly dead, its authorial concealments an artefact of aristocratic propriety. If cinema is legitimately to persist, it must reinscribe personhood, communality, the erotics of touch, and every other sign of human sensation an increasingly digitized commercial cinema schemes to neutralize.

The scarifying body politics that are part and parcel of Actionism inevitably conjure up a repetitious, even numbing art-world jargon, as the body, whether tormented or ecstatic, is invariably mapped, charted, marked, inscribed, reinscribed, excavated, engraved, regenerated, reframed, unframed, doubly or trebly framed, and so on. It is therefore refreshing to encounter the directness of EXPORT's nine-minute short film *Mann & Frau & Animal* (1970–73), a deceptively simple, three-part allegory of gender. The first section ('Man') begins with lengthy, languorous close-ups of a bath tub whose metallic knobs and snaking hoses later accrue phallic significance, even if the male body itself remains tendentiously invisible. In the second sequence ('Woman'), a female hand intervenes to activate the tub, turning the knobs to release not seminal flow but abluting water. When the shower head lets loose a thin, trickling stream, the film cuts to an unashamed, seemingly endless close-up of the filmmaker's vagina undergoing a masturbatory bathing, while the soundtrack groans with sounds of female elation. The spectacle is neither sacred nor titillating, however; the cleansing is as unassuming as EXPORT's unpreened, deglamorized body, and the spectator, witnessing a masturbation striking only in its mundanity, feels oddly cleansed as well.

With masculinity now reduced to sterile plumbing and femininity revealed without cosmetic enhancement, the third sequence ('Animal') begins. A fleeting image of a black (vaginal) triangle gives way to a new image of EXPORT's frontal orifice, first smeared with seminal glop and then sloppily with blood, the feminine groans in the second sequence's soundtrack now transformed into the shrieking, animalistic and altogether preposterous grunts of an imaginary male spectator. We then see the vagina lifeless within a photo, and then the image of a bloodstained hand, raining down upon the photographically reframed vagina. Maleness had already been exiled to the status of mere utilitarianism in the film's first sequence and reduced to libidinal, futilely voyeuristic snorting in the third. Now in the coda, the camera abandons its genital-centrism to focus on the ultimate tool, the hand, eminently capable of not only usurping the rule of the penis but transforming the sexual fixations of psychoanalysis into the outward, worldly interactions of EXPORT's 'expanded' cinema.

The bloody hand that bids adieu in *Mann & Frau & Animal* reappears more sinisterly in the digital self-mutilations of EXPORT's less humorous (and indeed more polemical) ten-minute short *... Remote ... Remote* (1973). Here, EXPORT, miming the pose of a despondent housewife, sits before a black and-white image of two impoverished children (the 'remote' children of the title?), a bowl of (mother's) milk cradled in her lap. The camera, now in long shot, reveals a box cutter in her hand, its blade readied. Preparing us for the sedulous flaying we know is to come, the film nervously crosscuts among EXPORT in medium shot, her ominous eyes, and the voiceless, frozen children. Wielding the box cutter, she begins to scrape her fingertips as soullessly as a hausfrau peels an apple or potato; the camera soon becomes more intimate, obsessing on the box cutter as EXPORT obsesses with carving her cuticles. She pauses to wash her hand in the mother's milk seen earlier, but, as in *Mann & Frau & Animal*, the gesture of cleansing yields no easy catharsis; on the contrary, the skinned, dripping fingertips only pollute the milk's pallor. The ritual resumes, slowly, methodically and above all stoically, as though her decortication were as bourgeois – and, indeed, as culturally humiliating – as cosmetic attendance to the wiles of the feminine nail. After another round of cutting, the camera moves in excruciatingly closely, fixating upon ripped cuticles that receive succour from neither a second dip in milk nor from EXPORT's own sucking lips.

As the camera focuses on the finger, something unexpected happens: we've seen the torn cuticle in such extended close-up that it accrues an uncanny appearance, and when glimpsed anew, the loose skin appears almost as a foreskin and the protruding nail as the tip of an uncircumcised penis. The masculine element that in *Mann & Frau & Animal* was a sterilely metal hose re-emerges as phallic flesh; yet the phallus is here the savagely torn remnant of a far greater, gender-neutral tool, the evolved human finger, that which separates us from the lower species and facilitates every technology and every movement beyond the narrow inheritances of nature. What is 'remote' in the film's title becomes the penis, mystified by a century of Freudianism and now revealed as a ragged sham. Our social strivings are not Freudian sublimations of phallic frustration – rather, the weeping phallus is an inferior sublimation of the technological, gender-superseding finger. This, truly, is EXPORT's feminism, suggesting that beneath the beautiful, adaptable, versatile finger is a degraded, savage totem better left to the ancients. Thus is EXPORT, for all her self-flagellation, not a psychoanalytic 'primitive' in the manner of Muehl but a modern who sees the truly creative appendage as the evolutionary finger, an appendage that must resist masochistic devolutions into bloody phallic tragedy.

Though concerned superficially with the fracturing of femininity, the unblinking, sometimes ascetic style (especially in *Mann*) of EXPORT's shorts opposes the film collaborations between Muehl and Kurt Kren, whose 'stroboscopic' style of rapid montage fractures the Actionist's singular act into quavering infinities of time-space. While Kren's anarchic montage seeks to disrupt (albeit temporarily) the monolithic masculinity of Muehl as actor, EXPORT's feminism, at least in the context of the avant-garde short, must assume the contrary position, reconstituting in lengthy, barely edited shots a female body that, in reality, has already been endlessly riven, economically, spatially and bodily. The female body's fractures become literalized in EXPORT's 17-minute *Syntagma* (1983), in which multiplying split-screens and superimpositions represent the working woman's 'divided' self, as variously seen through video monitors, mirrors and the reflecting windows of the shopping arcade the heroine – mainly viewed from the leg – relentlessly stalks. Most important in *Syntagma*, however, is its opening sequence, in which the two hands of the heroine, alternately confident and confused, push apart images of two leaders of celluloid such that she can better emerge from a cinematic centre. The liberated organism is again represented by the evolutionary hands, ones now unbloodied, literally rending the frame as the self-excavating hausfrau of … *Remote … Remote* once ripped apart herself, and undoing the mediations that have entombed her for far too long.

1   Brigitte Huck, 'VALIE EXPORT: Expanded Arts', liner note booklet, in *VALIE EXPORT: Three Experimental Short Films* (Austrian INDEX DVD release #004) 9–10.

2   Ibid.

3   E.M. Cioran, 'Beyond the Novel', *The Temptation to Exist*; trans. Richard Howard (Chicago: University of Chicago Press, 1998) 137.

Andrew Grossman, extract from 'Finger Envy: A Glimpse into the Short Films of VALIE EXPORT' (30 April 2012). (brightlightsfilm.com)

Dara Birnbaum
Cable TV's Failed Utopian Vision: In Conversation with Nicolás Guagnini//2002

Nicolás Guagnini In early video pieces, one structure repeatedly appears: camera/ body/monitor. It started as an interrogation of the self and moved more towards playing with the audience and defining social spaces, in pieces like *Wipe Cycle* (1969) by Ira Schneider and Frank Gillette, or in Dan Graham's works between 1973 and 1978. How did that development come about?

Dara Birnbaum From my own experience, I felt that early on there were two distinct developments evident. The one you first mentioned, camera/body/ monitor, is best seen in the early tapes by Bruce Nauman or Vito Acconci. They were coming out of what became known as 'body art' but also from a projection of an inner psychological state. But there was also another area of development, which was to create alternative forms to broadcast television. Here the concern was with relationships to and through the community, or a much more social 'self'. Both fields overlapped. With regard to the self and the body, many works were developed in the isolation of the artist's studio, such as Bruce Nauman's 1968 *Stamping in the Studio*, where he inverted the camera so that to the viewer he appears to be walking on the ceiling. Even though he repeatedly stamps in a rhythmic, almost primitive pattern, he is not really participating in any social or communal rite. He remains individualized in his own studio. Acconci's *Centres* (1971) has the artist pointing at his own image on the video monitor, attempting to keep his finger in the centre of the screen. He was pointing away from himself and to an outside viewer. In that work he introduces another aspect of video: using the video monitor as a mirror. The work also begins to take advantage of the self-reflexive potential of video by becoming more aware of the psychology of interpersonal relationships. Other artists, like Dan Graham, were producing works where this social awareness was evident, but they expanded this initial awareness by also providing for a way that the viewer could interact with their work, such as Graham's numerous delayed feedback/ mirror installations. *Wipe Cycle* incorporated the viewer's image into delayed feedback loops. In *Wipe Cycle*, again the importance was that the audience became participants by directly affecting the work and thus the viewer was no longer passive. Gillette and Schneider wanted to emphasize the process involved in a work. They were both members of Raindance Corporation, an alternative media collective that published *Radical Software*.

Guagnini The technical device that prompted the explosion of video art was the Sony Portapak, and the theoretical framework was coming from *Radical Software*. Feedback was one of the main topics. Among the writers for *Radical Software* was Paul Ryan, who came up with topological models for feedback, quite influential in the works of Graham. Another of Ryan's concerns was the application of those models to education. What was the relationship between education and the community concerns you mention in the early video groups?

Birnbaum What the Portapak brought in was a high level of self-awareness. In 1965 Nam June Paik bought some of the first consumer video equipment on the American market. In the following years, there were so many art pieces that came out of literally 'living with the Portapak'. There was a sense of amazement towards that apparatus that, unlike film, could reveal oneself in real time, or in slightly delayed time. Many pieces were diaristic and confined to a secure or isolated environment. The ones I am thinking about deal with being within one's home space. There was not really an extension outward. Think about Nauman's 'anti-gravitational' pieces, like walking on the ceiling; all these types of work were structured in an interiorized safeness. That is different from the methodology that Ryan applied. He seemed much more interested in pedagogical models and collective usages for video. Alternative television was trying to reach out, to permeate society. In addition, artists were discussing the portability of video, for example when Allan Sekula made reference to a group of workmen on strike – how they utilized a Portapak powered with car batteries, which allowed them to both record spokesmen's statements as well as to play them back again directly to the strikers who were assembled. That was more like agitprop. The most interesting experiment with education that I remember was done by students of the Irvine school system in California who were able to be tutored through open cable channels which linked different schools in the area. David Ross presented this at the Long Beach Museum of Art. It seemed natural to those students, who were then in high school, or grade school, to utilize the video systems like a telephone. […]

Guagnini […] Your early works *Pop-Pop Video: Kojak/Wang* (1980) and *Technology/ Transformation: Wonder Woman* (1978/79) brought upon you the appellation 'the pirateer of images'. You certainly pioneered the act of making copyright and distribution instrumental issues for the meaning and understanding of the work. How did you come up with the idea of cannibalizing television?

Birnbaum What happened to me when I started working with video in the late 1970s was that I saw two distinctive roots to video art. One was television, which was being ignored, and the other was an extension of other artforms like body art and performance art. There was a proliferation of writing, especially coming from Europe, such as *Screen* magazine, which looked at America though the language of film – countless articles and studies on Hitchcock and *Film Noir*, but nothing on television. And I felt that it was absolutely necessary to look into the most common language, and that was TV.

Guagnini Wasn't Warhol a model already for that kind of search?

Birnbaum I was deeply affected by his work, perhaps mostly by his use of serial reproduction and what it seemed to reflect about mass production and the neutralization of signification that comes with it. When I was in Berkeley everybody was carrying a little red book – Mao's red book – and when Warhol produced his portrait series of Mao in a very aestheticized way, it was a shock – a good shock. The type of imagery and portrayal that was present in mass media affected many people around me at the time, like Jack Goldstein. These artists began to utilize aspects of the mass media's forms and modes of production. However, they were translating these images into other mediums, like Warhol. For me, from 1977 on, it was important not to translate this vocabulary into other mediums. By turning the medium of video/television on itself, the real dislocation took place by altering the iconography of television through changing its original structure and context. At a time when there were no VCRs available, I could capture Wonder Woman and disassemble the 'her' from a seamless flow that provided viewers with the Pop glorification of her red-white-and-blue democratic iconography. Before the onset of home video recorders, that type of imagery was only coming one way at you. TV was strictly controlled. The idea was to grab these images that were part of my own landscape and not to translate their meaning by making objects, but to let it exist on tape or film. I wanted to place the work anywhere that it could permeate back into the culture. It was a way of talking back to the media.

Guagnini Was that idea of permeating the monolith of mainstream culture, rather than neglecting or resisting it altogether, related to artists using cable?

Birnbaum Yes. *Technology/Transformation: Wonder Woman* was put on cable TV opposite the 'real' *Wonder Woman* on network TV. So if you were channel-flipping, hopefully you could come across both versions – which I felt could destabilize the meaning and intention of the original network programme. The attempt to change context was very naive but very honest. We were trying to change things by permeating different territories. By 1979, Jenny Holzer and

Barbara Kruger were also working in that direction in their artwork, but they were not invading the territory of television. I thought that this was the most important territory to invade. In the early eighties, many artists working directly with video thought of cable TV as different from broadcast TV. It seemed less regulated and controlled, even though it was already developing into a big business. Its structure was different in relation to commercial advertising and how that affected programming. The regulations that demanded that colour camera studios for production be made available to the public, for local programming in the public interest, gave many people a basis for production without great expense. The other regulations that guaranteed programming time to such local and artistic production allowed a window for more experimental work and ideas. It was possible, for a moment, to live out a more Benjaminian ideal of becoming producers, rather than spectators. In addition, there was a terrible need for product – software – to temporarily fill the gap presented by these new spaces of transmission. Even though it was also a big business, at that moment it represented a potential space for art practice. Now it is much more difficult to tell cable and broadcast TV apart.

Guagnini Looking at it from today, do you think that works like *Technology/ Transformation: Wonder Woman* still have a critical potential? Or do they get absorbed in the logic of commodifying nostalgia?

Birnbaum Well, it marks a moment in time when I felt I had to capture that idealized vision of a woman, with a perfect body, wrapped in the American flag. This was a horrendous image for me. In the year that I made the videotape, Wonder Woman bathing suits were the hottest-selling items for girls. I couldn't go and join Lanesville's community television. I felt that I had to take on the task more directly. If Bush has his own 'axis of evil', then that image was mine. The reason why his recent quote of the 'axis of evil' is so immediately assimilated is because it has the potential to resonate in all of us, as based upon a historical past. For me 'the evil' was and is the industry – an industry that men dominated, where they could form a commodified, corporate image of women.

Guagnini The feminist politics of the piece are very much alive, but this still does not answer the previous question. Both Kojak and Wonder Woman are today a cherished part of many people's childhoods. The context of the piece evolved within the logic of the industry.

Birnbaum A lot of the artists working in the late 1970s and early 1980s had a need for immediacy. I distinctly remember when someone smashed the storefront window of Franklin Furnace, angered by the aphorisms that Jenny Holzer had posted there. At that time her work was produced on cheaply photocopied, standard 8 1/2 by 11-inch paper. That type of immediate reaction, that immediate provocation, was exactly what I was looking for. The urge for immediacy had a lot to do with being the first generation to grow up entirely on television. It was an apparatus that was introduced in our houses like a gun. It was a weapon, and that is how I wanted to use it. I think those pieces hold up as markers of a certain moment in time, not unlike the original series that they come from. They give you a window into a specific preoccupation we had with mass media – and our feelings of being controlled by it. We wanted to respond by breaking down the 'control' of the industry and to allow for a space for altering views and representations. It was important to talk back and resist the passivity of reception, both in relation to the mass media's dominant forms and its ideologies. Of course, like everything else in this society, years later the tapes I made came down themselves to be saleable objects, and that is the way they are distributed now. I did not escape my own copyright.

Dara Birnbaum and Nicolás Guagnini, extracts from 'Cable TV's Failed Utopian Vision: An Interview with Dara Birnbaum', *Cabinet*, no. 9 (Winter 2002–3) 35–8.

Yvonne Rainer
In Conversation with Mitchell Rosenbaum//1988

Mitchell Rosenbaum Some people have a problem with the flatness of the acting in your films. For example, the narrators of your films are quite monotone and without affect. However, this can be seen as a very natural kind of acting, because it's the way people talk in ordinary conversation, or as non-acting.

Yvonne Rainer Well, that's a style I have cultivated.

Rosenbaum Of course, some people take that for inexperienced or bad acting.

Rainer I have trouble with so-called 'bad acting' where nothing in the film tells you that the artifice of the illusion is supposed to be revealed. That's where bad acting interferes. In *Journeys from Berlin/1971* (1980), where the text is very non-naturalistic and it's obviously a surreal kind of recitation, then Annette

Michelson's non-naturalistic performance is totally appropriate. The setting tells you this is not a realistic film so you are going for something other than totally credible, believable acting. Still, a character is built. That is the amazing thing about film. Just the framing and focus on a person speaking creates this bond with the spectator, and it's that illusion that builds the character. I mean, it's a two-way thing: the audience, in identifying, is already constructing the character. It's a much more immediate process than the stage, which always requires the suspension of disbelief. The suspension of disbelief is there *a priori* in the cinema, with the dark room. It's this very atavistic kind of relationship to an image, which some theorists liken to the earliest experience of the infant at the mother's breast, watching shadows on the surface of the mother's skin. […]

Rosenbaum In [*The Man Who Envied Women* (1985)], you seem to have confronted the problem facing political filmmakers: that is, you don't so much preach to the converted as scold them.

Rainer Harangue them.

Rosenbaum Nobody on the Left gets away without a jab. In particular, artists – a group you're certainly counted among – take quite a beating.

Rainer Artists are seen as being in very compromised positions in the urban setting, and yet, in other areas, are trying to work in a progressive way. Which I think is the true state of things in New York-based artists today. I had to approach this problem from many different angles: political activism, housing and feminism.

Rosenbaum So what about feminism at this point? In this last film you seem to both praise and lampoon the current state of feminism. This is exemplified by the Jackie Raynal character – a *femme fatale* whose dialogue consists of poststructuralist feminist text.

Rainer Well, there again it's hard. You are expressing this question about what my position is on some of that material, which is very multifaceted. Nothing is resolved. I follow the debates on sexual difference and Women Against Pornography. I am personally committed to the abortion rights movement. What is expressed in *The Man Who Envied Women* is exactly what Jackie recites, this Meaghan Morris essay which points out where feminism makes these confusions between right-to-life and abortion rights. It's very complicated. I deliberately make the male character a feminist to show how a seemingly progressive position can be used for aggrandizement all over again. Just as I'm now reading about the history of the medical and scientific attitudes about women's orgasm and reproduction, how social theorists used to view women's organs as simply a version of the man's, like an inverted penis. Then when this was disputed around the turn of the century, and people like Havelock Ellis began to say women were biologically different, this recognition was used simply to say that women's place was in the home and to reproduce. So theoretical debates are all very well but can be used in repressive ways. Maybe that's reactionary. I've been called a combat-liberal by Maoists at some point, but I thought it was pertinent to these current debates which rage on in this academic realm and are very pertinent to problems of representation. Who in the film is uttering these kinds of doubts? It is a woman who is presented as a *femme fatale*. It seemed very appropriate that these debates, whatever they are, be keyed to these notions of imaging and sexual difference, or projections of male castration-fear, to open up one of the most pervasive and pernicious examples of male stereotyping in cinema history. [...]

Yvonne Rainer and Mitchell Rosenbaum, extracts from interview, *Persistence of Vision*, no. 6 (1988); reprinted in *The Films of Yvonne Rainer* (Bloomington: Indiana University Press, 1989) 37–40.

Johan Pijnappel
Partitions of Memory//2006

[...] It was certainly not for lucrative reasons or for recognition in the West that Indian video art started up at the turn of the century. Scarcely that. It was on 'Black Friday', 12 March 1993 that another bead on the string of violence hit the city of Bombay with a tremor that could be compared with 9/11 in New York. A series of explosions cut a swathe through Bombay, spreading terror and destruction. Starting at the landmark Bombay Stock Exchange, the blasts extended all the way across to Centaur Hotel in Juhu. The toll: 257 killed or missing, 713 injured, and a city in shambles. It was in this period of despair that especially women artists in this city, such as Nalina Malani and Navjot Altaf, broke out of the frame to expand their testimony to a wider public with installations and theatre performances that included the medium of video. These artists were not aesthetic rebels. It happened in the period in which India opened up to the international market and where one felt the loss of the crumbling Nehruvian dream upon which their grand narrative was constructed.

In contrast to the cynical postmodern feeling in the West, these artists felt there was still a value and purpose to offering hope. However, this was not a reawakening of political awareness as we have seen in the art of the West in the 1990s. Nor was there a feeling of doubt about the value of a critique on the society based on individual experience. For these artists the speed of change in their society made this 'time based' art the best equipment for making meaningful works. For them video was a medium par excellence, appreciated and understood by the masses and as such appropriate for political engagement and consciousness-raising. The NGOs in India had used it effectively in this capacity. Video was still seen as a possible catalyst for change. [...]

These artists are all from the fast developing mega-cities and they address issues regarding the position of the woman in the so-called modern metropolis that still continues to be a subordinate one. Tradition and orthodoxy are still strongly prevalent. These female artists are permanently confronted with the male gaze inscribed in everyday society and as well in the illusionary world of Bollywood that is fundamentally a traditional male one. In-depth work has been done on this by scholars such as Kumkum Sangari, Urvashi Butalia, and others. If only the world could be seen through the eyes of a woman as a cross-gender form of awareness, but in this social context it is said that India not only has a caste system but that being a woman is a caste in itself.

In the animation video *Memory: Record: Erase* (1996) Nalina Malani touches upon the desperation of unemployed women who, if they fail to fit into their own job categories, have to manage to earn a wage by subterfuge. The story is about a woman who impersonates a *chowkidar* (nightwatchman). Her disguise is discovered and she is caught by the police. In the introduction text: 'she continued to fight for her job while still in custody, needless to say without success. It was given to one of the countless thousands waiting for any vacancy, one whose legs chanced to have between them the organ recorded on his birth certificate. Thereafter she probably sank without trace into the ranks of that army of millions who are forced to earn their modest bread by selling themselves, wholly, in part, or to one another and who are, in short, lost, and if we are to believe the prevailing view, lost forever.' In the animation the artist unfolds the feelings of this woman – unsavoury experiences that one would want to erase from one's memory.

In *Stinging Kiss* (2000), Tejal Shah creates another cross-gender situation, where she turns the male Bollywood stereotype completely on its/his head. In her version 'when the hero doesn't come on time to save our heroine, the dacoit [bandit] arrives ...' In this kidnapping story it is Shah herself who acts as the male dacoit and Anuj Vaidya, the male co-producer of this video, plays the coy kidnapped girlfriend, in beard and sari. The hero is none other than the one and only Amitabh Bachchan, montaged from found footage of a Bollywood movie.

This cross-gender narrative turns rather risqué when the decoy forces a blowjob from Miss Pretty. This is probably the first time in an Indian 'movie', with its tradition of severe censorship, that a woman rapes a man. This provocative work was made in Chicago, and screening it in India has not been easy. One remembers only too well the incidents caused by the local right wing, which works like an ongoing cultural inquisition. In 1998 the famous Eros cinema was attacked as it was screening Deepa Mehta's 1966 movie *Fire*. [...]

Johan Pijnappel, extracts from 'Indian Video Art: Partitions of Memory', in *Cinema of Prayoga: Indian Experimental Film and Video 1913–2006*, ed. Brad Butler and Karen Mirza (London: no.w.here, 2006) 27–9.

Rob Mullender
The Haptic Optic//2010

Where is the part of us that understands outline drawing? Is it in the eye? In the visual nerves? Or is it in vision at all?[1]

What is the best way to record an object? This seemingly simple question probably represents a whole landscape of enquiry, rather than an avenue, so let me rephrase it. How can we come to know an object – its weight, surfaces, balance, temperatures, and so on – and is the capture of this information in the best interests of the object itself? (Or to put it another way, do we see it in its best light?) We know what the normal responses to these questions are: the camera holds dominion, then text description or drawing, and perhaps for some things, sound recording bringing up the rear; it depends on what our attention is turned to. So to focus further, I have been confronting the question: what is the best way to record a recording object, say, a 16mm camera? I'll readily admit that I find the paraphernalia of 'old style' filmmaking seductive, perhaps because they're tangible mechanisms – as opposed to digital ones – of a sort that are often beautifully engineered, usually from durable materials. Not only is this apparent in many hand-held film cameras, but even more so in the equipment needed for the printing, copying and developing of film. The imperatives of clarity within the recorded moving image – consistent speed, registration, stability, the absence of aberrations –serve to filter down through engineering strategies, to coalesce in mechanisms designed to direct exactly the correct amount of light at exactly the right time, in just the right place, on a moving piece of plastic substrate carrying photographic emulsion. Keyways and transport mechanisms, sprocket wheels, focus-pulls and locking levers all (hopefully) work just so … And then there's the interfaces and the surfaces: knurled knobs, striated lens rings, butterfly catches, covers, switches, pitted or reticulated thermoplastic coatings, rubber grips.

It occurred to me that maybe it was possible to allow something to write itself using itself; to offer all of its surfaces to the record using a kind of exploratory imprint. To this end, and a few others outlined below, I began using rubbing, or *frottage*. This trace of an activity is clearly neither a photograph, despite its autographic (self-writing) flavour, nor a drawing in the strictest sense, since the action of the mark-making device is coerced by the physicality of the object in a directly causal manner; rather it oscillates between these categories as well as others. It might equally be proposed that a rubbing is the record of a performative exploration of an object, in an operation of touch outside of the intended parameters, which are negotiated between the designers and users of these things.

In taking a rubbing of a complex object, I cover up the object that I am to record, for it to re-reveal itself as I work. In this sense the object makes itself anew but as a multi-sensory percept; it expands as a site of knowledge. This sensory land-grab is never complete since the barrier-medium (the membrane which is also a gulf) is inelastic, and must be endlessly manipulated and re-sited to perform its purpose in a saccadic exploration of cracks and crevasses.[2] Since the membrane is forced into this time-based relationship with a surface, each rubbing represents a set of micro-superimpositions, or even what might be described as a gestural palimpsest; the recursive quest for an impossibly complete knowledge of an object. In this way, multiple readings of time can be derived from its surface – either as a journey around the original object (or a set of decisions made by myself; a constant realignment of the recording surface to the imprinting one), or as a battered-looking and unreliable net.[3] As for the object itself – we might think of it as being refigured as a recording head, or imprinting mechanism, which works in two intercommunicating ways. Firstly, it is made active at one particular point on its surface; this point is the locus of desire for all elements present in the tripartite exchange; the hand of the artist, the recording medium, or membrane upon which he or she acts, and the original imprinting object. Secondly, if considered as a set of problems, to be negotiated using the imprinting medium as negotiating tool, the original object's surface complexity requires a continuously shifting train of actions on the part of the recordist in manipulating this 'skin'. These encode themselves as creases and cracks, particular and peculiar to the material; a skin to be scarred by its own folding …

Thin paper tears on sharp things, and in the list of features mentioned earlier, sharp things inevitably stand out. In searching for a membrane that would not tear in the way that paper did, I tried a few different materials, before hitting upon a particularly fine ivory-coloured nylon. This presented its own problems, in so far as it would simply slide around, or off the thing I was going to work on (in this case, a Bell & Howell contact printer). To counteract this, I tried coating a sample in shellac to stiffen it, and give the surface more friction. I began to see that this new translucent composite would take marks without the need for a second medium such as graphite, thereby embedding this act of frottage structurally within the material, instead of simply adding a pigment to a substrate. It feels to me now that the condition of making a cast has somehow been bestowed upon an unsuspectingly two-dimensional process, however tenuous or fugitive this condition may be. This latent dimensionality, encoded as process, permeates further through each crease and fold produced by the manipulation, folding and re-siting of the material. Also, I like the smell of shellac.

The idea of producing rubbings in part arose from a wish to articulate, however inexactly, the concept of the simulacra or eidolon, that peculiar but evocative vision of vision proposed by the Atomists (and latterly the Epicureans) as the means by which images transported themselves via the eye into the mind. The idea, put simply, is that objects throw off atom-thin skins in all directions, which flit lightning fast to the eye, all the while retaining their original form. [...]

[W]hat happens when we listen to light? This is not quite so peculiar a proposition as it first seems, since light predates both magnetic and mechanical media as a means to recording sound's traces, and has remained a constant, if somewhat marginalized presence in sound production ever since. But this essential nature, of a sound generated from a modulated luminous source – often by way of the scanning of graphical information – seems to be at once counter-intuitive (light is for seeing with), revelatory (that's what the flickering of my TV sounds like) and even mystical (there are voices coming out of that light bulb). How might the spectres of Lucretius' fecund imagination make light of this mixing of registers?

It turns out that this is a particularly filmic question, not least because the optical soundtrack of twentieth-century cinema was the premier site for exploration and experimentation into this process.[4] But equally, the clear implication of the Atomist model of vision – that reality is discontinuous, interstitial, indeed cinematic – resonates strongly with the peculiar condition of turning light into sound – particularly environmental light sources, both natural and man-made. The perceptual parameters that enable the artificial moving image to work (that is to say, our visual flicker threshold) are also what prevent us from noticing, for example, the 100Hz flashing of mains lighting, or the even higher tones of modern digital lighting systems, which use pulse width modulation to produce dimming effects. This flashing may not be visible, but by virtue of the ear's ability to resolve detail in the time domain – to hear faster than we see – it can be made audible. A photovoltaic cell pointed at a light source will generate a voltage in proportion to the amount of light it 'sees', and this can be treated as an audio signal for listening to on headphones. Ambulance lights crackle, LED display boards shriek and hiss; Piccadilly Circus is bathed in an electromagnetic storm. The glittering of the sun upon the sea, perhaps predictably, sounds pretty much like the sea, and the invisible flickering produced by a mosquito's wings as it passes through a beam of sunlight, even though it may be several metres distant, makes a sound very similar to that which you might hear as it hovered next to your ear as you lay in bed. even desirable – just a photovoltaic cell, a field recorder and headphones.

Listening to light is inherently synthetic as an experience – a category error, so to speak – and so it seems entirely fitting that a fantastical, or synthetic model of the world be brought to bear upon it. Moreover, it seems to me that an object's surface – the point of departure of its sensory output – is an interesting notional point of synthesis, through which different sense modalities may act upon one another. The world of flitting eidola sits neatly, if a little awkwardly, between our understanding of how sound and light actually do work; a wavefront theory of light, or perhaps light as a longitudinal compression wave. These successive images are certainly reminiscent of the compression and rarefaction at work during the transport of sonic energy. Perhaps I am overburdening these relatively demure objects, but I sense that these rubbings might be considered as analogues of the 'photophonic' exchange. They are in some way 'ghosts of ghosts' – eidolic shadows, or their fragments, which have been coerced into conforming to the materiality of nylon and shellac. And how strange that something as ostensibly mundane as sitting down and making a rubbing can contain all these possibilities.

1   J.M Kennedy and N. Fox, 'Pictures to See and Pictures to Touch', in O. Perkins and B. Leondar, eds,
     The Arts and Cognition (Baltimore: Johns Hopkins University Press, 1977) 118.

2   'Saccadic' refers to the way that the eye jumps from one point to another in twitching motions,
     or saccades.

3   In the mathematical sense – for example the simplest net of a cube is a cruciform shape made of
     six squares.

4   [footnote 7 in source] As soon as the optical film soundtrack appeared, artists, filmmakers,
     acousticians, and to a lesser extent, musicians began photographing, drawing or scratching
     onto it. [...]

Rob Mullender, extracts from 'The Haptic Object', *Sequence*, no. 1 (London: no.w.here, 2010) 4–7.

Jeremy Bailey
Performance for the Computer//2006

I often imagine a sequence of events, occurring sometime after the introduction of the portable video camera. A performer frustrated with the inability to judge one's own performance turns to video as a solution to his or her problem of self-documentation. The artist eventually learns to see a recorded performance differently, realizing that the grainy black-and-white image does little justice to the original act. Soon the artist realizes that the video image is a performance context in its own right, and invents what we know as the first Performance for the Camera, a magical place where the artist is able simultaneously to view and react to his/her artwork as it is created. Video art as we first knew it was born and flourished in this new self-reflective environment. Indeed, though other branches of video art have developed and prospered, performance for the camera has remained a consistent presence. I propose that in recent years Performance for the Camera has evolved into what I term Performance for the Computer. This development represents a large shift in thinking which challenges the efficacy and thoroughness of our prior understanding. In this paper I will seek to define the differences and unique properties of this new context.

Performance for the Camera is defined best in Rosalind Krauss's 'Video: The Aesthetics of Narcissism' (1976). According to Krauss, video centres the body between two machines that are the opening and closing of a parenthesis. The first of these is the camera and the second is the monitor that re-projects the performer's image with the immediacy of a mirror.[1] This immediacy makes the performer acutely aware that in seeing him/herself (recorded), 'it' is already over and he/she is enacting history. Time collapses visibly and editing happens during the making of the work in response to the camera's view.[2] Krauss is careful in her analysis to distinguish between reflective and reflexive states; where reflexivity creates the 'other' separate from Self, reflectivity implies the vanquishing of separateness. Where modernist reflexivity locates the object, the reflective feedback of performance for the camera brackets that same object out. Herein, the work becomes about the self, it enacts a condition of narcissism. This is typical in works from the period. Canadian artist Colin Campbell's *Sackville I'm Yours* (1972), wherein Campbell interviews himself on his own pathetic art celebrity status in small town Sackville, New Brunswick, hilariously and preemptively pokes fun at Krauss's formal arrangement.

Krauss outlines two tangential (yet contradictory) ways out of this psychological squeeze, the first are videos 'that exploit the medium in order to criticize it from within', and the second are videos 'that represent a physical assault on the video mechanism in order to break out of its psychological hold'.[3]

Perhaps in Krauss's ideal case the video device is behaving more as a tool, whereas in its exceptional form it appears to be acting more like a machine. Karl Marx distinguishes between the two as follows: that in the case of a tool, man is the motive power, while the motive power of a machine is something different from man.[4] In the former, the video instrument behaves as an extension of the human body, while in the latter the video instrument imposes its rhythm on man. Krauss specifically asserts that the video mirror acts against the 'other', therefore more like a tool, and yet rejects that the video mirror acts as an extension of the body and emphasizes psychological internalization. Despite Krauss's assertion, many artists at the time were experimenting in ways that forced the rhythm of the machine upon themselves. Joan Jonas' *Vertical Roll* serves as a good example. In her 1972 video, the machine is literally transposed upon her body in the form of a forced vertical roll, the result of desynchronizing the frequency of the tape. Peter Campus, the Vasulkas, Bruce Nauman and many others also made tapes that closely acknowledged the integral presence of the machine to their performance. Herein the mechanics of the video mirror are more than just an 'appurtenance', as Krauss dismissively asserts. Even then and especially now, the machine is everything.

The introduction of the computer was not the first, but has become the most important change to the reality of video since the 1970s. Slavoj Zizek proposes that the computer is a third, new stage in Marx's scheme of development. On one hand, he says, it is closer to a tool, in that it does not work automatically, and on the other hand, it is more independently active than a machine, since it works as a partner in a dialogue in which it questions itself.[5] In this scenario we begin to act toward computers, despite our better judgement, as if they are living things. The excitement a person has in creating a desired effect with his or her computer is similar to a hunter who has conquered a beast. Not surprisingly this perceived complexity has led us to refer to our own minds, nay our whole world, as a network of computers. Artists like Cory Arcangel have even begun releasing artworks along with how-to guides in the spirit of computer programmers' open source projects.

What happens to Krauss's narcissism in the presence of this new machine culture? Many artists, myself included, perform inside and alongside of computers. Herein any image that can be recorded can also be adapted in any multitude of imagined ways. Digital video is one piece of data among many. Where the mechanical analogue nature of the 1970s video circuit may still have appeared simple enough to be completely dominated by the artist, the new digital hybrid space appears to expand even as one tries to encapsulate it. Zizek suggests that the computer is an inconsistent machine, which, caught in a snare of self-reference, can never be totalized. Within this context we conceive of a world in which anything is possible; where we can arrange the rules arbitrarily. One may then assume that in a world where the computer is a social metaphor our psychology has undergone this same displacement.

I believe that the result has been a transposition of Krauss's narcissists' ego, from an internalized Self, to a Computer (Other). Indeed, the computer's vastness has resulted in a sometimes-misguided re-modernization of the artist's spirit. Artists like David Rockeby, who first began performing in the 1980s alongside computers and documenting the results on video, have invested the entirety of their egos into the egos of their machine creations. Indeed, software development cycles have taken the place of aesthetic movements. It is no longer cubism that leads to abstract expressionism, but rather the release of a more powerful computer or a new software program that dictates aesthetic development. Many artists have chosen simply to use machines to mimic aesthetic forms from the past.

> Our typical response to a disturbing new environment is to re-create the old environment instead of heeding the new opportunities of the new environment. Failure to notice the new opportunities is also failure to understand the new powers. (McLuhan)

Without a hint of irony one can find machine-made examples of John Cage's experiments with chance operations in composition, Duchamp's removal of the hand of the artist in his readymades, the rule-based work of Sol LeWitt or the system art of Bridget Riley. These are artworks that prioritize the process of codifying and executing the artwork through mechanical and logical procedures to make art less about the human and more about the machine. Today's artworks are the opposite, machines making art in some effort to appear, as Zizek suggests, more like humans. What does a machine-made painting in the style of Jackson Pollock suggest of our society, other than that we believe more in our machines than we do in ourselves?

Much of what we are seeing can be examined as a continuation of what Roland Barthes described in his essay 'Death of the Author'. For Barthes, the 'death of the Author' signified the 'birth of the Reader'. Indeed, as I have shown, the human author has been diminished significantly, present only in his or her evolving transition towards software programmer. Herein, the Reader is most obviously privileged and pleasantly obliged to interface with a growing number of interactive artworks. The role of the author is simply to plug in parameters for a reader to transfigure into any number of self-pleasing results. Any author who positions him or herself within these confines sees the ego diminished to the level of a 'user', to use a computer term. In effect the Author becomes a Reader, pathetically trying to peck out an understanding of his or her own fantastic creation. Here the only narcissist is the unwaveringly confident Machine. [...]

As Krauss asserts, the alternative to video art's narcissistic trappings is to 'exploit the medium in order to criticize it from within'. This is my artistic strategy for dealing with the contextual framework outlined in the above passages. I am a privileged white male video performance artist who uses computers to make art. I am the Dead Author, the flaccid male ego with a curved spine that pecks at his keyboard trying to understand the rhythm of the machine and the naive Reader who still believes in meaning. Of all of these trappings I am critical, for I am the solipsistic bastard child of a digital mirror. Ultimately the only way to overcome this tragedy is to laugh about it, and so I ask the viewer to laugh at me laughing at myself. Indeed, what greater way to subvert the machine than to exploit the subtlety of one of our most human and illogical traits, the ability to laugh at ourselves.

1   Rosalind Krauss, 'Video: The Aesthetics of Narcissism', *October*, no. 1 (Spring 1976) 181.

2   Peggy Gale and Lisa Steele, eds, 'Video Has Captured Our Imagination', *Video re/View* (Toronto; Art Metropole/VTape, 1996) 117.

3   Rosalind Krauss, op. cit., 186.

4   Karl Marx, *Capital* (1867) (New York: International Publishers, 2003) 352.

5   Slavoj Zizek, 'From Virtual Reality to the Virtualization of Reality', in *Electronic Culture: Technology and Visual Representation*, ed. Tim Druckrey (New York: Aperture, 1996) 291.

Jeremy Bailey, extract from 'Performance for the Computer' (April 2006) (www.jeremybailey.net)

Stanya Kahn
In Conversation with Grant Wahlquist//2010

Grant Wahlquist Do you see yourself as portraying or constructing a 'character' in your work, or do you understand what you're doing differently?

Stanya Kahn What people generally refer to as 'character' in my work I see more as a 'state of being', a metaphorical state, a representation or manifestation of issues, feelings, ideas, signs. In a literary sense, the word *character* is not so far off. In literature I think the symbolic has more play in terms of where it can reside, and 'character' is one of those places. A person in a novel can commonly be read as a vessel for all kinds of meaning. In theatre, performance and moving pictures, it's much more difficult to maintain the conceptual construction in the foreground of the viewers' minds because a moving, talking person in time and space always appears to be just that. A person. Not a set of ideas.

I include things that might foil the seamlessness or believability of character, I try to blur the line between myself and character, and I do a lot with sound and editing to try and break the spell of full cinematic or theatrical fiction. In some respects, 'character' in my work is an amplification of certain aspects of self, without ever really being about me per se.

The 'character' in *It's Cool, I'm Good* (2010) is as much a Deleuzian desiring machine as it is a physicalized version of my own interiority doubled with a broader concern about trauma. We are a country traumatized by corrupted and nearly non-existent promises of democracy and by our perpetration of trauma all over the world. Meanwhile, this 'character' is based loosely on an ex-boyfriend of mine whom I nursed through a gruesome death from AIDS. And then from this base springs a 'character' that is also a sign for the undisciplined (in the Foucauldian sense) citizen body exhibiting a kind of exuberance (albeit an ornery one) in the face of near destruction at the hands of the state. It is also an unruly fall guy for antidepressants – lonely and trying to go with the flow, hoping to get laid and find somewhere to plug in an excess of creative energy temporarily repressed by the effort it takes to make one's way in the world. And I'm all those guys.

Wahlquist In *It's Cool, I'm Good*, the protagonist changes the explanation of his injuries from scene to scene. This is a bit of a lowbrow reference, but in the most recent incarnation of the Batman franchise, the Joker does the same thing. How are the shifting explanations related to the concerns of the piece as a whole?

Kahn Funny you should mention the Joker. He never occurred to me as model for this protagonist, but I like that you offer the reference. He's a perfect parallel. The original Joker character was born out of trauma. He starts out as a chemical engineer who quits his job to become a standup comedian(!) but bombs at the comedy club. Then his wife and unborn child die in an accident. Then he falls into a vat of chemicals and is severely disfigured. The shock of his lousy luck makes him insane. I like to think it's the depth of his trauma that leads him to say, 'My past? I always remember it differently. If I'm going to have a past, I prefer it to be multiple-choice! Hahahahaha ...'

In *It's Cool, I'm Good*, I'm trying to deflect the viewers' search for the 'truth'. In part because trauma reorganizes truth, but mainly because with this work I'm more interested in how we *cope* with what has happened and less concerned with how or even why it happened. I want to confound the question of what happened so I can steer away from sentimentality and keep us in the visceral experience of surviving. I'm often suspicious of too much story. I want to stay in the speed of the body. In this case certain mechanisms take over in what might be an effort to stay alive: incessant joking, flirting, ruminating, recounting facts, exploring, driving, walking, being. This is exuberance; this is something like a cross between will to live and will to power.

Changing the story over and over is also a way to portray the emotional armouring that can come with trauma (hence the title). Which is funny because I recently tried therapy for the first real time. I said to the therapist, 'Look, I can tell you all kinds of horror stories, but the telling doesn't seem to change my problems.' I start in with the stories, and by the end of the session she's recommended a therapy called eye movement desensitization and reprocessing, a neurological approach developed during the first Gulf War to help veterans cope with PTSD. As the brain remembers the bad feelings, it starts digging up past traumas. And as the old source traumas emerge – the big, bad ones – eye movements neurologically transmit the memories to a different part of the brain so that you can recall what happened but you don't have to keep reliving the experience with the same level of fear and distress. Which is cool. I like my past to be multiple-choice too.

Another aspect of the post-trauma stage that interests me relates directly back to the issue of the Joker. His personal trauma shaped his social relationship to the world. It birthed a supervillain. I'm interested in the social aspect of what happens to us, how our personal experiences shape our responses to the world. We develop all kinds of neuroses, addictions, fears, phobias, antisocial behaviours. And doesn't that in turn impact upon what we do in the world, what kinds of projects we make, what kinds of organizations we form, how we steer our politics, how we fashion entire infrastructures? And if we take Foucault's position that madness is historically constituted, it makes so much sense that the Joker in the 1990s doesn't suffer from 'insanity' but from 'supersanity'. The protagonist in *It's Cool, I'm Good* is, in that respect, 'superinjured', able to persevere beyond what's reasonable exactly because there is no other choice. A sort of punk-rock PTSD supervillain ex-comedian but with no special powers and no enemies.

Wahlquist Speaking of cinema, how do you understand or position your own work relative to the role that narrative plays in traditional filmmaking?

Kahn I come to narrative via reading and writing, more so than watching, and yet it's the medium of film/video that allows me to privilege the experiential over the narrative arc. I do build story, particularly in my most recent work, braiding together strands for the viewer to follow. I want to provide some of the pleasure of story, but the pieces unpack more along psycho-emotional lines. The script is always punctuated by improvisation. Audio and visual information bear a significant load of meaning as well. Landscapes might function as *double entendre*. In *It's Cool, I'm Good*, the desert is really the desert, replete with issues of water politics and sprawl, for example. But it is also a psychological space, in a Beckettian sense. Music and sound are integral as 'texts' in their own right.

In live performance, you control almost everything with your body, timing especially and the rapport with the audience. I shoot and edit with the physical memory of what that's like. My live shows were driven in part by the desire to create an Artuadian catharsis and also maintain a Brechtian distance that would allow the audience to have autonomous, active consciousness. As a video maker, these concerns persist. The technology replaces the body, and I have to figure out how to make it 'sweat'. Vaudeville, stand-up, poetry, sermons, speeches, music, all inform the way I'm trying to loosen up narrative structure. I'm getting permission from histories of experimental filmmaking, video art, and documentary at the same time that I'm stealing from Hollywood. Recently, I'm revisiting Marx Brothers' films and noticing a renegade disregard for convention. The films are surreal, almost druggy, because they were born on stage and then folded into film. Time, along with the fourth wall, is interrupted regularly for wordless physical skits, non sequitur speeches, songs, dances, and the magical moment when Groucho looks right at you and winks.

Wahlquist Do you consider humour to be a theme or more of a strategy? Is it the idea of humour that you're trying to get at, almost as a subject matter? Or is humour a device that you're deploying to get at something else, a formal strategy?

Kahn Right. Both. Especially in this most recent work, I'm trying to do both at the same time. Like a tattoo of a butt on a butt (as Beavis says to Butthead). Humour has also been a central device in all the work I've made. I discovered its power in performance, specifically as a way to connect with the people. To establish camaraderie and give permission to laugh (because inevitably at some point the work also gets heavy). Once you're in, humour is freed up to start working on more complex levels as a strategy: upending expectations, disrupting norms, subverting meaning, interrupting hierarchy, critiquing the status quo. At its best, humour plays with lines of agreement while simultaneously relying on agreements: we laugh because we recognize. Freud says part of what gives us pleasure in humour is the experience of recognition.

In this recent work, I'm looking specifically at how humour functions as a survival mechanism and how it forms a language of its own, specifically in response to trauma. Here joking and humour are used likewise to mirror the way meaning is similarly upset by trauma. Trauma ruptures what we thought we knew.

Which leads me back to the earlier question about why my protagonist, like the Joker, keeps changing the story of the trauma. Kathy, the subject of my video *Kathy* (2009), says that repeating stories of traumatic events can traumatize the listener. While the Joker can use this as a sadistic tool, I find ways to sidestep the direct retelling. I want to exorcise my demons just as much as the next guy, but I don't need to drag you down with me.

Boy, this is getting really unfunny. Which is exactly what Freud says will happen if you have to explain a joke. Part of a joke's pleasure is its innate economy, the compression of meaning. Which is why I really like fast shorties like: 'What's brown and sticky? A stick.'

Stanya Kahn and Grant Wahlquist, 'Interview with Grant Wahlquist', *2010 California Biennial* (Newport Beach: Orange County Museum of Art, 2010).

Kaelen Wilson-Goldie
The Body on Stage and Screen: Rabih Mroué's
Photo-Romance//2010

The premise behind *Photo-Romance* (2009), a ninety-minute performance by Rabih Mroué and Lina Saneh, is the adaptation of a film that is never mentioned by name and only obliquely referenced onstage. Ettore Scola's *Una giornata particolare* (*A Social Day*, 1977), starring Sophia Loren and Marcello Mastroianni, takes place over the course of a single day in the spring of 1938, when Adolf Hitler pays a visit to Benito Mussolini in Rome. Loren plays Antonietta, a beautiful but long-suffering housewife, married to a card-carrying fascist and limited in her world view. Antonietta's entire family has gone to join the parades and celebrations marking the historic encounter, leaving her alone for the day. Mastroianni plays Gabriele, a radio broadcaster, recently sacked from his job and about to be deported by the authorities for harbouring not only anti-fascist but also homosexual inclinations, who happens to live in the same apartment block. The two meet when Antonietta's bird escapes its cage, flies out of the window and lands on Gabriele's ledge. They befriend one another, fight, form an unexpectedly intimate bond and feel, throughout the film, for the edges of each other's solitude.

As the background story of *Photo-Romance* goes, at some point during the conceptualization of the piece, Mroué sought out one of Scola's heirs to ask for permission to adapt the film – a gesture of courtesy more than legal compliance. To Mroué's surprise, the heir turned him down. Who knows what shape or structure the performance might have taken had Scola's heir said yes, but the refusal seems to have pushed Mroué and Saneh to peel back and reflect on their artistic practices and critical intentions. The result is a performance that sifts through the sediments of collaboration and the creative process. Constructed as a conversation about a script in progress, *Photo-Romance* questions what it means to make original work, what it means to adapt the work of others, to appropriate, alter, manipulate, craft and finesse a work into being. It also asks what it means to do so with a partner, in life as in art, in a manner that constantly needles the substance of the relationship, which itself exists in a context that invariably imposes its own ideas of what the substance of that relationship should be. That context is defined by the codes and mores of Lebanese society, by the machinations of the country's sectarian political system and by gender roles prescribed by a thin body of law, which – on matters of sex, marriage, family, inheritance and personal status – tends to revert back to the religious community to which one belongs, not as a matter of choice but by birth and paternal lineage. The piece represents the most densely layered articulation of a question that has preoccupied Mroué and Saneh's work for more than two decades: how to use the presence of the body on stage as a metaphor for the struggle to be a complex, multi-faceted individual in a sectarian state, and how to access a just, equitable and participatory experience of citizenship in a functional but deeply flawed democracy. [...]

The prop dominating the set of *Photo-Romance* is an enormous white screen that cuts the depth of the stage in half. [...] *Photo-Romance* does not so much adapt Scola's film as disembowel and reconfigure it, with each of the three characters transmitting different elements of sound and image onto the screen between them, which operates as a kind of public space, a site of contestation where opposing and competing visions may be played out. [...]

Saneh plays herself, in a manner of speaking. She steps onstage to present, explain, justify and defend the work on behalf of herself and Mroué. Mroué's character is more slippery, as he interprets both himself and his nemesis, namely, a censor tasked with advising an artist, from a position of ill-begotten authority, on what to keep and what to cut from a work she has made with her partner. In the script for *Photo-Romance*, Mroué's lines are interchangeably attributed to 'Rabih' and 'The Judge'. On several occasions, Saneh addresses Mroué and in the same breath says that, unfortunately, Mroué couldn't be there to partake in the conversation.

The doubling of Mroué's character is a nod to the process by which a theatre director in Lebanon must run his script by the censorship apparatus of the state before presenting his work to the public. Here, by inhabiting both the artist and the censor at once, Mroué directs attention to the worst consequence of that process, its internalization as self-censorship. It is worth noting that censorship is a rather arbitrary affair in Lebanon, a structurally weak and economically laissez-faire state. The laws tend to be loose and archaic, and their enforcement applied in unpredictable bursts, often for the sole purpose of scoring quick political points on the local scene. Censorship falls not under the Ministry of Culture but rather under the Ministry of the Interior, and so it is meted out haphazardly by soldiers. For artists across different disciplines, this leaves a lot of wiggle room in terms of what one can get away with, and how one can manoeuvre. But it also raises a number of prickly issues about artistic integrity and autonomy, particularly as those soldiers in the security forces often hilariously or sadly overstep their bounds in deciding what is appropriate for the public to see. […]

After some preliminary banter among the characters, *Photo-Romance* begins with Mroué asking Saneh; 'Okay, so what's the story?' She responds by stressing the need for them to go through and evaluate the work at hand. […]

Saneh explains that she is concerned about the relationship between their work and a certain film. Mroué asks for a description of their approach. A free adaptation? A source of inspiration? 'I cannot explain it this way', Saneh responds. Mroué asks for a broad outline and says, as an aside, that he has, in fact, seen the film in question, and found it very beautiful. From there, Saneh runs through the decisions she and Mroué made to distinguish their work from the film. First, they shifted the setting from Rome in 1938 to Beirut in 2007, placing their work in the context of Lebanon's increasingly tense political situation in the aftermath of the war with Israel in 2006. That war divided the country even more starkly into opposing camps – the ruling March 14 coalition and the opposition March 8 coalition – which were named after competing demonstrations that took place in downtown Beirut in the spring of 2005, on 8 March and 14 March, respectively. Instead of a meeting between Hitler and Mussolini, Mroué and Saneh imagine a reprise of the two March demonstrations, in their performance held in the same space on the same day, so that the entire population is out onto the streets at the same time, leaving the characters (played by Saneh and Mroué) alone, like Antonietta and Gabriele, for the day.

Saneh explains that in their adaptation the characters from the film have also changed. Lina is the female protagonist, a divorcee whose ex-husband, revealed to have been an abusive brute, has nonetheless taken custody of their children.

Since her marriage fell apart, Lina has returned to Lebanon from Saudi Arabia, and now lives with her mother, her brother and his family. Rabih is the male protagonist, a print journalist who lost his job for questioning the extent to which the war of 2006 was really a catastrophe. By sectarian profile, both characters are nominally aligned with the resistance and the 8 March camp. Lina's character limply follows the party line, but Rabih's character is more of an activist and political dissident, a former communist who fought in the resistance back when it was a leftist concern and was detained in Israel's notorious Khiam prison in South Lebanon. Like so many former leftists and communists in Lebanon, the character Rabih plays was politically marginalized and intellectually sidelined by the rise of Hezbollah as the entity that took charge of the resistance against Israeli incursions into Lebanese territory. He is also a somewhat enlightened figure in his understanding of how gender roles, and housework, might be more beneficially distributed.

As Saneh reads the script to Mroué (and, by extension, to the audience), she periodically cues visual material to be projected on the imposing screen. The first bit of footage is a mock documentary about the simultaneous demonstrations in Beirut. After that, she projects portions of the 'film' she and Mroué are in the process of creating. The film is in fact a stop-motion animation, which consists solely of black-and-white photographs. The conceit captures the very different strengths of Mroué and Saneh as intensely physical performers – Saneh seems to act from the core of her body and conveys meaning through grand gestures with her shoulders and hips, versus Mroué's far more microscopic shifts in facial expression – without capturing a single fluid movement. The film, of course, is silent, so Saneh, with great virtuosity, races through all of the dialogue from her seat behind the lectern. Haber adds the music to the mix, and Mroué, at Saneh's prompting, is called on to provide a few sound effects. In between the stretches of film, Mroué and Saneh discuss various aspects of it, with Mroué, in his role as the censor, occasionally declaring that bits of material must be cut lest the piece provoke sectarian strife. [...]

The significance of the setting portrayed in the mock documentary is key. Martyrs' Square, the physical and symbolic heart of Beirut, currently is little more than a long stretch of gravel, due to the fact that Solidere, the private real-estate corporation that has been managing urban renewal of Beirut's city centre since the mid 1990s, has largely ignored this patch of public space in favour of the more commercially lucrative plots that surround it. [...]

Despite the specification of the site, the blankness of Martyrs' Square, like the blankness of *Photo-Romance*'s imposing white screen, also represents a version of the public space Chantal Mouffe imagines as a site of agonistic confrontation, where an individual, 'inscribed in a multiplicity of social relations, the member of many communities, and participant in a plurality of collective forms of identification', as she wrote in *The Return of the Political* (1993), might reclaim his or her role as an active protagonist in political life.

A final component worth lingering on in *Photo-Romance* is the fanciful notion, explained to Mroué by Saneh onstage, that the camera used to produce the projected film is only capable of capturing individuals. It cannot detect communities or groups. Comparing two scenes from the beginning and the ending of the film, Saneh explains about her own character in the performance: 'And here, as you've noticed, we could still hear the family talking when she appeared in the image […] Because contrary to the first scene, where she doesn't appear, when she is still integrated in the communitarian discourse, here she alone appears. That's because she has started to feel herself an individual, distinct from her group. But this new found individualism will condemn her to solitude and anguish, you see?'

Kaelen Wilson-Goldie, [retitled] extracts from 'The Body on Stage and Screen: Collaboration and the Creative Process in Rabih Mroué's *Photo-Romance*', *Afterall*, no. 25 (Autumn/Winter 2010) 73–9.

Akram Zaatari
Scratching and Stretching Skin//2011

Every artefact has skin, even images. For more than 150 years, photographs have been rendered and delivered by silver particles bound to glass plate, gelatin film or paper. With Nicephore Niepce's invention, images became objects, artefacts that have a physical nature, a size and a weight that allow them be handled, manipulated and communicated. But while being artefacts, like every artefact they age. They get damaged. They get scratched, and may vanish. Photographs are fragile, and because an essential history of humanity in the past 150 years has been captured with photography, and because photographs as artefacts themselves present a record of the development of a practice, their preservation against all kinds of violence has become a pressing necessity, and a scholarly field.

We know that we live in a violent world. This is the reason why animals and humans look for shelter, and do their best to make home safe. We, animals and humans, were born with an agency to adapt to new risks, otherwise we wouldn't have lived and reproduced for that long. Those animals that couldn't withstand violence because of innate disability ceased to exist, and those who couldn't adapt to new forms of threats have gone extinct. Our primary protection is skin; that thin physical and elastic membrane that wraps around our bodies in various forms and colours, and protects us from a changing environment. But as threats are increasingly changing, and because humans love comfort, we upgrade and we develop all kinds of alternative and layered skins around our first skin, to protect it. We buy clothes, and wear an outside shell when it's cold and windy. We build a home, and we seek refuge in it.

We know that we live in a violent world, and we have experienced it. Violence has marked us because it is pain that we remember most. How would we not remember and therefore learn to recognize everyday pains such as a skin burn or a scratch, a wounded skin, or the pain that comes from a sick tooth or a headache? But there are many pains that we imagine without having ever experienced, like the pain of dying from a wounded body, or drowning, or while killed in a car accident or a plane crash. We have learned about dying in similar accidents, and our imagination is capable of transforming them into imagined pain that has become part of our human register. We have heard stories of violence, and we have witnessed others, and our register has expanded to include – besides what we have experienced – all that we have witnessed and have been told.

We know that we live in a violent world, and we have read it in the newspapers and have seen it on television, and more and more recently on the Internet while we sit comfortably in our safe homes. We have seen people throwing themselves from the upper floors at the World Trade Center on 9/11. We have seen the people dying while starving in Somalia. We have seen demonstrators killed while filming demonstrations. We have heard people scream through radio, cable and wire, and this has become part of our expanded imagination. We know that the media have normalized violence while telling us, showing us what has happened, and what is happening live, repetitively. And the more we see, the larger our pain register becomes.

What do we do with all of that?

In her piece *The Birthday Suit – With Scars and Defects*, made in the early days of video in 1974, Canadian video artist Lisa Steele undresses in front of the camera and shows the traces of every scar on her body, while citing the reason and date behind each one of her scars. She tells us that skin is our personal register of violence; in other terms, the violence that our body has been through. Steele's early black-and-white video is quite simple in its form. It is made with a camera fixed on a tripod, with a voice-over. It chronicles the violence in a personal history where a naked body becomes a war landscape.

Ali Cherri's work is born at the turn of digital production some 40 years after artists like Lisa Steele started using video to communicate the violence of urban centres in modern times. Ali's work engages in exploring violence, stripping it from both historical and personal accounts. His work embodies the imagination of various forms of violence without engaging in the politics or in the binary of victim/oppressor, or even engaging in the idea of justice, or human rights, often associated with the representation of violence. And his imagination involves a wide spectrum, from urban and environmental aggression to immolation as an act of self-inflicted violence.

In his work *My Pain is Real* (2010), Cherri presents us with a self-portrait video in which a computer cursor moves across the screen over the image, leaving scratches and bruises on the artist's face. At surface value, the cursor is either seen as a tool for applying make-up or as a knife that defaces the artist's face. With a second reading the cursor becomes a distancing device, the trace of a process within a digital practice, like a reminder of the skin of an image in digital times.

Between the first reading and the second is a major shift in the understanding of an artwork, once engaging in formal interpretation, and once in creative critical distance, and therefore discourse.

Akram Zaatari, 'Scratching and Stretching Skin', in gallery newspaper to coincide with 'Bad Bad Images – Ali Cherri' (Paris: Galerie Imane Farès, 2011).

Ryan Trecartin
In Conversation with Cindy Sherman//2011

Cindy Sherman How do you view your physical self in your work? Do you feel you disappear in the videos?

Ryan Trecartin I want ideas to translate from a place that isn't about the person that I am. But I can't entirely disappear, so there's always a struggle, and by-product friction and drama, which forces the physicality of character concepts to mutate, more so than a successful total dissolve would. It's important to me that the work invent new or alternate meanings in the context of something familiar, rather than merely demonstrate something already known.

It would be amazing if we lived in a post-information world where we could truly transcend form and habit. If we did, I would be exploring different ideas. Where we are today, even people who are excellent at mimicry have to deal with the limitations of the forms their body can assume and the behaviours they don as vehicles for transformation. I'm excited for a future when something like 'gait' is still perceptible underneath character, but rather than as form in action, it's present as something like reconstituted perspective as form.

In a similar manner, it's important to me that the traditional director-actor hierarchy disappear into the work. In the movies to date, I tend to play characters who orchestrate 'curatorial' personalities for themselves: they have editorial skills that lead them to make selections, pairings and contexts for others. I think I have been drawn to this by the dynamic of performing and directing at the same time, while also concentrating on maintaining enough openness in the shoot for other performers to have a degree of agency over their scripted lines and their own linguistic mannerisms. I want everyone to have authority in their relationship to being directed, which often makes my characters straddle a blurry line between being directed and directing.

Sherman Do people assume that your videos are some weird form of self-portraiture? (This is a comment I get all the time and I can't stand.)

Trecartin I think I haven't gotten very much of this because people approach movies and photos in such different ways. Also, artists like you have established the photographed body as a medium, and the idea that working with one's own body in this way does not automatically imply self-portrait or even self-reference. What I have to deal with more is people assuming that the movies are improvised parties. I spend a ton of the time scripting the work on many levels, and the process is choreographed accordingly. Everyone involved works their asses off! The improvisational moments are always contained within their own specific part of the script or intentions of a scene. I also find that people often read, reductively, the people I work with as a posse or collective, or that we have a [Warholian] Factory-style relationship, which is very different from the way we actually collaborate. In reality, those kinds of models can end up being uncollaborative because someone or something ends up overemphasized, and individual contributions fade from the record. The way Lizzie Fitch and I work with collaborators has grown out of a network culture perspective that sees authorship as a fluid space and collaboration as an inherent, connective reality. A collaboration doesn't necessarily need its own label, unless its purpose is to announce an autonomous concept. [...]

Ryan Trecartin and Cindy Sherman, extract from 'Cindy Sherman Interviews Ryan Trecartin', in *Ryan Trecartin: Any Ever* (New York: Elizabeth Dee/Skira Rizzoli, 2011) 143–5.

Luther Price
In Conversation with Aaron Cutler and Mariana Shellard//2012

What does the matter of film look like? A clean image transformed by nature; dust and stains that have never been washed off. Pieces cut and glued to other pieces, sculpting each other. Film can be seen as a cocoon that holds a life inside it; when its physical essence is manipulated, burned, buried, painted, and sliced, the cocoon is cut open to reveal a caterpillar and a butterfly posing together with the carcass and gathering ants and flies. The American artist Luther Price disfigures film to reveal the beauty of the process of putrefaction.

Price has been doing this for over 25 years, most recently in the form of handmade 35-millimeter glass slides. In these, he makes the matter of film into its content, exposing what is actually present in it and on it, rather than what is represented through it. Minute, infinite braids and strands appear calligraphically within a coil of hair framed by translucent film. Dead ants curl up inside holes cut into filmstrips that have been chemically dyed brilliant shades of pink, purple, red, yellow, and blue. [...]

Price began working with Super-8 film stock in the mid-1980s, combining found footage with original material to create films such as Sodom *(1989), a collage of gay male sex scenes accompanied by Gregorian chants. In the early 1990s he began mixing film projections with live performances, casting himself as figures ranging from a crank-calling foul-mouthed clown to a maggot to a bloody-faced Karen Carpenter. Personal tragedy led Price to abandon performance by the end of the decade in favour of films built around manipulating childhood family photographs. He moved from these into working exclusively with found footage, which he has done prolifically ever since.*

This conversation with Price was held over e-mail. We found his written voice to be a natural continuation of the way that he expresses himself in his film, visual, and performance art, and have preserved his style accordingly.

What would you like to say about your Views from the Avant-Garde show, 'A Luther Price Bestiary'?

I'm very excited........I will be screening new.......handmade slides.......*Utopia* (2012, 35mm)........and an archive of images from past films.........made from the tiny leftover scraps.............the splicer left behind...............I'm excited that we will be including static film work.............This is where my head has been this year......I'm editing handmade slides to send to New York last minute........ but I'm glad this is all coming together..........I have not completed a film since

January..........I have many films on my shelves waiting.........half-complete chapters...................old dusty films...................just waiting...................and new work....too...............about...............car crashes...tampons...crystal meth..........heroin................Jesus Christ...............the end of the world.................But I've put all my time into making slides...............and everything else is collecting dust....................I've spent the last few months making static films..................I love where they go..............They take on another chance that I like and find ways for me to see better...............I really only just try to find a better way to see and work that out...............I feel that with slide work I've accomplished ....a sight................and vision...... that I have not in film..........I would like to show what I've done this year with my handmade slides....................To me...it's sculpture and film..............but also shows how much I want to molest film.............

How did you begin working with glass slides, and how have your methods changed over time?

I'm much more a 3-D....guy......I like the tactile elements................of things and objects.........and even memory and thought........have a certain weight...... The library of our minds holds everything........and so much of it is jogged into all of us..............I know what a camel is........and I know what it looks like and where it comes from.......I know that it retains its own water..............and smells really bad....................but I've never seen a camel.............But I've seen a camel toe...In my mind...I know about a camel........This is something that interests me.............the fact that we have this huge world archive....... within all of us...............and in a way...............a vocabulary................ through which we all know what everything is................We copy .... translate.............and try to provoke......There is a layer of things in life............ that we may never unveil................but through time we unravel........and find a way to talk about it...............

You also work with found footage. How do you find it?

Back in the late 1980s when porn switched from film to video..........all the porn bookstores were selling packs of three Super-8 films for $10........Then they ended up in dumpsters..........So I did a lot of dumpster hopping..........and I ended up with a series of fleshy Super-8 films, including *Red Rooster* (1986, Super-8)...and *Sodom* (1989, Super-8).....But from the 1980s to 2002.........I also shot a lot of film..........and made very autobiographical work........or performance-related.........Like *Clown* (1990–95, colour sound Super-8)........or

A (1990–95)....A failed attempt to make a 70-minute.....black and white and colour narrative............about a suicidal......washed-up movie starlet wannabe.........I played 'Edie'.........I was in and out of it for five long years and was so happy for that to come to an end.........Then in 1996, three members of my family got cancer....so I made films about that..........I'm glad I did, but it took a lot out of me.............I hated working.......It only made me sad........I would be editing film and break down crying.......I've always worked with found footage.........but I think it was when I realized that I no longer wanted to be so autobiographical...that I switched completely to found footage.......Still talking about many of the same issues but in a way that wasn't as close........removed enough so that I wouldn't feel that pain that was eating me up..........But yes... I've had films come in the mail and then put them aside to look at a year or more later.........and find that they were postcards to my life..........predictions........of what was to come..........Many people know I think in repetition.....so friends will send me multiple prints.......or find reels of film at thrift stores.........Just recently.........I found a batch of over a dozen Super-8 porn films in the trash up the street from my house..........Medical footage also always finds its way to me somehow........And they all work their way into this non-real reality.........

How do you work with footage once you've acquired it?

I live and work at home, in a very small beach house on the ocean in Revere, Massachusetts, right outside of Boston......I have a small studio......I keep it very organized.............The shelves are filled with films that have been pre-dissected.........and edited into chapters......categories.......Right now.....I've got the *Sorry* chapters..............all set and ready to deal with........My process with *Sorry* was to............find these repetitive loops through multiple prints and edit together chapters that would become their own vignettes..............going by the myths and stories in them all........but finding ways to say a little bit more...... ..I've included flies and maggots in one chapter to perhaps talk a bit about who and what is the parasite.............and the idea of godliness is next to cleanliness... ....I'm not trying to make fun of anything ....It's an old story .....told over and over and over again...........I'm just telling it one more time....... So.........there will be a chapter on..........the blind woman......walking the cross..........the Last Supper..........on the cross.........after the cross........ Then....there is the *Biscuits* series.......again, made with multiple prints.............. there are as many as six more films to make from that series............The thing is, for the past few years, I've spent most of my thoughts on rotting films buried in my garden.....After they get to a certain point.........I dig them up or pull them from a salt water bath or spray them down with concoctions.....and then let them bake and dry and rot in the sun...........................Mostly now........I'm using salt and forms of bleach...........A lot of this footage consists of outtakes......... but also very controlled cut works...........I like to recycle film........so many of my outtakes.......end up in the garden or chemically manipulated......in some way.........And of course......the optical soundtrack is affected by this transformation as well.................For the past several months, I've been making handmade slides..........I've made several bodies of work this year.........like Utopia......mostly looking for human content........facial expressions..........We know that something is very wrong...............and we are living it.........and can we fix it?.....................Perhaps not, but the slides provide an attempt to at least ask a question......I'm liking making the slides as well.............I think I will make better films in the long run from setting myself aside......and thinking about the static frame...........that also moves through a projector.........at a different time rate..........I'm feeling how much I can explore even more......the tactile aspects.......of film.......and focus on single frames.............These are things that I've done before in my work.......but I'm really loving this marriage of static still composition.....with a different formal time-based projection........... from 16mm or Super-8...........I'm also more than ever loving colour............. and to explore that within one frame is rewarding.......I've been working on the Inkblot films.......for a few years............and feel I've established a relationship with the movement of paint and colour..........but with the static.......handmade slides.......I feel they transcend........and really begin to talk about the three-dimensional.......the object....These are all things I want to bring back to my filmmaking......... […]

Luther Price, Aaron Cutler and Mariana Shellard, extracts from 'The Hand Made Luther Price', Idiom (October 2012). (idiommag.com)

T.J. Demos
The Unfinished Revolution: Oreet Ashery's *Party for Freedom*//2013

In 'Geert Wilders Triptych', track 8 of Oreet Ashery's hour-long video *Party for Freedom/An Audiovisual Album* (2013), a man is shown chasing a woman around the grass, grunting 'Geert' as they go. Both are naked and on all fours. Tracking his female prey in this bizarre tale of sexual experimentation and political theatre – 'Geert' references Dutch rightwing politician Geert Wilders – the man kicks like a donkey, and eventually succeeds in grabbing her leg and bringing her down face-first on the ground, as a dog looks on and appears miffed by the curious display. Reminiscent of the scene of the nude chase in *The Idiots*, Lars von Trier's 1998 comedy-drama film in which characters attempt to get in touch with their inner-idiot in a related critical acting-out of European libertarianism-become-libertinage, Ashery's ribald allegory of humans-become-animals offers a subversive mimicry of Wilders' extreme-right Partij voor de Vrijheid (Party for Freedom). As such, her moving-image work, constituting ten interconnected tracks, reveals what Fredric Jameson would call the 'political unconscious' of rightwing political discourse, exposing its underlying 'problematics of ideology, of the unconscious and of desire, of representation, of history, and of cultural production.'[1] [...]

One key reference for this cycle of works, and which is particularly significant for Ashery's *Party for Freedom* video, is Vladimir Mayakovsky's 1918/1921 play *Mystery-Bouffe*, which relays the story of the Clean and the Unclean, updated by Ashery, as per the Russian playwright's wishes, to the political context of the moment. In her creative appropriation, the play is made to respond to the current-day struggle between European neo-conservativism and the perceived threat of the influx of Islam, contextualized by the populist demagoguery of racist nationalism, and the recent murders of outspoken politico Pim Fortuyn and filmmaker Theo Van Gogh, events definitional to Holland in the years following 9/11 and the politicized rhetoric around terrorism, western values, and the clash of civilizations. The video also explores connections between the current-day defence of freedom and its relation to earlier twentieth-century movements around nudism and sexual emancipation. It does so by drawing together a diverse range of references, recalling the history of counter-cultural naturalist movements, select moments in body art (such as that of the Viennese Actionists, who worked through the trauma of World War II via controversial, staged rituals of bodily punishment), and visceral musical forms like punk, introduced in the video by those parts of the soundtrack written and performed by the all-girl band Woolf. In each case, aesthetic forms – such as DIY video, avant-garde nude performance, naturalist photography, and hardcore music – are shown to be highly unstable politically, all overdetermined sites of paradoxical values. [...]

Rather than rely on direct footage of the likes of Fortuyn, Wilders and Van Gogh, Ashery's video introduces their intertwined political positions via coded playful allegories and performative displays of psycho-sexual drama and physical game playing. These translate into revelations of the deep-seated elements of rightwing ideology that at once celebrates individual liberties in the realm of sexuality (being gay, displaying the naked body, engaging in unconventional sexual practices), and expresses a racist resentment of immigrants, with their alleged attempts to 'take over the house' and ostensibly install their own theocratic culture based on Islamic Sharia law. The resulting paradox of freedom and repression is dramatized throughout Ashery's video, where 'freedom' is shown to be a relational and deeply conflictual practice, according to which the freedom of some is inextricably tied to the unfreedom of others. The point that Ashery develops is clarified by political theorist Wendy Brown: 'freedom is neither a philosophical absolute nor a tangible entity but a relational and contextual practice that takes shape in opposition to whatever is locally and ideologically conceived as unfreedom.'[2]

In Ashery's video, this tension unfolds in relation to the body, approximating what Van der Veer terms the 'contradictory politics of desire' as it pertains to Dutch rightwing cultural and political discourse.[3] The site of boundaries and portals between inside and outside, the body is selectively opened up and controlled, transgressed sexually and violated politically, in Ashery's work. In various sections of the video, figures are seen, for instance, playing naked games in groups in the green space behind the twelfth-century country church in Suffolk that serves as the set for much of the piece. They dramatize a hippie, psychedelic, out-of-doors love-in, undergo a nude séance in order to attempt to communicate with Van Gogh's and Fortuyn's spirits with the aid of a Ouija board, assume softcore sexual positions in twos and threes, and adopt postures and movements that suggest animalistic transformations of the human body. These scenes of animality, primitive ritual, group sex, childlike games, and insane theatrics are at once desublimatory of conventional relations to the body, transgressive of heteronormative and couple-dominated sexuality, and sacrilegious of religion-based ethics.

The 'Piano Rim' sequence of track 6 is the most avant-garde and sexually explicit, showing a young man standing while playing the piano as he tongues the ass of an androgynous figure positioned on hands and knees before him, while a young woman sits nonchalantly occupied with her laptop on the piano in the background. Boundaries between human and animal, self and other, public and private, normative and unconventional sexuality, are here violated in this act of freedom.

Meanwhile, a corresponding and opposite desire for the annihilation of the body of the Other – approximating the phantom-object of rightwing resentment regarding the non-western Islamic immigrant – transpires in scenes such as the fourth vignette, 'Untitled (Fantasy).' The passage shows a group of bloodied Arabs, one wearing a traditional keffiyeh headdress, others with religious skullcaps, all lying dead on a public bench outdoors. As if victims of neo-fascist violence, they are objectified in a state of complete domination, a scene resonant with the anti-immigrant brutality that has taken hold in European countries from Holland to Greece, France to Italy, in recent years. A few moments later, the actors emerge from their lifeless slumber and wash off the fake blood, revealing themselves to be white European-looking actors dressed in costume, thereby exposing the constructed basis of the fantasy. In this regard, Ashery's engagement with migration and politically-attuned performance recalls the artist's past work, for instance, *Portrait Sketch* (2006) for which she inhabited stereotypes of Jewish and Islamic identities and had herself drawn by street-based portrait artists in Delhi. Similarly, her concern for immigration and displacement continues her past investigations into the politics of citizenship and border regimes in her native Middle-Eastern context, as in *A Gathering* (2006) for which she held a banquet in London for Palestinians prevented from returning home by Israeli restrictions; and *Welcome Home / Memorial Service* (2006) a collaborative performance project for which three Palestinian voices recited the names of 369 Palestinian villages that were destroyed during the war around 1948 when Israel was created.

As in these works, and especially in the related projects of *Naked as a Jaybird* and *Monkey Bum Factory*, it is the body that is shown to be one of bare life: a site where sexual depoliticization and political exclusion collide, exposing an oscillating paradox of freedom and unfreedom, the one built on the other.[4] The contradictory politics of desire ascribed to the Party for Freedom exists in the sense that one type of freedom (individualist, liberal, sexual) excludes other kinds of freedoms (those of migration, multiculturalism, religious freedom), yet each appears constituted by the exclusion of its other. As a result, sexual freedom, tolerance of difference and democratic principles are revealed to inspire an opposing state of control, flipping into intolerance, repression and illiberal governance. […]

While Ashery's critical mimicry clearly attacks the Party of Freedom, it is not simply, in my view, a deconstructive dramatization of the underlying psychology that drives rightwing ideology. Ultimately, by inhabiting past forms of avant-garde transgression and emancipatory politics, the project returns to sexual liberation and multiculturalism as unfinished revolutions, which await an eventual reckoning, if not ultimate resolution. Its transgressive elements – particularly its sexual experimentation and gender-questioning playfulness – might yet be re-radicalized, the video suggests by re-animating these forms, which points toward the embrace of a post-heteronormative, pro-polymorphous perversity. As such, the project identifies the progressive elements of a potential state of pluralist living-together, albeit in a non-programmatic way, although it provides no answer to the thorny question of what a reconciliation between the freedoms of sexual liberation and religion would mean or look like, or even if the artist would support such a reconciliation.

A further key is the project's grassroots distribution form, according to which institutions, businesses, and groups of a minimum of ten people are invited to host *Party for Freedom*'s live performance event, *Party for Hire*, which includes nude displays and screenings of the video. [...]

The performance exerts a seductive invitation to the audience to join in and get naked themselves, even while the video reveals the overdetermination of the body as a contradictory and unstable site of freedom – both as a white, heteronormative, and youthful privilege (exemplified in Ashery's typological determination of the actors' body-types and identities to correspond to a select range of appearances), and coded within radically divergent ideological formations, including emancipatory libertarianism, counter-cultural subversiveness, fascist purity, neo-nationalist xenophobia, and murderous hate speech. The viewer, then, comes to inhabit the affective site that rotates between desire and disgust, attraction and repulsion, as s/he witnesses the spectacle whereby the illusion of nude abandon reveals how the body is situated within relations of power, and where freedom itself crumbles as an innocent pleasure or essentialized category. Sexuality is thereby denaturalized, becomes radically unstable, and as a result, viewers experience a state of estrangement from their own body, and that of others, which precipitates a powerful questioning – at once critically conceptual and viscerally affective – of sexual dynamics, nudity, and their relations to freedom claims, especially as the final track delivers the short history of the modern transformations of that discourse. [...]

1   Fredric Jameson, *The Political Unconscious: Narrative as a Socially Symbolic Act* (Ithaca: Cornell University Press, 1981), 13.

2   [footnote 3 in source] Wendy Brown, *States of Injury: Power and Freedom in Late Modernity* (Princeton University Press, 1995), 6.

3   [4] Peter Van der Veer, 'Pim Fortuyn, Theo van Gogh and the Politics of Tolerance in the Netherlands', *Public Culture*, no. 18 (2006).

4   [5] See Giorgio Agamben, *Homo Sacer: Sovereign Power and Bare Life*, trans. Daniel Heller-Roazen (Stanford, Stanford University Press, 1998).

T.J. Demos, extracts from 'The Unfinished Revolution: Oreet Ashery's *Party for Freedom*' (May 2013), in *Oreet Ashery: Party for Freedom* (London: Artangel). (www.artangel.org.uk)

Roddy Schrock
The Internet in Our Bones//2014

While airplanes of today have never been able to fly more perfectly directly, from take-off to touchdown, runways have become damaged due to wheels landing repeatedly at exactly the same spot. Micro-precision is thought to lead to a better tomorrow. Countless activities are monitored at hyper-granular levels in order to squeeze out the most potent data, which is in turn used to make machines less brutalist and more balletic and predictive. We have apps that measure every step and heartbeat; stock market trades are recorded in milliseconds. But at the end of the day, the euphemistically labelled cloud, storing so much of this information, is formed from acres of gigantic metal, glass and plastic warehouses, absorbing megatons of environmentally unsound energy to keep machines cool. The intensity of the race for immediate precision in all things is leaving scratches and scars. The seemingly seamless perfection of data-driven everything sometimes has unseen liabilities – the worn-down spots on runways are allegories for the scars being created in our collective digital psyche.

In this current transitional period, when technology begins to reside commonly in and around us, systems and frameworks of machinic perfection are overlaid onto the messy and dense tangles of people, feelings and objects that make up life. The notion of leaving bodies behind, transferring consciousness to a cybernetically-enhanced 'matrix' as naively imagined a decade ago, never came true. Rather, the inverse has occurred, we can nearly feel the internet in our bones.

There is a preponderance of the usage of the word 'disruption', as a potential means to recalibrate systems through technologically-enhanced radical efficiency, both in the marketplace and in governance. This notion carries with it an ahistoricism and unawareness of very real, large and entrenched power structures – it seems to have the political and ideological dimensions sucked out of it. Late twentieth-century notions of 'intervention' and its historical belief in high-level structural understanding are being replaced by ground-up micro-actions, working under the guise of disruption, that are assumed to result collectively in change. This move to a disruptive practice, as opposed to large-scale intervention, is still underway, and in the end may be a more effective means for quantifiable change, but the tally of what is being lost in this approach has not been tabulated; a net gain in efficient action doesn't equate to an increase in happiness.

What new definitions of machinic pleasure are being created and how many are being forgotten? How many terabytes of data are contained in a single smile? The imposition of algorithmic corrections distorts what were once uniquely human domains; an internet-of-everything mentality acts as a kind of anti-endorphine. Experiences are tempered to a point where individual eccentricity is smoothed to a statistical anomaly. I sometimes imagine airline pilots being bored as they fly the most sophisticated technology ever conceived across expansive oceans and through the most uninhabitable conditions, nearly a mile above the earth, engines functioning nearly perfectly day after day. And yet, as the glowing 'heads up' monitor display ticks off every micro-detail of change in the plane's operating system, bouncing digital hand-shakes through interstellar satellite systems back to Boeing's headquarters in Seattle, the pilot flying yawns, and maybe even nods off for a few minutes. Essentially we are witnessing the laying to rest one of humanity's most instinctual excitements – that of rocketing through the clouds – through systems of predictive mechanics and on-board algorithmic environmental taming. [...]

Roddy Schrock, extract from 'The Internet in Our Bones', text to accompany 'Slipped Gears' group exhibition, Usdan Gallery, Bennington College, Vermont, 2014. (www.rddy.im)

Jumana Manna
In Conversation with Omar Kholeif//2014

Omar Kholeif The issue of proximity is key to your work. In your video *The Umpire Whispers* (2010), for instance, you negotiate an intimate relationship with your swimming coach.

Jumana Manna In that work, I revisited massage sessions between me and my coach during my teenage years as a competitive swimmer in Jerusalem. I was interested in the borders of intimacy and the dynamics of power between coach and athlete, within this context of sport and nationalism. I have a need for physical and mental closeness to my materials and subjects. But when trying to understand events or characters within their broader context, a certain distance is also needed. This is one negotiation of proximity. I grew up as a Palestinian in Israel, making me both a member and an enemy of the state. I later lived in different cities: Oslo, Los Angeles and now Berlin. I speak their languages and experience their realities, but seem to always have one foot somewhere else. This ambiguity is something I have always lived with.

Kholeif Blessed Blessed Oblivion (2010), is part homage to Kenneth Anger, part exploration of a group of male thugs in East Jerusalem. Again, the proximity to your subjects is essential: you don't fetishize the young men but, in a sense, become embroiled in their chaos.

Manna I wanted to make a film about the unflattering men in my hometown with whom I have a great sense of empathy. I met Ahmad, the protagonist of *Blessed Blessed Oblivion*, through my hairdresser. He opened up to me, and I followed him on his nightly adventures. Even if he was performing his idea of a powerful man, we had a certain shared desire and mutual vulnerability. I didn't feel like I was exploiting his trust but that we were both exposing and negotiating our positions. This understanding allowed me to get close to, and capture, a world I wasn't otherwise a part of.

Kholeif How do you choose the subjects for your films?

Manna It's always intuitive. Usually, it's an encounter with an individual, dead or alive, who I need to get closer to. I am haunted by the past, but allergic to nostalgia. Sometimes I need to rid myself of a fear. Other times, broadly, I'm trying to understand what brought us here. I'm never satisfied by one position, so I layer things and trust that connections will be drawn, since they grow out of my experiences.

Kholeif A Sketch of Manners and The Goodness Regime (both 2013), made in collaboration with Sille Storihle, reimagine historical acts. However, it strikes me that there is something anti-monumental in how you portrayed these histories.

Manna The Goodness Regime was prompted by my concern about the way Norway brands itself as a benevolent nation through peace and conflict negotiations, and the dangers of its assumed neutrality. Our case study was the Oslo Accords, a peace treaty signed between the Palestinian Liberation Organization and Israel in 1993, as a result of a secret nine-month back-channel facilitated by Norway. We cast children in the film to play the roles of national heroes. We were being satirical, but the decision grew out of an allegory; a translation of the image of Norway as small, young and harmless. We realized that by responding critically to this ideology, and instructing the kids to perform its myths, we were perpetuating this 'regime of goodness', which sees itself as self-aware and critical. So the semi-bored enactments by the children were both a way of deflating the coherent, heroic national narrative and also a way of incriminating ourselves.

Kholeif Why is satire so important to you?

Manna I think it can be a tool of resistance that doesn't carry the same weight as activism nor the weariness of *realpolitik*. It's playful, which allows it to reach broad audiences, but it's also deadly serious. Importantly, it's not cynical. I think cynicism is one of the biggest problems of our time. Satire can be simultaneously conspicuous and empathetic.

Kholeif You work in sculpture as well as in film. How does one medium relate to the other for you?

Manna I've often thought of my sculptures as condensations, or extractions, of the narratives I explore through time in the moving image. Sculpture is a place where I can explore abstraction – where specificity is withdrawn in favour of more constant principles or truths – more precisely than in film. Film can be abstract, but I also want to tell stories with it, unrolling images and narratives. I find sculpture more apt for exploring the spirited aspect of materiality, and the physical relationship our bodies negotiate with objects, spaces and materials. I am interested in how objects are carriers or agents, just as our bodies are vessels of subjectivity.

For a recent project in Norway, for example, I made three casts of the pillars of the government building that the right-wing Christian extremist Anders Breivik bombed on the 22 July 2011. I was interested in the role of these pillars in this attack, as guards and anchors, which both protected the high-rise from collapsing, but that also served as forms into which memory and ideology were embedded. In my show earlier this year, 'Menace of Origins', at SculptureCenter, New York, I created a series of works that explore the political dimensions of material culture in Silwan, East Jerusalem. I juxtaposed archaeological forms and the relics of male thug culture in order to reflect upon how materials and goods come to fashion identities and reify performances of power in the neighbourhood.

Sculpture is elevating and emancipatory, but sometimes it's painful, too. I don't always like the labour, and it's lonelier than filmmaking. I've tried to stop doing sculpture completely, in favour of filmmaking, in the past but I have never managed it. The ideas culminate and nag at me and I have to relieve myself of them. It is a kind of exorcism. Then I can make way for the next film.

Jumana Manna and Omar Kholeif, extract from interview, *frieze*, no. 164 (June–August 2014). (www. frieze.com)

THE POOR IMAGE HAS
BEEN UPLOADED,
DOWNLOADED,
SHARED, REFORMATTED
AND RE-EDITED

IT TRANSFORMS
QUALITY INTO
ACCESSIBILITY,
EXHIBITION VALUE
INTO CULT VALUE,
FILMS INTO CLIPS,
CONTEMPLATION INTO
DISTRACTION

THE POOR IMAGE
TENDS TOWARDS
ABSTRACTION:
IT IS A VISUAL IDEA
IN ITS VERY BECOMING

Hito Steyerl, 'In Defence of the Poor Image', 2009

MATERIALIZATION

George Kuchar
In Conversation with Charles Bernstein//2009

Charles Bernstein [...] From when you and Mike [Kuchar] started in 8mm, and onward, how did you feel about each of the mediums you worked with and the differences that they allowed you?

George Kuchar Well, you know, I'm happy to jump mediums, and in fact it's kind of like the Frankenstein monster, sometimes you can make a movie ...

Bernstein The film is the Frankenstein monster and you're Dr Frankenstein?

Kuchar They can actually get a disease, they have that vinegar syndrome, and then in order to prevent that you have to have, like, a facelift. And so, you can put it on digital – you can digitize all of your pictures. I guess in the old days they used to put the movies onto paper. [...]

Bernstein Are there particular things working with 8mm versus 16mm versus video that you liked? Let's just talk about those three.

Kuchar Oh yeah, well with 8mm the image was small, my eyes were better. And so I was able to edit, even without a viewer.

Bernstein You edited direct? On the film?

Kuchar Oh yeah, for sure.

Bernstein That is tiny.

Kuchar Very tiny, and of course I wear glasses now. That may have helped – you know what I mean – my deterioration of the eyes. But anyway I used to work with that and I enjoyed it. And then you had a little chart when you bought the film and it said ... if it was bright sun you put on F16 and then hazy you put on F8 and stuff, it gave you simple instructions. So I used to like the simple way you had to make a movie. [...]

Bernstein So in films of that period, there's really only the original edited version – there's not a work print?

Kuchar No, no work print. [...]

Bernstein Now a lot of filmmakers of your generation felt a kind of regret at the loss of the projected image in 16, going to digital. You don't seem to feel that way.

Kuchar No, because you can project video now. [...]

Bernstein But there must be a number of things that you do in video that you don't do – that you couldn't do or didn't do – in 16, and vice versa.

Kuchar Yeah, you know what? When people are looking in the wrong direction you can flip them without the damn thing getting blurred. Because when you flip the film, the emulsion was on the wrong side. And also you can turn the stupid thing upside down ... the image ... and if people look particularly ugly, you can make them look uglier, and therefore when people see them in person they look better. I once did an interview myself and I looked so hideous and I saw the footage and I decided to split the image in half, and so my Adam's apple was up near my chin. It was horrible, like monster footage. But somehow it was more acceptable. [...]

George Kuchar and Charles Bernstein, extracts from 'George Kuchar with Charles Bernstein on Close Listening (2009)', in *Whitney Biennial 2012* (New York: Whitney Museum of American Art, 2012) 172–3.

Bill Viola
In Conversation with Michael Nash//1990

Bill Viola [...] When I started making videos I was caught up with the current issues of the day, structuralism being probably the most dominant. This was in the early 1970s. A lot of my work ostensibly started out by trying to prove something, much like a scientist. You start with a premise or hypothesis or an observation and you want to create an arena that acts as a symbolic representation of that aspect of the world in you. The idea of the controlled experiment, which I think a lot of early performance and conceptual art was very much taking on, that kind of pragmatic positivistic approach of the experiment that exists in a kind of rarified state outside of normal existence. But video would not let me do that, because the camera, as it was evolving, became better and more portable, and all of a sudden you could take this thing outdoors instead of working within the confines of the electronic studio. I found that you could just take a camera outside, walk down the street, bring it back, and then integrate it into this electronic domain. You would just take life as it comes, which is what happens when you take the lens cap off.

I'm moving away from that kind of empirical scientific paradigm. The stuff I did when I was still in art school and right after was literally modelled on that approach, and the influences were obvious. I was interested in the 'body artists' – Vito Acconci, Terry Fox, Dennis Oppenheim, and others – who used that device to frame experience. It was one of these rare historical moments that artists find themselves in from time to time, incorporating experience itself directly into what was being called a work of art. It was a major shift, not making something about an experience, but making something of an experience, like when Acconci blindfolded himself in 1969 or 1970 and had someone he didn't know well lead him around the pier on the Hudson River in New York, not knowing if he was going to be led to the edge or not. That's a very real experience. I found myself being influenced by that. Living within the frame is living within the experience. Art has to be part of one's daily life, or else it's not honest. [...]

Michael Nash Could you talk about the matrix in which the work operates, its relationship to the context of art, television and home videos, and how you see the future of the video medium in general in relationship to these venues?

Viola After I went through an early infatuation period with the technology, I obliterated it – literally and metaphorically – in 1973 in a piece I called *Information*. I've chosen to work with images of the real world, camera images, recorded outside on the streets or in the mountains, images that obviously are representations, and those issues now are very current. I think we were aware of them back in the early 1970s. They've now been articulated quite eloquently by people like Baudrillard. They are representations, and that leads to a whole other set of issues. Nonetheless, they have been taken for the truth, as Baudrillard mentions, they've become what they represent. One becomes what they behold. For that reason there is a kind of cultural currency with these images, as they are part and parcel of the mass media.

There was always the physical possibility for people to understand my work outside the confines of the specialized issues of the art world. That for me solved a lot of problems I was having at the time with Clement Greenberg's theories, and a lot of those approaches that seemed to be about narrowing down and limiting discourse and dialogue to a group of the initiated that finally turned me around, from the time I was in art school and detested anything I made that my mother would praise, to coming completely full circle and understanding that I had to make work that my mother could get something out of – not understand, because that is a very tricky word, but get something out of. The context changes the work, obviously, we know that not only from contemporary art theorists, but from people like Heisenberg, that the observer and the observed are this interactive system. [...]

Bill Viola and Michael Nash, extracts from 'Bill Viola. Long Beach, California, 30 June 1990', *Journal of Contemporary Art.* (www.jca-online.com)

George Barber
Scratch and After//1988

As a rule, in video art, technology is often characterized as self-evident or passed over as a 'given'. Usually this is simply because artists are too egotistical to want to share the credit with machines and, not unrelatedly, artefacts seem to be devalued once it is known 'how' they were made. 'Oh, you mean you just fiddled with button X to get that?' ...

Hopefully, from the point of view of the audience, the ideas in video art should be more interesting anyway. Video art is primarily a technological form and thus one is easily able to date and make links between the visual solutions chosen by artists in particular periods. If artists rarely used dissolves in the early 1970s, one is aware that the 'look' of their tape is not so much to do with their 'vision' but frequently, merely a byproduct of what they had access to. Specifically, in Scratch, a mid eighties genre of video art, technology played a huge part, not just in a 'making' sense but also as a delimiter of an emerging visual language. However, before elaborating the role of the edit suite in this, I would like to outline a historical context for the genre.

In the eighties, as far as the fading corpse of British avant-garde film and video art was concerned, strung out on the operating table, mouth agape, body limp, there were two blips on the screen where something stirred – the New Romantics and Scratch. The first, pioneered by John Maybury and Cerith Wyn Evans, centred on Super 8 film's image characteristics and mostly involved attitude and a novel no-holds-barred policy on narcissism. The second, Scratch, was more impersonal, throwaway even; it mostly used television companies' product, taped on the newly rentable VHS format, to be re-cut and re-presented with zap-happy glee. Neither of these oscillascope 'highs' had much political or ideological task to which 'weight' might have been attached. And, as it transpired, neither had much chance of living longer than that *certain moment* – except in the world of commercials, there to be hooked up neatly into the visual vocabulary of hip advertising directors, and 'Youth' television programmes. But like all the best eighties products, the New Romantics and Scratch *felt* good – the independent scene's equivalent of jogging and Walkman culture.

For Merleau-Ponty, a fundamental of vision is that, with open eyes, one doesn't *choose* whether to see or not. Vision is an enjoyment in itself, there are no set premises to be fulfilled, even in boredom one cannot help registering 'sights'. Ultimately, seeing has a fascination within itself. Part of the holding power uf moving images – film and video – is this flow, technology creating a meta-fascination, one like life itself. Both the New Romantics and Scratch concentrated energy at this mesmeric level, they never really offered anything that would draw one in – other than this eye contact – or go past it. They stayed on the surface. Indeed, frequently the images engendered a feverish passivity that was quite different from the more earnest expectations of what had gone on before in the independent scene. At the time, this kind of approach seemed fresh, weirdly unpretentious in some ways, enragingly so in others. Part and parcel of the eighties high points was that they ignored the independent 'establishment'. They made their own context, pitching themselves successfully at pop magazines and papers who, in typically English style, were actually sick of pop – their very *raison d'être* – and only too pleased to write about something else. Yet the rupture with the past, conceived in these terms, has been most misleading for criticism.

In fact it now seems that the New Romantics and Scratch inherited and drew in quite a logical way from the past, even if the makers never troubled themselves to find out much about it. The New Romantics explored the myriad permutations of how 'beautiful' one could make a film image – lace, snow, reflections, over- and under-exposure, wind machines, flowers etc; while Scratch, with its customary light-fingered approach, spent more time hustling the rules of how pictures go together, searching for aesthetic moments that had gone underrated and unappreciated when the stuff was first broadcast on TV. Furthermore, both movements concentrated almost exclusively on shots containing people. But in retrospect, it appears that the New Romantics especially only ever had formal concerns. In this sense, it could be claimed that these were the *same* ones as those of the previous generation of film makers, say of Peter Gidal or Nicky Hamlyn. Whereas one group searched the smallest matrices of their chairs or bathrooms, the next generation did much the same with the faces of their best friends. Plugholes in virtual silence gave way to pretty pouts, to Maria Callas.

In terms of artistic methodology and ideology, both the New Romantics and

Scratch felt very European, very French in fact – Baudrillard would perhaps be pleased but probably he'd be more so with the go-ahead entrepreneurs of television that have now perhaps inadvertently taken over the mantle of the avant-garde. They alone have realized the full power of fragmentation, the full force of modernism – just pictures from all over the world, all the time, all day, all year. And as far as any television or video goes, never mind the avant-garde or otherwise, it's all about pictures referring back to other pictures. Specifically about Scratch, he'd probably see it as the condensed version of an evening's entertainment, the collapsed version, and he would be right. Seeing things faster than they go on in real life was Scratch – the same old impatience as that shared by Fillipo Marinetti, James Dean or, more contemporarily in Britain, the country-based BMW-driving lager lout.

Nevertheless, both the New Romantics and Scratch have often been seen as just a reaction – as much in their profile and swanky confidence as anything else – to the stodginess of the British late seventies independent scene. If anybody can agree about anything, it would be this characterization. For example, from Mick Hartney, an amusing anecdote epitomising the scene then: Hartney once had his work rejected by David Hall – the Iman of British Video and co-founder of London Video Arts – because he committed the cardinal sin of using music 'and it was Brian Eno as well, who was pretty cool then by any standards, but music was just "out". […]

George Barber, extract from 'Scratch and After: Edit Suite Technology and the Determination of Style in Video Art', in *Culture, Technology and Creativity in the Late Twentieth Century*, ed. Phillip Hayward (London: John Libbey, 1990) 111–13 [footnotes not included].

Jean Fisher
In Living Memory: Archive and Testimony in the Films of the Black Audio Film Collective//2007

In his 'Theses on the Philosophy of History', Walter Benjamin questioned the ethic of history as a tool appropriated by powerful ideological forces and driven by the concept of 'progress'. However, a more productive basis for thinking history was not as linear progression but as intersecting constellations of the past and the 'now' – the present as the chiasmus of past and future.[1] To borrow a Bergsonian formula, the present is pure becoming; it is not, but it acts. The past, on the other hand, no longer acts but it has not ceased to be.[2] Among the casualties of mediated technology, as Benjamin related in an earlier essay, is transmissable experience, figured in the reciprocity of storyteller and listener.[3] The violence of History lies in its disavowal of this tradition, the testimony of those subordinated peoples without representation or political agency whom Deleuze describes as 'missing' – no longer existing, or not yet.[4] Testimonial memory is the ghost that haunts the interstices of historical discourse. […] [T]hrough a radical re-articulation of the historical archive with testimonial memory, the films of the Black Audio Film Collective (BAFC) disclose the intersecting constellations of the past and present, where memory is to be understood not as a dead past waiting to be excavated but as a product of the present.[5] What emerges is the possibility of rethinking black subjectivities through the reinvention of storytelling whose passing Walter Benjamin had so lamented.

Giorgio Agamben's gloss on Benjamin's essay specifies 'state of emergency' (or 'exception') as the suspension of the law.[6] In the 'tradition of the oppressed', dispossessed of belonging to place, language, culture, the law is always in suspension. Deprived of any ground from which to speak and narrate itself in the world, the dispossessed self, haunted by the trauma of loss, is reduced to the biological state of the 'inhuman', bereft of the past and the will to imagine new possibilities of the future. To reclaim will and agency means negotiating a passage out of the impasse of the traumatic effects of separation and loss, between the compulsion to remember and the need to forget. It concerns re-founding a place of dwelling and links the body intimately to language: to be 'at home' is first to be at home in a language capable of forging a meaningful existence.

That the postwar British African and Asian diasporas lived under an alienating 'state of emergency' is one of the primary disclosures of BAFC's early films. A new language was required, one capable of imaginatively redrawing the discursive contours of a society as yet unreconciled to the changes in its internal dynamics produced by its diasporic communities. This language was to come from the young African, African Caribbean and Asian artists emerging into the turmoil of race politics in the early 1980s, among them the founders of BAFC, John Akomfrah, Lina Gopaul, Reece Auguis, Avril Johnson, Edward George and Trevor Mathison, soon to be joined by David Lawson. As BAFC's films demonstrate, language had to divest itself of the old rhetoric of lament and recrimination, too easily pacified by a few concessions, and invent a poetics of affect, beyond the scope of documentary media, that could penetrate beneath surface symptoms to the deeply buried psychic economy of race and belonging. The challenge and the exhilaration was to negotiate a new language from – to borrow a phrase from Deleuze – the impossibility of speaking, the impossibility of not speaking, the impossibility of speaking in the language of dominance. BAFC understood that what was required was a transformation of traumatic memory, to listen to its melancholic soundings and translate them into a form of critical reflection that could start the work of cultural mourning. More than most, the work of BAFC demonstrates the insight, acutely felt in trauma, that the present 'is not, but it acts', while the 'past never ceases to be'.

BAFC emerged with *Signs of Empire* (1983), an innovative slide tape, textual and sonic work, whose elegant typographical image overlays announced the discursive space that their films were to open up: 'In the beginning – the archive – imperialism – the hinterlands of narrative – the impossible fiction of tradition – the treatise – in national identity – the decentred autobiography of Empire – the rhetoric of race …' A slow dissolve of archival photographs of colonizers and 'natives', many of them more typical of intimate family albums than official historical records, are sparingly interrupted by short film clips – Asian tea pickers, black industrial workers, the fires of urban riots. Series of images cut to details of public monuments in angled shots that undermine the stability and permanence that such sculptures are intended to invoke. Throughout, repeated extracts from two political speeches expose the distance between myth and reality: one eulogizing the multiracial unity of the British Commonwealth, the other expressing anxiety at the alienation of diasporic youth. In this way *Signs of Empire* presents an extraordinary, condensed soliloquy on a mythic British national identity that, constructed in the confidence of Empire, was now fragmenting under the uncertainties posed by the presence of diasporas reaching for their own sense of identity and belonging. The audio-track spatially extends the sombre trajectory, moving between an intimacy and distance resonant with the emotional ambivalences between whites and their black neighbours, beginning with an electronic *basso-profundo* that one might imaginatively locate in the bowels of a ship at sea, it segues to the fragmentary refrains of a classical orchestral piece and a melancholy chorale.

The work opens up a dialogical space of pure images and sounds through a constant framing and de-framing, a structuring to which slide dissolve particularly lends itself. Slide projection, an artistic and pedagogical medium, rests ambiguously between an animated still photograph and a decelerated film sequence, and relates to the more theatrically derived *tableau vivant*, which also privileges the image. In conventional film it is precisely the image we 'lose sight of' as it becomes sacrificed to a diegetic flow in which each successive shot cedes to the logic of its predecessor and to the overall logic of dialogue or commentary. By contrast, in *Signs of Empire* momentary arrest and periodic repetition pose the image as both a seduction and an opacity, disclosing the impenetrability of both the photographic referent and the historical context from which it derives; while each image, autonomous from the next, undermines spatial continuity to produce the radical anti-narrative narrative that was to characterize all BAFC's films. By sampling the colonial archive, the historical discourse derived from it is dis-assembled, realigning the dismembered body of the past with the constellation of the present to 'decentre the biography of Empire'. The work closes with a black field bracketed by bands of blue then red, which, we subsequently learn in *Testament* (1988), are the Ghanaian colours of mourning, as if to announce a shift away from the disabling melancholy of separation and loss. [...]

1   Walter Benjamin, 'Theses on the Philosophy of History', in Benjamin, *Illuminations*, ed. Hannah Arendt, trans. Harry Zohn (New York: Schocken Books, 1968) 257.

2   Gilles Deleuze, *Bergsonism*, trans. Hugh Tomlinson and Barbara Habberjam (New York: Zone Books, 1988) 55.

3   Walter Benjamin, 'The Storyteller', in *Illuminations*, op. cit., 89.

4   Gilles Deleuze, *Cinema 2: The Time-Image*, trans. Hugh Tomlinson and Robert Galeta (London: Athlone Press, 1989) 216.

5   See Stuart Hall, 'Constituting an Archive', *Third Text*, no. 54 (Spring 2001) 89–100.

6   Giorgio Agamben, *State of Exception*, trans. Kevin Attell (Chicago: University of Chicago Press, 2005) 1–10.

Jean Fisher, extract from 'In Living Memory: Archive and Testimony in the Films of the Black Audio Film Collective', in *The Ghosts of Songs: The Film Art of Black Audio Film Collective 1982–1998* (Liverpool: Liverpool University Press, 2007) 16–30.

R.V. Ramani
In Conversation with Pallavi Paul//2014

Pallavi Paul What do you think independent documentary is? And do you think the Emergency [imposed by India's prime minister Indira Gandhi in 1975–77] marks a turning point in the history of what independent documentary meant?

R.V. Ramani No, I wouldn't place the Emergency as a turning point. I know a lot of people would, but I wouldn't. This is because I know that for documentary maybe you can say the Emergency was important, but for filmmaking as a whole the Emergency was irrelevant. There were people making really independent films even before that and who are continuing even today. For example, *Bhuvan*

Shome (Mrinal Sen, 1969), is an absolutely amazing and independent work. Which for me is a major reference point, that someone can make work like that. When you say 'independent', it is also a kind of activism. You are trying to be independent of some established norms. You are trying to question them, reinterpret them. [...]

Paul Do you think format had a bearing on independent practice?

Ramani There were things like import permits, etc., but again I look at them as incidental issues. If one was stuck with the idea that all film must be shot on 35mm then that's another kind of issue, it no longer remains a question of independence. In the market today there are so many things one can pick. It just becomes about subversion with whatever tools you have. I left working on film because I had to make documentaries. To make a documentary I did not need 35mm film. My films were never going to theatres and 35mm would have been a waste. 16mm cameras had started to become more and more problematic and there would be many niggles in them. Also the processing and developing became a major issue because most of the labs in India did not have large orders for 16mm stock. So because of all this it was not a very stable proposition to work with film. There were issues like scratching of negatives, etc. It's like if you go a to a place which doesn't make samosas and insist on eating samosas there, what will you get? In my experience I have seen these things change. In 1982 when I joined FTII (Film and Television Institute of India), people were talking about 35mm. Even within that there was a hierarchy between Arriflex and Mitchell cameras, where Mitchell was considered to be a better camera, even though they were both using the same format film. Then by the time I was in the second year people were talking about 16mm and by the final year U-matic/Low Band had become a real possibility. But these hierarchies never used to affect me. From the beginning if something was easily available in the market and had good functioning for me, I would take it up. These things change so quickly. You name any format and I have worked with it and therefore I can make this statement to you easily that formats have nothing to do with independent practice.

Paul How did you place yourself, vis a vis your contemporaries, on these questions?

Ramani To think of it, it was not from film contemporaries, but I learnt this from friends who were artists and painters. The fun of mixed media. They use anything and everything. Acrylic, oil, charcoal, pencil. So I was learning a lot from there about my practice.

Paul Where did you imagine your films would be shown?

Ramani There were places where you had to create the possibility for screenings, because nothing like that existed. There were a few organizations, like Max Mueller Bhavan, that were open to showing Indian films, new filmmakers and interesting works. Max Mueller Bhavan was one my staple venues. Whenever I used to make a film, Max Mueller would show it in Chennai. Therefore Bangalore and Delhi would also show. I would hold on to that link. The Alliance Française and the American Centre were also venues. They had nice auditoriums and projectors. And other than these there were a few non-commercial entities with a projector and a hall. I would approach them and they would also be happy to show my films. In fact I have never catered to an audience of more than a hundred people. Sometimes it would just be a few friends. I don't even think of large audiences now, I don't even need them actually. I like small audiences. I like showing my films to a few people and having a nice feedback and talk. I don't even like to show my films on television.

Paul Why do you feel television is unsuitable for your films?

Ramani For television perhaps one needs to make different kinds of films. For the way I make my films, they are not really suitable for that medium. People may like them, but I'll still be uncomfortable, and cinema halls are totally impossible. But there was this one film that was made by me and my friend Soudamini (also a graduate from FTII); it was called *Interested* and was shown on TV on a one-time royalty. This was in 1990 and the film became the taste of what independent could be for me. That film was made largely because I wanted to make some other film in Bombay. I was generating various kinds of resources to make that film on an expedition to Mount Kanchenjunga. I was supposed to be the filmmaker travelling with the team, but the project never happened. So whatever I had raised for that, we eventually decided to do a film with that. We lived in two villages in the South and the concept was that we were looking for lost songs, forgotten songs. We would go from village to village, meet elders, meet people and ask them what they remember. It is a very short film of 22 minutes, but it was a wonderful experience. It was shot on a camera that nobody would use, etc., and since there is no sound on the film, we used an ordinary tape recorder, but it was a lot of fun.

Paul Do you think there is something that can be called a documentary aesthetic?

Ramani No I don't think it can be said that documentary has a separate aesthetic.

Is there anything in the world that is without aesthetics? In fact everything is in aesthetics, documentary is just a set of parameters that you're working with. Basically documentary is that you don't give dialogues. [...]

Paul [W]as it ever a struggle in your practice, to arrive at a documentary form rather than place yourself within it as a historically informed choice?

Ramani (*laughs*) No, it wasn't really a struggle, because I don't think of fiction as fiction. Our common ideas about fiction come from literature, because things are rendered and written in a certain way. But fiction need not be limited to that. Any thing can be fiction, no? Fiction is a way of talking, one recognizable act, there is nothing essential about it. Actually, frankly speaking, I am a fiction filmmaker, I work with fiction. My parameters are a bit strange; that's why my films seem weird. I just don't give people dialogues, but other than that there are characters, there are songs there are situations – everything is there. I work with all those things. It's juxtaposition, the energy levels – all of it comes together to create fiction. Putting two shots together is fiction for me. I work against the notion of information, so if I am working with that as a principle then what is it that is making me choose one shot over others, and put them together while editing? In documentary filmmaking information becomes a predominant tool for a lot of people. I don't work like that, I am interested in experience. So when I work with experience everything becomes fiction. I keep saying that my films offer an experience of fiction, even though I work with documentary as a plane.

Paul Would you call yourself a political filmmaker?

Ramani Absolutely. My politics comes from being personal and empathetic. That's very political. People's criticism of my work is that it is indulgent and that I'm making films only for myself, etc., but that doesn't bother me. Sometimes people are looking for social messages, or what exactly the film is offering to someone. In fact a friend of mine was asking me yesterday, Why is it important that you show your film to others? So I got very zapped by that question and began to think, really why is it that I show my films to others? Like today I am showing *My Camera and Tsunami* (2011) in JNU (Jawaharlal Nehru University). I'm thinking about why it is important to show it. I mean, of course it is very important, because something else happens when you show. How the image is perceived becomes palpable. Since I'm working against the commoditization of the image this activity of seeing together in this way is necessary. I contest the commoditization of images by making them more porous, less definitive, less judgmental, and therefore more democratic. There are not authoritative positions or self-righteous decisions, there are just voices, and I hope together they can work towards a better world

R.V. Ramani and Pallavi Paul, extracts from interview, *Wide Screen*, vol. 5, no. 1 (February 2014).

Rebecca Comay and Michael Newman
Ghostly Medium: James Coleman's *Charon* (MIT Project)//2001

What if we take the sense of medium literally – not simply as the material specificity of an artform but as a modality of transportation or passage: a mechanism of transition and transience? Does the apparent collapse of medium-specificity in a digital age expose a truth about medium that becomes visible only at the end of its epoch, and at a point where photography has begun to refract itself through other mediums? If photography could never be counted as one more medium amongst others, this is because photography had from the outset challenged the very idea of medium.[1] Photography in the mid nineteenth century had already begun to pose its own questions. In challenging traditional notions of the medium as an instrument for the externalization or expression of interiority it had exposed a movement which is not that of inside to outside. And in capturing the fleeting passage of time within the stillness of an image it had pointed towards a movement irreducible to a vector oriented towards determinate ends. Giorgio Agamben, following Walter Benjamin, speaks of medium as the apparition of pure gesture: 'means without ends' – a morsel of movement detached from every linear continuum.[2] This would block any teleological determination of the artwork, whether as instrumentality (means towards ends) or as aesthetic autonomy (ends without means).

In *Charon (MIT Project)*, 1989, James Coleman poses a series of questions about photography in a medium which is conspicuously not quite that of photography proper. It is crucial that here, as elsewhere, Coleman never presents photographs simply as photographs. Projected, doubled and superimposed, Coleman's images are presented in the extended temporality of the slide-tape, constructed according to cinematographic principles, and displayed according to the shot by shot arrangement of a storyboard. His 'photographs' make explicit the durational aspect of the image, however 'still' it may be, as if photography may only be grasped in its precipitation into slide, film or video. This is not to make a teleological point about the inevitable self-overcoming of photography within the expanded field of cinema. It is, however, to understand that the transience embodied in photography also here directs itself towards photography's own transience, its special pastness or ending.

Charon as we have it is composed of fourteen discrete episodes, thematically connected by a preoccupation with the vicissitudes of photography, and formally unified by the continuous voice-over of the commentator, whose slightly unctuous diction evokes both documentary cinema and the corporate slide-tape. *Charon* is narrated, in the third person, from the omniscient standpoint of a speaker whose emphatic use of style indirect libre seems to transcend the manifest differences of gender, race, age and class of the various photographers whose fears and fantasies he relays. Whilst the genres of photography discussed are conspicuously utilitarian and overdetermined by palpable economic, political and social fantasies – advertising, fashion, real estate, documentary, didactic, family snapshot – the work does not simply attempt a critique of ideology. Nor is it attempting to sublimate a vulgar 'anaesthetic' medium within the purer medium of art. It does, however, raise the question of the persistent imbrication of phantasmagoria and redemption within the disenchanted medium of photography. The ambiguity of the title, with its curious blending of ancient myth and modern progress, points to this inescapable redoubling.

The title asks to be read literally. In the original myth, Charon ferried the shades of the dead across the River Acheron to Hades. His real function, however, was less the actual transportation of souls (they came equipped with wings, and at least prior to the fifth century flew over unassisted) than the regulation of the boundary separating the living from the dead: his job was to prevent the living and the unburied dead from crossing over into the underworld, and to prevent the dead from returning to the land of the living. Coleman exposes the terrifying porosity of this border. Photography inserts the living prematurely into the world of the dead and resurrects the shades as ghosts and nightmares.

The work is thus perhaps more Dantean than Greek. Each episode involves a harrowing journey or descent, each self-enclosed, the discontinuity between each episode echoing the discontinuity between each slide, whilst involving a similar layering, a deferred transparency, not dissimilar to the staggered propulsion of the *terza rima*. Unlike in Dante, however, there is no obvious deepening or narrative progression – no eschatological horizon of fulfilment – although there are structural or syntactical transformations suggestive of the infinite productivity of myth itself to mutate into ever more complex configurations. Coleman's concern, however, is not just with myths of passage, but with the possibility of a passage beyond myth as such: can one escape the phantasmagoria of the dream world by means of the apparatus of the dream world?

It is notable that *Charon* hardly deals with that aspect of photography which has received so much attention in recent years, partly under the pressure of digitalisation, namely, the character of the photographic image as index or imprint. Coleman is, rather, concerned with the implication of the photographic image in scenarios of power and desire – the construction or staging of a certain kind of representation. His work explores the various scenes of photography and uncovers a substratum no less traumatic than that of the imprint.

The elaboration of the space of representation finds its *locus classicus* in Foucault's description in *The Order of Things* of Velázquez's *Las Meninas*: the spectator stands in the position of both the sovereign who models and the painter who is the author of the work.[3] By putting all three into the picture, Velázquez makes visible the normally invisible conditions of representation. Whilst Coleman's *Charon* describes the various crossings – whether literally or in fantasy – between the photographer (as well as the spectator) and the space of the image, it is notable that, unlike Velázquez, he resists introducing the means of representation into the representation itself. Nowhere in *Charon* do we see an actual camera. (That this almost happens in one episode, when a timer mechanism is said, but not shown, to crash onto the stage, only emphasizes this exclusion.) Nonetheless, the physical presence of the slide-projector in the gallery, so evocative of the magic lantern, suggests the phantasmagoric character of the various projections the work both depicts and literalizes. At its limit, the desire to cross into the photograph – to identify with the frozen image – is revealed as the impossible desire to experience, whilst living, the trauma of one's own death. This is registered as the desire to see oneself dead – as image, corpse or simply absence.

Charon tells the story of the photographer's failure to control the space of representation (for example, by conflating the positions of sovereign, artist and spectator, as in *Las Meninas*). The blind spot shows where that effort at control fails: it blocks the identificatory movement which the work itself initiates. There is a literal dimension to this blockage. The slide projector physically obstructs the illusion of identification which photography invites and cinema simulates. Squarely placed within the installation space, the machine literally prevents the viewer from occupying the centre of identification. The work will explore an escalating attempt to recuperate this blockage, by appropriating blindness itself as the condition for its own insight. Blank screens and blindfolds will come to literalize a blindness at once feared and desperately desired. [...]

1   For an influential discussion of medium in a post-medium age, see Rosalind Krauss, 'A Voyage on
      the North Sea': Art in the Age of the Post-Medium Condition (London: Thames & Hudson, 2000);
      and on the idea of James Coleman's slide-tape works as inventing a medium, see her '... And Then

Turn Away? An Essay on James Coleman', *October*, no. 81 (Summer 1997) 5–33.

2   Giorgio Agamben, 'Notes on Gesture', in *Means Without End: Notes on Politics* (Minneapolis: University of Minnesota Press, 2000) 49–60.

3   Michel Foucault, *The Order of Things: An Archaeology of the Human Sciences* (New York: Vintage Books, 1973) 3–16.

Rebecca Comay and Michael Newman, extract from 'Ghostly Medium: James Coleman's *Charon (MIT Project)*' (paper for Tate symposium, London, 2001), in *James Coleman* (Madrid: Centro de Arte Museu Nacional Reina Sofía, 2012) 35–8.

Jonathan Crary
Olafur Eliasson: Visionary Events//1997

[…] Much current art practice, in these fin-de-siècle years, seems caught between two equally restricted avenues of development. One is appropriate to this particular historical moment of decadence, in which art is posed as an activity that perpetuates itself by playing out its own exhaustion. It becomes an endless recycling and reappropriating of the flux of myriad cultural signs and gestures, while simultaneously fashioning an ironic and self-reflective relation to already discarded aesthetic strategies. The other major arena of activity is perhaps more suited to the symbolically weighted passage into a new century and new millennium: art shakes off older and obsolete paradigms to engage a new technological pragmatics of information and communication within electronic networks and image processing systems. Of these two paths (which of course overlap at times), the latter might superficially seem to be more affirmative in its assumptions about the possibilities for cultural and aesthetic creation, and during the past five years or more we have heard many times how new electronic media are dramatically expanding the limits and possibilities of human perception, through a wide range of new machinic and prosthetic capabilities. For many, the vast possibilities of digital imagery and global telematics signal the opening of a new historical regime of visuality and of aesthetic experience. But curiously there has been little questioning or critical challenge to the many extravagant and often dubious claims being made about cyberspace today. Instead there has been a generally passive and obedient acceptance of the idea that significant cognitive and perceptual innovations will inevitably be within the wired terrain of cyberspace, computer graphics and communication systems. […]

Clearly, the work of an artist like Olafur Eliasson can be understood as staking out in a crucial way a kind of third path. Eliasson's work is exemplary of thinking which believes in the importance of expanding and exploring human perceptual capacities but which pursues such experimentation independently of any contemporary technological imperatives. What is at stake now is the very meaning of the idea of the 'visionary' and of creativity. Since the end of the nineteenth century there has been an acceleration of the transfer of various functions of human knowledge and perception into a wide range of information and image machines. It is part of a larger historical process in which the texture of thought, memory and sensory experience has been reshaped and externalized by its increasing embeddedness in powerful technological systems of many kinds. It was once thought that modernity was characterized by the separation and autonomy of the spheres of art, science and ethics. Now as Jean-François Lyotard and others have observed technoscience is becoming a new master paradigm which is increasingly determining the nature of art, knowledge, politics, morality and community.

But significantly, even amid the installation of such a paradigm and related processes of global homogenization, marginal and alternative spaces of innovation and experiment flourish. I refer not to any attempts to return to some impossibly pre-modern or supposedly 'natural' conditions of subjective experience, but rather to work founded on a richer and more imaginative conception of what machines are capable of and a far more probing investigation of how various technical (in the richest sense of this word) procedures and interventions have the potential for transforming and enhancing human perception. Eliasson's art, from a certain perspective, might seem to be about the evocation of phenomena derived from what we used to refer to as Nature: mist, waves, atmosphere, rainbows, arctic moss, and so on. But what is crucial about his work is that these elements are only partial components of a larger machinic set-up. That is, his pieces cannot be understood in terms of a distinction between a biosphere on one hand and a mechanosphere on the other. Instead a nature/culture duality is dissolved within a single field in which machine and organism are not separable. Thus it would be a mistake to find anything nostalgic in his work; rather it is grounded in a historical understanding that 'visionary' experiences have always been the product of various technical procedures and material practices, that 'nature' is never apprehendable in some pure state but is always mediated or incorporated through practices of use, ritual, observation and assimilation. Eliasson's work must be seen as part of a counter-tradition of machinic production in which the dominant contemporary values of storage, speed, productivity, uniformity are discarded in favour of techniques for the creation of singular and non-recordable phenomena. [...]

To cite Aldous Huxley: 'Our perception of visionary objects possesses all the freshness, all the naked intensity, of experiences which have never been verbalized, never assimllated to lifeless abstractions.' Clearly, so-called electronic virtual reality is just the opposite: its synthetic images are fully derivable from algorithms and simulation models which necessarily preclude the disclosure of anything not already formalizable.

In this sense Eliasson's work is about a field of events in which nothing objective is produced, in which conditions are set in play to allow a zone of virtuality to hover at the edge of actualization. It is a question of mobile and non-hierarchized relations between spectator, apparatus and milieu – elements out of which a non-identifiable and non-localizable phenomenon coalesces and subsists. Unlike some of the well-known artists (for example James Turrell) with whom he has been associated, Eliasson does not engage in any concealment or mystification of how specific effects are fabricated. In this sense we could term his work anti-phantasmagoric – the word phantasmagoria of course refers back to certain early nineteenth-century magic lantern displays which used back projection and concealed mirrors to keep the audience unaware of the means used to create illusory images. Eliasson's pieces are resolutely transparent in their exposure of the usually simple and straightforward functioning of the machine components. Thus while there is this distinctly de-mystifying character to the practical and mundane concreteness of these elements, it is paradoxically at odds with the highly evanescent and even sublime effects that these elements produce. The material and the dematerialized co-exist within the same charged field. A horizon of transcendence then is fully embedded in a world of immanence, a world of finitude and from which the absolute implied, for example, in the work of Caspar David Friedrich, Mark Rothko or Robert Irwin is evacuated. For the neo-romantic Eliasson, transcendence is driven back into the actual world and made to serve an immanent function in terms of the creation of effects, desires, epiphanies and temporalities which are embodied in a social and human world. [...]

Jonathan Crary, extracts from 'Olafur Eliasson: Visionary Events', in *Olafur Eliasson* (Basel: Kunsthalle Basel, 1997) 60–66.

Vivian Sobchack
Nostalgia for a Digital Object//2003

Whenever I watch QuickTime 'movies', I find myself drawn into someone else's – and my computer's – memory. Faced with their strange collections, moving collages and juxtapositions of image-objects whose half-life I can barely remember, I tend to drift into a reverie not quite my own. Indeed, the form usually evokes from me the kind of temporal nostalgia and spatial intensity I feel not at the movies but before American artist Joseph Cornell's mysterious boxed relics. Both QT movies and Cornell boxes preserve 'under glass' fragments of a 'read-only' memory that is, paradoxically, 'random access': that is, dynamic, contingent, associative. Both also refuse mundane space-time, drawing us into enclosed and nested poetic worlds far more miniature, layered and vertically deep than we usually find in cinema. Both also salvage the flotsam and jetsam of daily life and redeem it as used material whose re-collected and re-member presence echoes with traces of an individual yet collective past. And both also construct 'reliquaries' – cherishing 'the ephemeral object as if it were the rarest heirloom'.[1]

Both QuickTime movies and Cornell boxes contain 'intense, distilled images that create a remarkable confrontation between past and present'[2] - a confrontation furthered by QT's stuttering attempts to achieve 'real-time' movement, or to embrace the spatio-temporal lacunae that visibly mark its expressions. While cut-out statues and matted silhouettes float gracefully like collaged dreams across photorealist backgrounds that effortlessly warp and melt, 'live-action' balks and stiffens in contrast. Strangely static and consequently moving, full of gaps, gasps, starts and repetitions, QT movies intensify our corporeal sense of the molecular labour of human becoming – evoking not the seamlessly-lived animations of real-time and live-action movies, but, rather, the half-life of certain time-worn kinetic objects: wooden puppets with chipped paint, forsaken dolls with missing limbs, Muybridge-like figures in old flip books hovering with bravado and uncertainty between photography and cinema, images of nineteenth-century strong men hand-cranked into imperfect action by old Mutoscopes relegated to the dark corners of amusement arcades.

Given the pleasure I find in their fragmented temporality and intensely condensed space, I have no desire to see QuickTime movies get any quicker – or bigger. I don't want them to achieve the 'streaming' momentum of real-time and live-action – measured against the standard and semblance of cinema. Indeed, precisely because QT's miniature spatial forms and temporal lacunae struggle against (as they struggle to become) cinema, they poetically dramatize and philosophically interrogate the nature of memory and temporality, the value of scale, and the meaning of animation. In sum, I don't want them to become 'real movies' at all. Nonetheless, they will – and have. It was just a matter of time, compression, memory and bandwidth. Thus, it is a shame that QT movies were called 'movies': so named, their extinction as a specifically computergraphic form of aesthetic expression was virtually preordained. Although QT is a 'multimedia architecture', most developers and users quickly reduced it: 'In QuickTime, a set of time-based data is referred to as a *movie*'.[3]

Long ago, André Bazin argued in 'The Myth of Total Cinema' that before the technology that made it possible, cinema was *preconceived* 'as a total and complete repre-sentation of reality … the reconstruction of a perfect illusion of the outside world'.[4] Unfortunately this realist desire remains in force despite the emergence of a new medium– one that digitizes, integrates and transforms all others. Belief in the myth of total cinema has led not only to the realization of sound, colour and relief, but also to the *primacy of cinema*, even as it is transformed into something else by a new medium. Thus, the aesthetic values of QT 'movies' are measured against those of 'cinema' – and the true computer graphic novelty of QT works becomes historically inverted as a false cinematic 'primitivism'. Hence the desire to make QT movies quicker and bigger rather than stopping to privilege the stalled and uncanny momentum of their animation and the poetic intensity condensed by their miniaturization and framing.

Indeed, I would have much preferred calling QuickTime works 'memory boxes' rather than 'movies' – for 'memory box' evokes not only Joseph Cornell's work, but also the essential fundament of QT's existence: *the computer*. As well, referring to diverse containers from reliquaries to shoe boxes filled with photographs or souvenirs, 'memory box' draws our attention to memory's historical transformations and the material conditions of its preservation. After all, in our technological moment, what is the computer but a fathomless 'memory box' – one that collects, preserves and allows for the conscious retrieval and visible re-collection of memories, all 'cached' in an enormous, unseen network of past images, sounds, and texts. […]

1   Kynaston McShine, 'Introducing Mr Cornell', in *Joseph Cornell* (New York: The Museum of Modern Art, 1980) 11.

2   Ibid., 9.

3   'Introduction to QuickTime', *Developer Documentation for QuickTime 3* (Apple Computer Inc., 1997) n.p.

4   André Bazin, 'The Myth of Total Cinema', *What is Cinema?*, trans. Hugh Gray (Berkeley and Los Angeles: University of California Press, 1964) 20.

Vivian Sobchack, extract from 'Nostalgia for a Digital Object: Regrets on the Quickening of Quick Time', in *Future Cinema: The Cinematic Imaginary after Film*, ed. Jeffrey Shaw and Peter Weibel (Cambridge, Massachusetts: The MIT Press, 2003) 29–30.

Trinh T. Minh-ha
In Conversation with Alison Rowley//2010

Alison Rowley [You have spoken] of the implications of the move from analogical to digital technology for your work of imaging and sound recording the complex locations of transcultural encounters *in time*. In addition it seems to me that in [your film] *Night Passage* (2004) you are using the technology to explore as well the complex *spaces* of transhistorical encounters. [...] A commitment to the 'analogical' limits of the pro-filmic event at the level of image is an obvious way in which *Night Passage* does not square with the out-of-body utopian rhetoric of some digital imaging and theorizing around virtual reality.

Trinh T. Minh-ha Yes, that rhetoric is widespread and quite misleading. Largely based on the deep-seated duality between mind and body, spirit and matter, it's easily recognizable in certain reactions from viewers, programmers and critics who seem to know what digital is all about. Although it's commonplace, linking exclusively the corporeal to the analogue seems rather illusory and needlessly reductive. For me, the more cutting-edge studies of digital media focus precisely on the vital role of embodiment in our experience of reality – manifested in its manifold forms, both phenomenal and virtual, to use a dysfunctional binary. [...]
   Yet, as in a spiral, the move forward in novelty is also a leap back in time, for this is where new technology potentially meets the ancient Asian science of living, whose spiritual praxes refer not to one but to seven bodies in a human: the physical, emotional, mental, astral, etheric, celestial and ketheric. Here the physical body is only one among others, whose centre channels the earth's energy, grounds us in the material world, and is located at the base of the spine. It can be viewed as being at the end or beginning of the human body, but what about the rest? Seven and yet one. The term *body* itself is used very differently in this context. We have a lot to learn of ourselves, for we do not live in eternity; eternity lives through us. When spirit and soul are indivisible, there's no separation between higher and lower; as the part of us that takes in the obtrusive and the dark of matter, soul is what makes the rest of the world 'real' and is made

real by the world. Interestingly enough, rather than achieving immersion through the illusionism of virtual reality spaces that characterizes mainstream VR researches, artists' media projects today often privilege the unfolding behaviour and bodily movements of the participant.

Some of the ideas developed at the initial stages of installations that I've made in collaboration, like *L'Autre-marche* (2006–9, at the Musée du Quai Branly in Paris) and *Nothing but Ways* (1999, at the Yerba Buena Center for the Arts in San Francisco), call for full interaction between human body and technology to determine letters' mobility in their projections, on the one hand, and to produce sound through motion sensors and contact microphones, on the other. For financial reasons, the mutual inter-affect called for in the former project was not realized as conceived (partly because of the costs raised by the very large scale of the installation). But these are two examples among many in media arts. As you have acutely noted, far from removing experience from materiality and embodiment, technical and cinematic mediation in *Night Passage* makes use of the flexibility of digital technology to feature the (spiritually) interpenetrable relation between human and machine, intermittently inscribing the human-computer interface in the transient formation of its images. [...]

In realizing a film event, I work less with digital per se than with the ways of the digital. It's not a question of producing a non-human, automated vision, nor that of turning every live-action image into data for manipulation and special effect purposes. Understanding what is radical to digital imaging allows one to work differently with the experience of film and imaging, while soliciting from the viewer *a new seeing*, one in which the human, although all too visible, remains an other among others, no longer superior to the machine in terms of sight and speed, for example. In other words, we would have to learn to see wide into the depths of time, and hence to see not with our ordinary eye. [...]

Trinh T. Minh-ha and Alison Rowley, extracts from 'The Depth of Time', interview with Alison Rowley, in *Digital and Other Realities: Renegotiating the Image*, ed. Antony Bryant and Griselda Pollock (London: I.B. Tauris, 2010); reprinted in Trinh T. Minh-ha, *D-Passage: The Digital Way* (Durham, North Carolina: Duke University Press, 2013) 101–12 [footnotes not included].

Ed Halter
The Matter of Electronics//2010

Digital and Material

I would like to consider a notion that I have felt was intuitively true but have never explored in depth: that the 8-bit or 'low-res' aesthetic of much contemporary electronic art can be thought of as a form of digital materialism. By employing the phrase 'digital materialism,' I draw upon a specific term that has circulated within the sphere of avant-garde filmmaking from the 1970s onward. In this context, materialism describes a sensibility, most explicitly theorized in the writings of London-based filmmaker Peter Gidal, in which the physical materials of film technology are made visible within the work itself, and thereby become decisive components of a reflexively cinematic but predominantly non-narrative experience. Materialism reverses the usual Hollywood practice of hiding the mode of production so as not to disrupt the suspension of disbelief necessary to enter into a staged, fictional world.

One example of materialist filmmaking would be Malcolm Le Grice's *Little Dog for Roger* (1967), created out of a home movie originally shot on an obsolete format, 9.5mm film, which has the unusual distinction of bearing its sprocket holes in the middle of the frame rather than on the sides. Le Grice transferred the original 9.5mm film onto larger 16mm, using an optical printer to shift the images forward and back and side to side, exposing the full shape of the frame. As viewers, we thus examine the original footage now less for its photographic content than as a physical object unto itself – a shift that is punctuated, in this case, by the source format's obsolescence.

The idea of a digital materialism might at first appear to present a paradox, We have become used to imagining new media as quintessentially non-physical, virtual, immaterial. This concept may be traced back at least as far as 'Les Immatériaux', the seminal exhibition curated by philosopher Jean-François Lyotard in 1985 that dealt with new relationships of science, art and technology. One finds related vocabulary in Maurizio Lazzarato's typification of the work of the information economy as 'immaterial labour' (language that carries over into Michael Hardt and Antonio Negri's *Empire*, 2000) as well as in the title of a 2001 conference at the Guggenheim in New York on archiving electronic media: 'Preserving the Immaterial: A Conference on Variable Media'.

This supposed contradiction evaporates when scrutinized. The editors of the recent collection *Digital Material: Tracing New Media in Everyday Life and Technology* have critiqued this longstanding notion as 'the myth of the immaterial,' noting that 'software for instance cannot exist by itself but is intrinsically embedded in physical data carriers. In other words, as stuff which may defy immediate physical contact, yet which is incorporated in materiality rather than floating as a metaphysical substance in virtual space'.[1]

Thinking about materialist film provides a workable parallel for a digital materialism, a means to appreciate new media's corporeality. After all, cinema too has frequently been thought of as something without substance – a dream, a fantasy, a psychic projection, a weightless vision. Materialist film resituates the concept of cinema back to its physical, technological basis. In *Against Interpretation* (1965) Susan Sontag observes that the goal of the art of her time had gone from the aesthetics of mimesis or representation to the practice of subjective expression. Materialism adds a third mode of experience: the contemplation of and interaction with a recalcitrant physical reality, an objective world. Materialism is anti-solipsist, counter-transcendent.

Materialist filmmaking is sometimes understood as an attempt towards 'pure film', and therefore merely another iteration of the longstanding modernist interest in essentialism – the Greenbergian impulse that artworks should explore the constitutive elements of their given medium. But Gidal rethought this concept specifically in light of the Marxist theory of dialectical materialism. So as Gidal explains in his essay 'Theory and Definition of Structural/Materialist Film': 'The dialectic of the film is established in that space of tension between materialist flatness, grain, light, movement and the supposed reality that is represented.'[2]

The primary concern of materialist film is therefore not simply the existence of the artwork as a thing-in-itself, but rather the quality of the encounter between the viewer and that object. It describes an experience of tension between perceiving the form and the content, the graphic and the photographic – between looking at the projected image, like the flatness of an Abstract Expressionist painting, or looking *through* it, as if it were a window, towards a 'supposed reality'. In cognitive psychology, such vacillation is known as multistable perception. Ludwig Wittgenstein described a similar mental flip-flopping as 'aspect seeing' in *Philosophical Investigations*.

A digital variant on this phenomenon can be seen in Gijs Gieskes's *Eye*, made by outputting video from a Game Boy Camera using a mode of his own invention. Gieskes includes images of female fashion models, apparently from magazines, rendered by the Game Boy's low-res capabilities into near-abstract arrangements of fat black pixels. In these moments are the contradictions between graphic and photographic parallels found in materialist film. Like *Little Dog for Roger*, *Eye* encourages us to look more closely at the surface manifestations of an outdated form of media, made more visible to us than before thanks to the alienating effects of time on old technologies, recouped as a form of pleasure. The effect recalls an observation by Rosalind Krauss of 'an imaginative capacity stored within this technical support and made suddenly retrievable at the moment when the armouring of technology breaks down under the force of its own obsolescence.'[3]

A similar quality can be found in the moving images produced by the *VinylVideo*™ project. Here, an analogue video signal is stored in the grooves of a vinyl LP. When played, the sounds from the LP are translated into a video signal by a proprietary digital processor, then displayed on a black-and-white television set. Unlike *Eye*, which employs and references a real artifact of past technology, *VinylVideo*™ combines two old technologies – analogue video and the phonograph – in a way that might have happened, but never did. It presents a counterfactual technology, a physical manifestation of alternative history. Here again we look to the image not simply for content but form: the occasional jagged diagonals that interrupt certain moments reflect the project's fancifully impractical process of storage and retrieval. The 'space of tension' noted by Gidal occurs between the unusual materiality of the signal and the video image it carries.

Seeing Materially

Eye and *VinylVideo*™ provide particularly suitable comparisons to materialist filmmaking because, like film, both use images originally produced by cameras. However, Gidal's dialectic appears to be an insufficient means to describe a materialist experience for anything but photographic media, unless one expands upon his system. I would therefore suggest that a materialist aesthetic actually involves tensions between three possible modes:

(1) the technological index: seeing the image as a record, a mark, of the specific technology used for its production.

(2) the representational index: seeing the image as a direct representation of the reality recorded by the camera.

(3) form: seeing the image as a two-dimensional composition, as one would a flat abstract painting or other graphic artwork.

Here I borrow the terminology of 'index' from philosopher Charles S. Pierce.[4] Following Pierce's use, Gidal's 'materialist flatness, grain, light, movement' functions indexically because these signs point to the existence of something that physically produced them. Pierce's index is like a footprint in the snow or a scratch on a wall; it contains a readable trace of its own causality. It has become common in critical thought to talk about the photograph as an index, but it is rarely noted that photographs actually point to two sources at the same time: not only what was in front of the camera, but the apparatus of the camera itself. Consequently, we look at the images in *Eye* and see them in three simultaneous ways: (1) as records of the Game Boy Camera's particular processes, (2) as records of objects placed in front of the Camera and (3) as formal compositions.

Thinking this way allows for a materialist aesthetic without photographic representation: it could occur as a tension between modes (1) and (3). Take for example the video *Look & Listen* by Mike Johnston/Mike in Mono, produced under the *nom de band* of the ZX Spectrum Orchestra. *Look & Listen* consists of a series of sounds and images made by Johnston with a ZX Spectrum, an 8-bit personal computer popular in the United Kingdom in the 1980s. Watching *Look & Listen*'s strobing stream of abstract planes and lines in primary colours involves no photographic images, but cannot be fully appreciated as merely a set of animated forms: we look at them as the products of an early home computer system with what now strikes us as an extremely limited memory and processing power rather than, say, mock-ups of the same produced in Flash, and would experience them differently otherwise. The same can be said for the work's audio component: our knowledge of its process of production is as essential to the experience as the form itself. [...]

1   Marianne van den Boomen, Sybille Lammes, et al., 'Introduction', in *Digital Material: Tracing New Media in Everyday Life and Technology* (Amsterdam: Amsterdam University Press, 2009) 9–10.

2   Peter Gidal, Theory and Definition of Structural/Materialist Film' (1975), in Gidal, ed., *Structural Film Anthology* (London: British Film Institute, 1976).

3   Rosalind Krauss, 'Reinventing the Medium', *Critical Inquiry*, vol. 25, no. 2 (Winter 1999) 304.

4   Charles S. Pierce, 'Logic as Semiotic: The Theory of Signs', in Justus Buchler, ed., *Philosophical Writings of Charles Pierce* (New York: Dover, 1955) 98–119.

Ed Halter, extract from 'The Matter of Electronics', in *Playlist: Playing Games, Music, Art* (Gijón: LABoral Centro de Arte y Creación, 2009) 70–72.

Hito Steyerl
In Defence of the Poor Image//2009

The poor image is a copy in motion. Its quality is bad, its resolution substandard. As it accelerates, it deteriorates. It is a ghost of an image, a preview, a thumbnail, an errant idea, an itinerant image distributed for free, squeezed through slow digital connections, compressed, reproduced, ripped, remixed, as well as copied and pasted into other channels of distribution.

The poor image is a rag or a rip; an AVI or a JPEG, a lumpen proletarian in the class society of appearances, ranked and valued according to its resolution. The poor image has been uploaded, downloaded, shared, reformatted and re-edited. It transforms quality into accessibility, exhibition value into cult value, films into clips, contemplation into distraction. The image is liberated from the vaults of cinemas and archives and thrust into digital uncertainty, at the expense of its own substance. The poor image tends towards abstraction: it is a visual idea in its very becoming. [...]

The poor image embodies the afterlife of many former masterpieces of cinema and video art. It has been expelled from the sheltered paradise that cinema seems to have once been. After being kicked out of the protected and often protectionist arena of national culture, discarded from commercial circulation, these works have become travellers in a digital no-man's land, constantly shifting their resolution and format, speed and media, sometimes even losing names and credits along the way.

Now many of these works are back – as poor images I admit. One could of course argue that this is not the real thing, but then – please anybody – show me this real thing.

The poor image is no longer about the real thing – the originary original. Instead, it is about its own real conditions of existence: about swarm circulation, digital dispersion, fractured and flexible temporalities. It is about defiance and appropriation just as it is about conformism and exploitation.

In short: it is about reality.

Hito Steyerl, extracts from 'In Defence of the Poor Image', *e-flux journal*, no. 10 (November 2009); reprinted in Hito Steyerl, *The Wretched of the Screen*, ed. Julieta Aranda, Brian Kuan Wood, Anton Vidokle (Berlin and New York: Sternberg Press, 2012) 31, 44.

Steve Reinke
On *Disambiguation*//2011

[James Richards' work] entered into me like some kind of dream material, a specific kind of the uncanny: not my dream material, the material of another, but deeper, more compelling than my actual recollections or notions or desires.

A residue that sticks. A residue that sticks because it seems to have once been known and then forgotten, or repressed (a residue from the past). A residue that sticks because it is utterly foreign, but corresponds to a particular psychic hole or lack (a residue from the future). A residue that refuses to move forward, that holds contraries – desires that are undesired – in ambergris suspension. A residue that moves like an amoeba through hostile psychic territory, restless but patient, contingent yet purposeful.

I don't know how our working method developed. An exquisite corpse is a kind of blind (or dead) assembly. The structure may be predetermined, but it is left to chance how the individual components relate. This contingency of arrangement, of montage/collage: delirium. But I don't think either of us had any interest making an exquisite corpse. I cannot speak to James Richards' beliefs, but I will anyway: we had no trust in surrealist delirium, in the idea that something interesting, some unconscious content or structure, would emerge. Perhaps we can even go so far as to say: there are no accidental deliriums. One must actively work to produce such a thing.

Also: fuck the subconscious. It is not your friend, and it is not your helper. There is no art there, only rot and slaughter churning against any future. The only delirium is a blind trust in such a thing. A pool to be tapped by some giant straw of fucked-upness that can suck some of that unconsciousness to the surface. There is no straw and there is no milkshake. Nonetheless, the idea that we were merely assembling an exquisite corpse was useful: all contingency, no pressure. So we burned files to DVD and posted them. That is, we actually put them in little padded envelopes, walked to the post office, bought sufficient postage for overseas airmail, and sent them off. I'm Mac-based and use Final Cut, so I sent QuickTime files. He's a PC, uses Premiere. I forget what his files were. WAVs? Whatever they were they were PAL rather than NTSC, which was once a great technical impediment, but in this strange digital age our respective timelines took every file format, like previously incommensurate slime moulds finding themselves layered happily in some primeval swamp. [...]

Steve Reinke, extract from 2011 statement on *Disambiguation* (with James Richards, 2009).

Ed Atkins, Melanie Gilligan, Anja Kirschner, Ben Rivers
In Discussion with Dan Kidner//2011

Ed Atkins While structural film is very important to me, there are key elements in my work that are crucially digital, in that it concerns the mediation of cinema and TV – this is about new media as a mediation of prior categories rather than as a third category. The model of making everything with one camera and a laptop is central to this; unlike structural film, my work can't be exposing the mechanisms of its making because I don't know the mechanisms. I don't know how to programme this software or how to decrypt these acres of binary. But, while the media is incorporeal, things like high-definition, 3D and surround-sound are – for me at least – all concerned with the privileging of material and surface. These preoccupations are often embodied by the subject matter of my videos. In *Death Mask II* (2010) and *III* (2011), for example, cadavers are figured as both abjectly physical and spiritual.

Melanie Gilligan For me it's not about making reference to already existing forms, but finding a form that's appropriate to the kind of communication that I want to make. I intend my work to give an ongoing commentary on the political events of our times, but through fictions and quasi-fantasies, as if the TV news were being relayed as a drama-satire-horror-play. For example, my film *Crisis in the Credit System* (2008) is a drama about the financial crisis, while Self-Capital (2009) and *Popular Unrest* (2010) both focus on how the subsequent austerity measures and biopolitical lock-down would change the political landscape. In these, and some earlier performances, I intended for the work to have a shelf life and to expire once the political moment had passed. Television has a very different set of boundaries now: it's not for the living room; people often watch it online, and that's increasingly the case with film. My work is made for that online audience. I guess I share the ethos of some very early video practices that picked up television as a way of commandeering a medium that's in the public realm but that is owned by corporate interests. Making my own low-budget television programmes is an attempt to challenge the cultural monopoly of how world events are told.

Dan Kidner Black boxes and monitors in galleries are now ubiquitous. They're used not only to present contemporary works of film and video but also to present historical works, and often films that weren't specifically made with this mode of presentation in mind. I'm thinking in particular of the presence of the work by people like Chantal Akerman, Yvonne Rainer, Harun Farocki and so on in art galleries – what you could call the exhibition of avant-garde or experimental cinema. It's into this context that all of you are presenting your work, and you're all making films that now exceed 30 minutes, and that are, it seems, getting longer and longer. These works call for higher levels of attention, and require the viewer to be present from beginning to end, which is a new development for films screened in a gallery context. It would be interesting to talk about the tension that arises between the length of the works and the modes of attention required to view them, and the gallery visitors who – certainly in the 1990s and through to the 2000s – may not have expected to spend more than five minutes per film as they moved from one black box to the next.

Gilligan One of the main ways I show my work is online, where the mode of attention is probably a bit distracted – not to mention that it's anytime and on demand, which I like. I made my first film, *Crisis in the Credit System*, to be shown only on the Internet because I was focusing on reaching a broad audience. While my videos were initially episodic so that they could be distributed and shown online, soon after I also began to show them in exhibitions, where I've started spatially separating the episodes. With *Popular Unrest*, for example, the installation has five different booth-like areas, each containing one of the episodes on a plasma screen, and to watch the work you move around the space, wearing infra-red headphones that work for all the monitors. It's more than 60 minutes long, but you can watch in parts and even stretch it over several visits. And, of course, the gallery-goer could also continue watching at home.

Kidner Is the fact that the episodes are shorter than the typical length of a TV programme a critical element of your work? In as much as they condense what would be an hour-long episode into a ten-minute segment?

Gilligan One of the reasons I've been drawn to TV is its ability to develop a narrative over many sittings, the way a novel can develop characters and a plot, which requires more than just ten-minute episodes. Though I'm not trying to replicate TV's hour-long shows, I am currently working on a programme with much longer episodes, which I'm also planning to put online. Up until now I've been making my own websites, but more recently I've been trying to figure out a better context for putting things online. [...]

Kidner Ed, at first glance your work doesn't appear to be the kind of thing that you have to watch from beginning to end, but your films have very strong narratives. I'm not sure if they're constructed from beginning to end, but they have a 'built' feel – a sense that the film has been assembled chronologically.

Atkins A lot of the graft with my films is in accumulating stock which, because I'm using digital technology, is potentially endless. Part of what I'm interested in is creating a stock – in the way that Getty Images creates it, through a keyword search, or through arbitrary or free-associative methods – and then simultaneously editing the sounds and images I've amassed. In terms of audience attention, I often have a kind of didactic filmmaking in mind: the kind of television that would feed into this might be something like a *Sesame Street*-type educational programme, where the 'lesson' is delivered using phonics and synaesthetic techniques; it might also be in the duration, the length of a lesson. Through this, the video both teaches you its own peculiar grammar and how to decipher it. If it works, then the duration isn't really a problem if you're showing a film in a gallery: the captive aspect is perhaps more to do with a mode of address than the physical space itself.

Kidner Aside from the more standardized modes of display, is there an ideal format of presentation, which perhaps isn't actually available to you at the moment?

Atkins I quite enjoy the discomfort or irresolution of a gallery becoming a cinema – of it sitting on the cusp of one thing or the other. For me, this in between space is the more interesting one. A perpetual problem is trying to find places that have all the right equipment to show films in full HD, with loud, defined sound. But, in a way, that fits quite nicely with the method: it's a transitional technology I'm using, so the mode of presentation can potentially also be transitional. It moves towards something unknown while looking back at that analogue inheritance and those conventions of cinema and the gallery space. […]

Kidner [E]conomic pressures are, in part, what have drawn people like Harun Farocki and others to the gallery space. It's a pragmatic thing – that's where the commissions are coming from. Ben, Anja's wanting lots of people to see the work in whatever form or format it came to them would seem to run contrary to way you present your work. The medium of film still seems very important to you. I can't imagine that you would be very comfortable with your work being shown on DVD or being dispersed as an MPEG?

Ben Rivers I have shown digitally, though I preferred not to until more recently now that digital projection has got so much better. While I agree with Anja in terms of 'anyone who'll take it', for me that doesn't necessarily mean any way of showing it. I'm less interested in numbers of viewers: my film *Slow Action* is online in four parts but I'm not really interested in hits. I like the idea of specific screenings where you have some sense of community and feedback. For example, I've done a number of tours, on my own and with an American artist called Ben Russell, around Australia, New Zealand and the US, and we're talking about doing one in China. In each town we found different spaces – galleries, universities, community centres, underground cinemas – where we would just set up a projector. The exciting thing about this is that you get an immediate conversation after showing the work.

Kidner In the last five years there does seem to have been an identifiable shift towards a new kind of professionalism in artists' film in London, and in the UK in general. Artists here are increasingly using large crews, working with producers, employing Directors of Photography, and so on. I'm thinking here of all of your practices, as well as the work of Duncan Campbell, Emily Wardill and many others.

Atkins LUX's Associate Artists Programme has been running for about that same period of time, so there's maybe a good parallel to draw there; I'm taking part in it now, and Anja did before, alongside lots of other very good moving-image artists. My experience at art college in London was that moving-image or time-based media was the awkward or irresolute thing to do. On my BA at Central Saint Martins it was called '4D' – something that maybe alludes to its awkwardness. If you were interested in politics or critical theory, but felt resistant towards painting or sculpture, then you would probably study moving image. Also, of course, in terms of recent economic developments, it's very cheap to make and show videos, to download them and copy them and screen them. [...]

Kidner [N]arrative cinema may not be inherently ideological, but I think it was more that subverting narrative, or subjecting it to scrutiny, was seen as a way of questioning certain ideologies and power structures per se. Of course, there was an earlier 'return to narrative' in the 1970s and 80s – some of these films were christened 'new talkies' by Annette Michelson, a term that was taken up by Noël Carroll in the 1980s.

Rivers One of my earliest influences was George Kuchar, who – in terms of his engagement with narrative, in films like *Hold Me While I'm Naked* (1966) and *A Reason to Live* (1976) – was really quite separate from the other 1960s experimentalists. This helped me come to terms with the idea that you could use narrative in a way that managed to also be satirizing narrative in relation to dominant ideologies. I'm of the school that is against plot, which is ideological in its own way. My films are full of narrative, though not in the traditional cinematic sense – I believe in the idea that when you put two shots together you are creating a narrative. I just finished making a feature film, *Two Years at Sea* (2011): it's 90 minutes long and is going to show at film festivals, and then I hope, in some way, to conventional cinema-going audiences. But what I'm very interested in is a fragmented view of looking at the world; there's no resolution to my films. [...]

Atkins I think of the fragments in my films as micro-narratives that function as a kind of bait. This is an inherited form of address: lure someone into the belief that the film will follow a standard path, and then interrupt or distort that expectation – or perhaps even completely fulfil it. I want to emphasize that the work is a construct, but that doesn't remove the possibility of enjoyment. [...]

Gilligan It's often argued that the immersive quality of narrative cinema is one of the main things that makes it 'ideological', in that it prevents critical distance. But for me it's important to make a kind of critical distance possible that isn't separate from affective and even emotional responses. Narrative is one way to bring an audience into a space where affects and emotions can happen in conjunction with thinking through ideas

Ed Atkins, Melanie Gilligan, Anja Kirschner, Ben Rivers, Dan Kidner, extracts from 'More than a Feeling', round table discussion, *frieze*, no. 142 (October 2011). (www.frieze.com)

William Kentridge and Peter L. Galison
In Conversation with Margaret K. Koerner//2012

In the installation The Refusal of Time *(2012) five films are projected on three walls of an industrial space near the Kassel train station. A large wooden structure with moving parts – it resembles something like an accordion and an oil rig combined – occupies the centre of the room; this is the 'breathing machine (elephant)'. Intermittent sounds of Kentridge speaking and music (most memorably tubas and singing) are transmitted through silver megaphones, one at each corner, each with a different soundtrack. The projections are sometimes in sync, but usually they run contrapuntally: a row of metronomes mark time at different speeds; Kentridge repeatedly walks over a chair; maps of Africa flip past in an old atlas; a torn-paper figure performs arabesques; more torn black paper, blown by a current of air, gathers to form a coffee pot, is blown away, becomes a coffee pot again; strings and stars animate a charcoal sky; twin Kentridges move almost in unison; vignettes set in Dakar (1916) and the clock room in Greenwich (1894) end in an explosion and a climactic serpentine dance; Duchamp's inverted bicycle wheels spin in negative like an animated Rayograph. [...]*

Margaret Koerner You had both been working on the subject of time for many years. How did *The Refusal of Time* come about?

Peter Galison We were both fascinated by this late nineteenth-century moment when technologies wore their functions on their sleeve, so to speak; they hadn't sunk their structure into chips and black boxes. One of the things that has made working together so appealing has been that we were both interested in this notion of embodied ideas, of very abstract things worked out in the material world.

Koerner Can you tell me what an 'embodied idea' would be in your case?

William Kentridge There are certain objects which I have come to as someone making drawings, objects that meet the drawing half way. If you take an old Bakelite telephone, its blackness is already half way to being a charcoal drawing. But more than that, once you are drawing it, there is a set of associations that come from old, manual, mechanical switchboard telephones. If you think of a switchboard, there is a cord that would connect the caller and the receiver, and the representation of it looks like a black line drawn across the holes of the switchboard. In my case, of drawing and animation, something that is now perhaps invisible – connecting people across phone lines across continents – is rendered in a very visible way, and may even be a description of an obsolete process. It is not so much being fascinated with the ideas of the late nineteenth century, but that it was still such a 'visible' era, in a way in which an electronic era is not. Even if one is talking about contemporary phenomena, very often an older representation is a better way of drawing it. [...]

I'll tell you a story. A German scientist, Felix Eberty, had come to understand that the speed of light had a fixed speed and wasn't instantaneous, and he worked out that everything that had been seen on earth was moving out from earth at the speed of light, so instead of having space as a vacuum, he described it as suffused with images of everything that had happened on earth. You would just have to be at the right distance from earth to be at the right moment to see what had happened in the archive – to see anything that had happened – so if you had to start 2000 light years away, in his terms you could see the crucifixion.

If you were 500 light years away, you could see Dürer making his *Melancholia* print, which is 500 years old now.

I was intrigued with the idea of space full of this archive of images that was spreading out. I thought of that in terms of a ceiling projection with all these images…[But] it was jettisoned because it was very complicated in terms of the physical projection. How would you see it? Would everybody have mirrors to look at the ceiling to look from down below (which I had done before)? At one stage we had a whole Room of Failures, which was all the things that didn't work, which we still could have done. […]

Koerner Some of the material in *The Refusal of Time* installation appeared in your Norton Lectures at Harvard this spring. How are they connected?

Kentridge The sixth Norton lecture took the process of making *The Refusal of Time* as an example of what the lectures had been talking about: of thinking through material, of allowing the impulses of an image or a piece of work to hold sway and see where they led. Live music was allowed to come into the lecture form at the end of the sixth lecture. The lectures, which started with Plato, end with a black hole. Even though we weren't starting with Plato in *The Refusal of Time*, the shadow procession came back as well, and it also ends with a black hole … The image you see at the end, those white holes going down and down, that's the roll from a player piano. It is both music and information.

Galison One of the debates of modern physics is whether information disappears in a black hole There is a giant black hole in the middle of our galaxy, and eventually everything will end up in it. Will there be something left? … The side that wants to believe there is something left behind seems to have won, because of the development of string theory. It means that all of the information that falls into that hole would leave something on the surface – a kind of holographic image of the thing that had fallen into it. If that is so, then some trace of memory remains. […]

William Kentridge, Peter L. Galison and Margaret K. Koerner, extracts from 'Death, Time, Soup: A Conversation with William Kentridge and Peter Galison', *The New York Review of Books* (30 June 2012). (www.nybooks.com)

Chris McCormack
Moments Not Remembered//2014

An image of a Robert Mapplethorpe photograph has been indelibly scuffed with wire wool to remove what would be an erect penis central to the composition. This is being swallowed by another man who covers his eyes with his palms. The pose part of a blinkered 1981 self-portrait of Mapplethorpe affects a resistance to being identifiable but also questions whether it is an attempt to foreclose the act from being 'witnessed' into existence. An action which overwrites the torn page so that the image and action are blinded and made to be blind. The neutered remains exist on a Japanese library bookshelf and continue to be distributed in this way, stemming from a nearly 150 year ban on overseas propaganda and sexual imagery. (I am also, during the course of trying to find out the title of this Mapplethorpe image, subjected to the minor sadism of having to view these books at a separate viewing table in the British Library in London.) The visceral and yet awkward strikethrough of the image forms part of a repeating sequence in James Richards' video *Rosebud* (2013). Here, amid a shot that incorporates the open book, the camera tripod and distorted background noise, we see the paper's torn surface, and, with slow incremental revelation, that someone has handled this page and delicately, but deliberately, removed what was once there. Richards reorganizes the otherwise 'locked' aspect of the photograph's temporality by filming it; pushing us back against the perceivable movements and hair-like triggers of meaning that have dressed this image in the material world. Tight cropping reveals a mark that scratches the upper section of the man's hand: an aimless, incidental and singular stroke. One driven perhaps by a moment of fatigue, frustration, or just lack of concentration – like a misplaced piece of chewing gum stuck to a poster on a subway platform. The rogue mark characterized by its ability to produce a legible absence in the picture. In the third successive framing of this image, Richards positions the tripod so that it is in view over the photograph – appearing forcibly to reinsert the structure of the image's construction directly into the open mouth of Mapplethorpe. A framing that indelibly lays bare the latent violence otherwise obscured within the photograph's circuits of distribution. Indeed, it is these limits of foreclosure or disavowal within the structure of visibility that are delayed by the emotional costs therein – in terms of both economic and social legacies – that are meted out with a studied and derailing effect by Richards, and which have underpinned aspects of his practice to date.

    The sequences crafted in Richards' video works are largely driven by a number of interlinked, discrete pieces of either found or made footage. This footage can sit on his hard drive for several years; being held and re-held in calibrations of thought before being placed into a 'finalized' piece – as a result, certain sequences echo and reoccur across works. By weaving sensual, haptic sways of material together, Richards reveals how 'ourselves' – the appearances of humanity – seem to have been rendered in the past tense, as series of images to be objectively studied and reviewed. Vagaries and fog-like encounters between individuality and the 'civic' world – increasingly enmeshed, shaped and informed by technological spheres, from touch-screen interfaces, multi-user or post-gendered attachments or re-attachments and endless social media expressions – rise up over these spaces with a haunting sense of melancholy. Subjectivity has lost even 'intuition's assurances', as Lauren Berlant [in her theorization of precarity] has observed. However, these 'losses' are not so much reconfigured in a positivized sense as felt or glimpsed at. *Rosebud* is formed by the appearance of a number of shallow 'surfaces' which create an often tight and claustrophobic world, contra to that of the digital deep and the potential of a transcendentalism that is easily induced by it – we are breathless and statically held in rhythmical loops. *Rosebud*'s associative interplays of thought are built through such recurring structural elements of seemingly disparate surface textures, where filmed or found images appear with alarmingly shifting, high-definition focus pulls.

During the Enlightenment era the 'eye' stood as an emblem of truth and insight: a renunciation of the more magical leanings of the sacred and terrifying omen that it once stood for. In *Rosebud*, the extremely tightly cropped, slightly fearful-looking eye is that of President Hamilton, waxy, wrinkled and scored into the surface of a well-used ten-dollar bill. This withering eye feels shorn from any such symbolic histories. If an eye might have once 'looked', or 'looked for us', Western late capitalism instead stares outward, blankly lost. An empty repository of deadening demands and draining needs. In Mapplethorpe's covered, blinded viewpoint, this appearance of an eye from a dollar bill, or a sequence where an anus is gently stroked by elderflowers and blinks with a muscular blindness, competing desiring and economic surfaces are captured and revealed. We perceive two mirrored 'looks', one that looks outward and the other inward. By expressing what feels like an inalterable, internalized juncture between draining capitalism and the pensive melancholy of remembered intimacies – casual, multiple or singular – the film evokes the otherwise invisible, and perhaps lost, histories shared and exchanged in 'touch'. Indeed, it is the slowly repeated, delicate and joyous movements of tiny flowers that pucker the skin – or the extended examination of a finger which, having turned from pointing towards a Venetian gondola, becomes the 'thing' viewed – that are redolent of the linguistic caesura caught in the moment between touch and being touched. In turn, Richards establishes inconsolable intimacies that exist between touch and the temporalities therein, and marks them with the breach between the annihilated, the dead and the ponderous stasis of a disembodied present.

The combination of images and sequences, grouped and regrouped, might suggest a representation of *bricolage*; punctuated and conferred by a poststructuralist position of the decentred self – a self endlessly unmoored and floating in an anti-hierarchical terrain – but they also produce different and more politicized returns of what might surprisingly be considered 'essence' and 'unity'. These lacunae, according to Katerina Kolozova, are the 'cracks of absence in the voice of the "I", in the incapacitated and silenced uttering of an "I" that is too awkward and too inarticulate to substitute or fit into the conceptual structure designed for in the name of the "subject"'.[1] By cutting the image and revealing its limits in vision, or by reflecting back to us the means by which the image is made, the glue that binds the subjective marginal condition of the 'self', or the 'structure of feelings' otherwise stranded and overlooked in society, is revealed, or at least hinted at. Richards in turn treats such notions of experience and its 'material thicknesses' as overflowing states of rhythmic dissolution and collapse.

1   Katerina Kolozova, *Cut of the Real: Subjectivity in Poststructuralist Philosophy* (New York: Columbia University Press, 2014) 27.

Chris McCormack, 'Moments Not Remembered', in *ars viva 2014/15* (Ostfildern–Ruit: Hatje Cantz, 2014) 124–77.

Basel Abbas and Ruanne Abou-Rahme
Statement//2014

In art, in science, in philosophy and culture, in any production of knowledge where data can be gathered, where information can be extracted from it, and where in that information new possibilities for the world are produced, there are hackers hacking the new out of the old. While hackers create these new worlds, we do not possess them. That which we create is mortgaged to others, and to the interests of others, to states and corporations who control the means for making worlds we alone discover. We do not own what we produce – it owns us.
– McKenzie Wark, *A Hacker Manifesto* (2004)

A call to hack moving images by way of
the guerrilla open access manifesto/
the hackers manifesto/
the situationists/
and the post situationists
the invisible committee

To hack moving images is to create out of a fossilized language the potential for a new language and with it the latent possibility of a new world.

To hack is to abstract. To hack is to steal, to rip, to pirate, to free images from their reduction as commodified information. To hack is to free information, to destroy the information economy.

To hack the image is to disrupt, to displace, to denaturalize the production of knowledge as private property. To hack is to refuse private property, to destroy private property.

To hack the image is to free the archives,
to free the archives is to hack collections
to un-curate
to un-collect
to un-possess

To hack the image is to turn the language of spectacle in on itself.
To hack the image is *to be* the image.

To hack is to puncture, to rupture the magic of the state
using its codes

To hack is to infiltrate.
To hack is to activate, encrypt and disseminate.
To hack is to permeate existing structures
to imagine
new forms of being

To hack images is to be in everyday revolt
to become manifest as a hacking class
to repossess ourselves,
to reclaim our labour
as labour
to detonate the scarcity economy
to be *anonymous*
to *reappear* as many figures
to have many *returns*

Basel Abbas and Ruanne Abou-Rahme, Statement, 2014.

Christa Blümlinger
What's at Play in Harun Farocki's *Parallel*//2014

Harun Farocki has spent decades working on an archaeology of contemporary visual culture. Even when he leaves the cinema for the museum, his thinking is shaped by film; he deduces epistemological and cultural-historical dimensions from the most marginal, utilitarian images. While Farocki's *Eye/Machine I–III* (2000–3) and *Serious Games* (2012–14) focused on the use of virtual spaces, automated vision machines and digital prostheses in military and civilian life, the four-part video installation *Parallel I–IV* (2012–14) explores the visual forms of digital games as part of a tradition of representation that reaches back to antiquity. Architecture, rather than the art of storytelling, appears to be the driving force behind these innovations in the gaming world.

In an impressive oeuvre of archival research, Farocki and his co-creators have assembled thirty years of computer-generated game interfaces whose designs range from schematic raster graphics and charts to photorealistic depictions. We see simple figures constructed from basic geometric objects, next to vector models and complex computer animations – as are used in meteorology today. Farocki's series of two single and two double projections demonstrates how strongly the visual aspects of so-called new technologies originate in drawings and cartography. In the vein of comparative image analysis, *Parallel* explores a fundamental question: to what extent do computer games today seek to follow, even transcend, the aesthetic experience of cinema?

A significant aspect of the installation series is its horizontal montage – a matrix of film exhibited in the museum space and adapted to it. The first and third instalments of *Parallel* make use of double projections that emphasize the comparison between two visual worlds through performance. Here, once again, Farocki creates the impression of an editing lab, where the observer is invited to follow the image analysis. His approach does not mimic a video game, but situates the viewer according to the laws of cinema. There is no joystick inviting the observer to intervene in the montage of images, as there is in the world of gaming. Rather, the logic of the parallel montage – as a vertical or horizontal association – is expanded via a simultaneously focused and speculative commentator's voice (the artist's voice, in the German version) emitted from precisely arranged sound columns, directly in front of the respective projection. Picture montages and acoustic mixing are presented in parallel, gradually over time; through the process of watching and listening, a film is composed – a continuation of cinema by other means.

The conditions of visibility and knowledge relationships, what Michel Foucault called an *episteme*, change over time. With them, the way we represent and describe objects, or convey similarity, also changes. 'The fundamental codes of a culture – those governing its language, its schemas of perception, its exchanges, its techniques, its values, the hierarchy of its practices – establish for every man, from the very first, the empirical orders with which he will be dealing and within which he will be at home', Foucault wrote in *The Order of Things*. *Parallel* presents specific animated images as central figures of this episteme, such as windswept leaves and grass, a roll of waves, cloud formations: motifs that have stood, since the invention of film, for cinema's mimetic power. Live-action film's symbolic forms and representational schemas serve as a scale of comparison for Farocki's speculations about the visual world of video games. They are used to measure more than the degree of graphic abstraction, which has transformed with historical developments. Simple stick-drawings are as instructive as photorealistic models in examining how the logic of synthetic animation distinguishes itself from the cinematic principles. Instead of a scenic breakdown or codified camera angles, users can interactively steer themselves along a number of paths. However, the spatial continuum of digital animation is not without limits: the game world is a 'flat plane'. Farocki's commentary describes the architecture of the growing field as if it were a film set or theatre stage. 'The virtual camera can dive under these waters, but there is no ocean floor to be seen. The rocks float on the water's surface.' […]

Christa Blümlinger, extract from 'Was bei Farockis "Parallel" auf dem Spiel steht/What's at Play in Harun Farocki's *Parallel*', *Berlin Documentary 3* (Berlin: Haus der Kulturen der Welt, 2014) 182–5.

THE
MUSEUM
BECOMES
A
CINEMA
OF MULTIPLE POINTS OF VIEW,
ITS CONTENT THE VERY NEXUS OF ITS MEANING

MEDIATION

Jacob King and Jason Simon
Before and After UbuWeb: A Conversation about Artists' Film and Video Distribution//2014

Jason Simon From Fall 2008 through Spring of 2009 I was living in Paris and teaching in Copenhagen, and I reviewed a show by a Danish artist named Pia Rönike for *Bidoun*. The show included her film *Facing*, from a Kurdish story, a black and white art house style dramatic featurette, which screened continuously in a Paris gallery. Although it wasn't a new phenomenon, I had never been more struck by this displacement of cinematic aesthetics into a gallery environment, and this started a long, slow percolation of questions about shifts in infrastructure.

At that time, UbuWeb was gathering extraordinary attention and dividing communities along lines of access and rights to historical and contemporary artists' media. It was in the range of responses to Ubu that I saw new positions being formed. How institutions and artists felt about Ubu in 2008 told you a lot about where things were going. I came back to the US and my job at the College of Staten Island, where I teach with the media scholar Cynthia Chris, someone who also has an extensive pre-academic and professional history with artists' media outlets like Women Make Movies, Video Data Bank, and Printed Matter, and we decided to pursue some of these questions together. [...]

The two initial questions I had in mind when I returned to the US were: what accounts for the differences between European and North American distributors in their relationships to non-academic partners like UbuWeb, galleries and museums; and how does one see a video after it shows in a gallery? These are medium-specific questions about infrastructure, which are different from the more interpretive discussion that accompanied video's wholesale migration into fine art exhibition venues. In Europe, pre-recession public money permitted non-profit distributors who grew out of an education market to adapt quickly, to embrace UbuWeb, to partner with galleries in placing and supporting editioned video works in collections, and to stream their catalogues. In the US, meanwhile, you had distributors resisting both Ubu's free-access model at one extreme and the galleries' economy of scarcity at the other extreme. This [economy based on scarcity] was clearly not sustainable, and since then, in the global recession, you could almost say the worlds have reversed: public money has disappeared from so much of the European non-profit video world, while the legacy American distributors, at least the ones that are left, have been steadily adapting. As a topic it mushrooms enormously, but Cynthia and I managed to conduct interviews in this time of transition with artists and distributors and gallerists, which were useful for us, if quickly dated.

Jacob King I sense that much of the uncertainty you describe stems from a conflict between two economic understandings of a film or video: on the one hand, the cinematic model, where a fee is paid to screen a work (either in a single screening or 'looped' in an exhibition); and on the other hand, the model which comes more from photography, where a work is 'editioned', with the purchase of an edition of a film or video generally conferring unlimited screening and exhibition rights to the owner of the work (or to whomever the owner might 'lend' his or her edition), without the payment of any fees to the artist. In film, this distinction is material: in the former situation, what is exchanged is a print of the work, while in the latter, it is a dupe negative, from which prints can be produced in perpetuity for the purposes of exhibition. But with HD digital video, no such material distinction exists – one digital file is just as 'original' as another and can be copied indefinitely.

The overlap of these two models can result in some strange, seemingly arbitrary situations. For instance, a museum or small non-profit that borrows a work from a distributor like Lux or EAI would have to pay screening fees, while a commercial gallery that exhibits the same work, and offers it for sale in an edition, might pay no fees. I wonder, do you have a sense of when film and video began to be editioned? Or in the case of 16mm, when artists and galleries started selling negatives and not just film prints?

Simon Those two economic understandings you point to can be mapped according to how far or close the contexts are from both cinematic and pedagogical structures. The second contradiction you point to (that the non-fee paying venue has greater access to original or master quality sources) is yet another anecdote in just how byzantine and unregulated the art market is. The entire economy of gate-keeping distributors is rooted in analogue, that is, pre-digital, culture. Breaking that mould without destroying their economy is the puzzle, and perhaps the solution lies somewhere in subscription streaming portals.

As for finding early examples of editioning media works, this is a popular scavenger hunt: most recently Erika Balsom, but others too, have been looking at this and other questions related to early video and artists' films. When Cynthia and I were at the Castelli archives at the Smithsonian looking at the distribution business papers, we saw a few instances in the 1970s where pricing of video works had interesting evolutions. The Chicago dealer Donald Young had an influence on the process, which you can see in his exchanges with Leo; Donald was a pioneer video dealer, and in his case I was very interested in the later evolution of Bruce Nauman's *Good Boy Bad Boy*. That piece is from 1985, the year that Castelli-Sonnabend Film and Videotapes closed, and is an edition of 40. The gallery staff were very helpful in determining with me that it was Nauman's first editioned video piece – but even saying that is fraught. Nauman had many unique moving image works and installations that preceded *Good Boy Bad Boy*, and he had an earlier vinyl LP of a video sound track that was a limited edition. And even *Good Boy Bad Boy* was initially part of a larger unique installation. But I would still say that it is his first editioned video work: in 1985 it cost $1,000, by 1989 it was $4,000, and by the last time I asked at a booth showing it at an art fair it was $250,000. Art/tapes/22, from the mid 1970s in Florence, Italy, was also a hub for arte povera videos, videos coming from the Castelli-Sonnabend Videotapes and Films catalogue, and Bill Viola was actually working there. I didn't know much about them, but I saw sales certificates for tapes, some as unlimited editions for $200 or less, some as editions of 20 for $1,000.

Important to me about *Good Boy Bad Boy* is that its release coincided with the closure of the Castelli-Sonnabend video catalogue and its dispersal to Electronic Arts Intermix and the Video Data Bank. The main reason for the hand-off was that Castelli-Sonnabend Videotapes and Films could not keep up with either the institutional demand or the changes in technology. EAI and VDB were just better equipped and prepared to handle the business, and built into that business was the fact that the necessary generational loss between an analogue original and an analogue copy was also a security; a bit of piracy protection and salesmanship that facilitated rentals of screeners and sales of heavier-duty archival sub-masters. But that security has been taken away by HD digital technology, and at precisely the moment at which these distributors were given the rights to a historical archive which could serve as a reliable source of revenue, artists started to distribute their works as editions, sold by galleries. Your example, that a work distributed by Lux or EAI could be obtained by a gallery for free and then sold by the gallery as an editioned work, is a particularly suggestive sequence of events; I would be interested in seeing new contracts or licence agreements designed to connect distributors more with editioned works. [...]

So many of the artists showing with Leo Castelli and Ileana Sonnabend in the 1960s and 70s made films and videos that were central to their practices, and the galleries supported them by creating a spin-off enterprise to handle that work: to manage the tasks of making and sending out copies and developing the catalog into its own business. That business followed the non-commercial film distribution model of lower cost rentals and sales for single screenings, at schools and libraries and museums and art spaces. Artists were paid royalties from the typical fees of $50 to rent a tape for a night or two, or $250 to own it. If you bought it, by the mid 1970s, you got either a reel-to-reel videotape, or (a little later) a 3/4" U-matic cassette, and in the case of a film you received a 16mm release print. If any individuals were collecting these then, it would have been rare; rather, most of the clients were non-profits or libraries.

The catalogue itself became a significant document of video's centrality to a conceptual vocabulary; it was three-hole punched and unbound, so it could be updated with supplements for new works that you added into your own binder. At first just the Castelli or Sonnabend gallery artists like Nauman and Vito Acconci and John Baldessari were included, but gradually it expanded with more filmmakers, especially more women. By the 1980s, the catalogue was widely circulated to art and film departments at schools, as well as all the museums and sites where this work could be programmed: it was a standard reference. When I finally got a copy, from Bill Horrigan at the Wexner Center, the writing jumped out at me for its unadorned and attentive style. A number of writers covered the 16mm film entries, but all of the video entries were written by the filmmaker Lizzie Borden: she seemed never to use an adverb, and instead reproduced the observational style of the videos themselves when describing what goes on in the tapes. I was interested in the literature of video art publications generally – rental and sales and exhibition catalogues that took video's medium-specificity for granted, with all of the political, aesthetic and technological assumptions intact. So many of these catalogues – the CSV&F, The Donnel Media Library, the Filmmakers Co-Op giant red book, Canyon Cinema, V Tape and Art Metropole in Canada, and the dozens of others that were standard reference volumes – now have this Rosetta Stone quality as the last printed compendiums to list and describe [artists' film and video as] a fairly contained culture before it exploded into an unfathomable ubiquity of artists' media. […]

King Your recent show at Callicoon Fine Arts in New York included a facsimile of the complete Castelli-Sonnabend Videotapes and Film catalogue which you produced as an artists' book. Alongside this you also presented a photograph of a 16mm film canister of Chris Marker's 1962 film *La Jetée*, which was distributed by McGraw-Hill Films for educational screenings, and the three *Video Against AIDS* VHS tapes from 1989, which are actually reproductions that you produced by scanning the covers of the original videotapes, now nearly impossible to locate (let alone purchase) because so many libraries and archives have trashed their VHS collections wholesale … Each of these items functioned as an invitation to consider a superseded structure of film and video distribution, and a corresponding site of reception: the cinema, the classroom, the home …

Simon I mark 1989 as the year that film and video began to share screens, or, more precisely, venues, and as the beginning of the end of a self-contained media-art culture more or less independent of the art market. *Video Against AIDS* is also from 1989, and proved more and more fascinating as it proved harder and harder to find. The story behind these tapes is that Bill Horrigan (who is a regular source of inspiration for me), and John Greyson were commissioned by Kate Horsfield at the Video Data Bank to co-curate an ambitious programme of AIDS activist media art. Important to understand about the context is the degree to which ACT UP and AIDS video was changing the landscape of film and video culture in general: you couldn't stand on the sidelines of the culture wars, and AIDS video was suddenly the prime shifter of media art culture. And with that programme too, you had this booklet that accompanied the tapes, entitled *Using Video Against AIDS*. Like Lizzie Borden's description of the earlier videos in the Castelli-Sonnabend binder, or like the discussion prompts printed on the inside of the film can for *La Jetée*, these are writings addressing teachers. In all three you find this directed, intimate, discursive bond between avant-garde art works and a pedagogical economy. [...]

Once I found out just how lost [this programme] was, each element became supercharged and somehow necessary to declare in the show. It wasn't part of any early plan and I'm not trying to make it sound heroic – it was more just compulsive. [...] The more systemic problem, that video is reduced to a mere index of itself in exhibition culture, is rampant and a consistent price for its inclusion in that context. It is also why I was focused on the education market in both my show and in the research with Cynthia Chris. It was the demand from schools that ultimately closed down Castelli-Sonnabend Videotapes and Films: they could not keep up with the interests of teachers and librarians, but because VDB and EAI were meeting that demand and could continue to do so, they handed the whole collection over and got out of the business. I believe that that choice was really about how to do right by the works, how to keep them alive, and it worked wonders. Now there is an open question about how galleries respond to that same demand ...

Audiences can be created in all of these contexts, but there is a difference between an audience being created by awareness and an audience created by experience. In a gallery, distracted as we are and ruled by multiple levels of awareness, content gets sacrificed, as you've said. That makes the availability of these video preview options a mercy – maybe a mercy that gets abused, but understandably so. In my show at Callicoon, I was interested in proposing an origin myth for this imagined golden age of avant-garde moving image practices: finding a denominator in the education market as the material condition that made the avant-garde possible. It's a bit facile as a fact, like saying the Russian avant garde was about selling tractors and textiles, until you make the connection with this as a precondition of content.

Jacob King and Jason Simon, extracts from 'Before and After UbuWeb: A Conversation about Artists' Film and Video Distribution', *Rhizome* (20 February 2014). (rhizome.org)

Erika Balsom
Original Copies: How Film and Video Became
Art Objects//2013

Over the past two decades, as the popularity of film and video in contemporary art has soared, the limited edition has finally proved itself as not only a viable model of distribution but also as perhaps *the* model of distribution for moving-image art. Today, films and videos are regularly sold as art objects, most often in an edition of three or four plus artist's proofs. Though still nowhere near the salability of more traditional art objects, film and video are attaining a new market viability that has drastically changed the ways in which moving-image art is bought, sold, valued, and seen. […]

The widespread espousal of the limited-edition model represents a reining in of the inherent reproducibility of moving-image media and its wholesale recuperation into the symbolic economy it once compromised, that of the unique work of art. Authenticity – a concept that had never mattered much to film and video – becomes paramount. For some, this represents a betrayal of the specific qualities of film and video and the utopian hopes invested in them; for others, it represents the only way that film and video will be taken seriously as artistic media, and the most viable economic model to support the livelihood of moving-image artists. […]

When one buys an edition, one purchases a rather curious combination of rights, content and technical support – the specifics of which are all closely regulated by the contracts accompanying the acquisition. This makes the accession of film or video into a museum collection distinctly more complicated than would be the case with most traditional artworks. Though moving-image media do possess a kind of objecthood, it is crucial to recognize that what is for sale is less this object per se than a set of permissions, privileges and responsibilities concerning the exhibition and guardianship of a given work over time. […]

After roughly sixty years of existence at the margins of the art market, what accounts for the ascendance of the film and video limited edition in the 1990s? Three factors of varying importance worked together to create market viability. The first factor is economic. Noah Horowitz [in *Art of the Deal: Contemporary Art in a Global Market*, 2010] emphasizes the crash of 1990 as instrumental in the creation of a new market for video. He writes, 'Galleries increasingly began exhibiting video largely because, according to Barbara London, associate director in MoMA's Department of Film and Video, "they had nothing to lose"; sales had dried up and the opportunity cost of showing video and other alternative practices diminished.' While the new viability of cheaper, less object-oriented work may be ascribed in part to the severe price deflation at this time, other key factors were at play.

The second factor is linked to technological innovation and changes in the speed and facility of image reproduction and circulation. While the mainstream adoption of the Internet in the early to mid 1990s spurred a significant artistic trend of remaking and recycling existing cultural forms, it also resulted in a qualitative leap in the transportability of images and sounds that induced a crisis of authenticity comparable to that of the late nineteenth century. Just as was the case for printmaking and bronze sculpture in the late nineteenth century, the film and video limited editions that emerged at the turn of the millennium were attempts to reconstruct authenticity and (near) uniqueness amidst a new proliferation of copies. During this period, edition sizes shrink dramatically: while Castelli-Sonnabend Tapes and Films offered editions of twenty in the early 1970s, by the 1990s this number had dropped to fewer than ten and often as few as three. At a time when images were more mobile than ever before, the limited edition provided a way of guaranteeing that the work would circulate only within authorized channels and would be seen only in the proper setting. While it was, of course, always possible to duplicate videocassettes, the 1990s and 2000s heralded a qualitative shift in the ease of moving-image reproduction. Jack Valenti of the Motion Picture Association of America had cause to assert that his organization was fighting its 'own terrorist war' against copyright infringement – a war it continues to lose. Unlike the film industry, the art world had access to radical measures that would successfully ensure the integrity of its product. Rose Lord, director of Marian Goodman Gallery, has stated, 'All our artists want their works to be shown under very specific circumstances, where every aspect is carefully calibrated. That's why we have collectors sign purchase agreements that insure that the works will be shown as per the artist's wishes.' [...]

The third and perhaps most important factor in the rise of the limited edition is again a matter of technological change, but also one of institutional politics: it concerns the advent of high-quality, low-cost video projection and its tremendous institutional endorsement from the early 1990s onwards. The moving image might have once challenged the traditional museum, but in the 1990s, endowed with a new, large-scale mode of display, it was recruited by museums to secure relevance in an increasingly competitive marketplace demanding breathtaking, immersive experiences. And where institutions go, the market follows. Institutional endorsement can have a profound effect on the price of an art object, a fact clearly demonstrated by the controversy surrounding the New Museum for Contemporary Art's 'Skin Fruit' exhibition of trustee Dakis Joannou's private collection in 2009. In the case of photography, the J. Paul Getty Museum's 8 June 1984 purchase of five major private collections of vintage prints for a reported twenty million dollars forever changed the market possibilities of the medium.

While no single event comparable to the Getty purchase may be cited in the case of moving-image art, the 1990s and 2000s saw an institutional investment in film and video without parallel in the history of art. The cavernous spaces of newly opened or newly renovated museums, many of which are devoted exclusively to contemporary art, called for colossal installations and big box-office receipts. The turn away from monitor-based presentation and toward projection resulted in a greater sense of monumentality and an increased assertion of presence in the space of the gallery. It pulled video art away from associations with television and its domestic banality, and instead aligned it with a medium by then possessing increasing cultural cachet, the cinema.

The increased visibility of the limited-edition model has brought with it increased criticism. For some artists, such as Martha Rosler, the solution is to opt out, to continue to issue unlimited editions that will be distributed through organizations such as EAI and VDB. For others, the popularity of the limited edition is something to be attacked outright. […] Certainly, the aura of rarity that surrounds the limited-edition film or video is an artificial construction – but it is one with real effects, both positive and negative. Editioning is no more 'fake' than the convention of delaying the DVD release of a film until after its theatrical run has been completed; it is, like the delayed DVD release, a mechanism to generate value. These are conventions that are agreed on by market actors, conventions that possess a certain truth despite their status as historical constructs. […]

Erika Balsom, extracts from 'Original Copies: How Film and Video Became Art Objects', *Cinema Journal*, vol. 53, no. 1 (Fall 2013) 97–118.

Pip Laurenson
Vulnerabilities and Contingencies in Film and Video Art//2009

[...] Time-based media are vulnerable to two types of change. They can be stripped away from the medium in which they were made and they can be divorced from the conditions and technologies of their original display.

Whereas traditional artworks rely on physics to bind them to their supports, the relationships that tie time-based media works to a particular set of parameters are constructed. The material support of a work of art has traditionally been the focus of fine art conservation. Charged with the responsibility of minimizing loss and damage to the material elements of a work of art, the suggestion that conservation might need to broaden its sphere of interest sits somewhat uncomfortably, as a threatened loss of clarity to its traditional remit. Within the conservation of modern art, the formalism characterized by Clement Greenberg, with its reductive focus on the physical medium, was in accord with the concerns of traditional conservation. However, in the art that reacted to Greenberg, the relationship to the materials changed, rendering the material form, as Robert Morris famously put it, 'less *self*-important', with aesthetic terms of reference existing as 'unfixed variables that find their specific definition in the particular space and light and physical viewpoint of the spectator'.[1]

When artists employed found or industrially fabricated objects in the creation of their works, their relationship to and interaction with their materials changed radically. However, despite this, an object remained the result. This enabled conservation to carry on as if the conservation object had not undergone this radical change.

Lying somewhere on a continuum between performance and sculpture, the time-based media installation lacks a material object that can be identified as 'the work', undermining the traditional notion of what constitutes the object of conservation. The relationship between the particular aspects of the medium and the identity of the work is not given, but is both constructed and uncovered in the development of the identity of the work. This process has a particular relationship to time. Given that time-based media works are dependent on technologies that become obsolete, the myth of the timeless art object is quickly exposed. The work's identity comes rapidly into question as external pressures for change take hold and decisions as to what can change and what must remain have to be made. For example, a once ubiquitous piece of equipment like a slide projector is now an object for specialist enthusiasts, and a technology that once symbolized a connection between art and the everyday is now obsolete. In the conservation of artists' installations that employ time-based media, the fact that the work only truly exists in its installed state refocuses the conservator's attention on the intangible and the temporary. However, this temporary quality may not have been apparent, or of interest, to the artist when making the work, since installing it in the gallery gives the illusion of completing it in a form that will persist. [...]

1   Robert Morris, 'Notes on Sculpture' (1966); reprinted in *Continuous Project Altered Daily: The Writings of Robert Morris* (Cambridge, Massachusetts: The MIT Press, 1993) 17.

Pip Laurenson, extract from 'Vulnerabilities and Contingencies in Film and Video Art', in *Film and Video Art*, ed. Stuart Comer (London: Tate Publishing, 2009) 146.

J. David Bolter and Richard Grusin
Remediation//1996

Immediacy is, however, a one-sided determination; thought does not contain it alone, but also the determination to mediate itself with itself, and thereby the mediation being at the same time the abrogation of mediation – it is immediacy.
– Hegel

And, as always, coherence in contradiction expresses the force of a desire.
– Derrida

The Double Logic of *Strange Days*

'This is not like TV only better', says Lenny Nero in the futuristic film *Strange Days*. 'This is life. It's a piece of somebody's life. Pure and uncut, straight from the cerebral cortex. You're there. You're doing it, seeing it, hearing it … feeling it.' Lenny is touting a black-market device called 'the wire' to a potential customer. The wire is a technological wonder that deserves Lenny's praise. It fits over the wearer's head like a skull cap, and sensors in the cap somehow make contact with the perceptual centres in the brain. In its recording mode, the wire captures the sense perceptions of the wearer; in its playback mode, the device delivers these recorded perceptions to the wearer. If we accept the popular view that the role of media is to record and transfer sense experiences from one person to another, the wire threatens to make obsolete all technologies of representation. Lenny mentions television, but we can extend his critique to books, paintings, photographs, film, and so on. The wire's appeal is that it bypasses all forms of mediation and transmits directly from one consciousness to another.

Strange Days itself is less enthusiastic about the wire than Lenny and his customers. Although the wire embodies the desire to get beyond mediation, *Strange Days* offers us a world fascinated by the power and ubiquity of media technologies. Los Angeles in the last two days of 1999, on the eve of '2K', is saturated with cellular phones, voice- and text-based telephone answering systems, radios and billboard-sized television screens that constitute public media spaces. And in this media-saturated world, the wire itself is the ultimate mediating technology, despite or indeed because the wire is designed to efface itself, to disappear from the user's consciousness. Two scenes, in which Lenny coaches the 'actors' who will appear in a pornographic recording, make it clear that the experience the wire offers can be as mediated as a traditional film. And if the wire itself is cinematic, the whole of *Strange Days* is also conscious of its own cinematic tradition, with its obvious debts to films from *Vertigo* to *Blade Runner*. Although Lenny insists that the wire is 'not TV only better', the film ends up representing the wire as 'film only better'.

Strange Days is a compelling film for us because it captures the ambivalent and contradictory ways in which new digital media function for our culture today. The film projects our own cultural moment a few years into the future in order to examine that moment with greater clarity. The wire is just a fanciful extrapolation of contemporary virtual reality, with its goal of unmediated visual and aural experience; and the proliferation of media in 2K LA is only a slight exaggeration of our current media-rich environment, in which digital technologies are proliferating faster than our cultural, legal or educational institutions can keep up with them. In addressing our culture's contradictory imperatives for immediacy and hypermediacy, the film enacts what we understand as a double logic of 'remediation'. Our culture wants both to multiply its media and to erase all traces of mediation: it wants to erase its media in the very act of multiplying technologies of mediation.

In this last decade of the twentieth century, we are in an unusual position to appreciate the double logic of remediation – not only because we are bombarded with images (in print, on television, in films, and now on the World Wide Web and through other digital media), but also because of the intensity with which these two logics are being pursued in all these media. 'Live' point-of-view television programmes show us what it is like to accompany a policeman on a dangerous raid or indeed to be a skydiver or a racing car driver hurtling through space. Filmmakers routinely spend tens of millions of dollars to film 'on location' or to recreate period costumes and places in order to make their viewers feel as if they were 'really' there. Internet sites offer stories, images and now video that is up-to-the-minute, all in the name of perceptual immediacy. Yet these media enact another logic with equal enthusiasm: websites are often riots of diverse media forms, including graphics, digitized photographs, animation, and video – all set up in pages whose graphic design principles recall the psychedelic 1960s or Dada in the 1920s. Hollywood films, like *Natural Born Killers* or *Strange Days* itself, routinely mix media and styles. Televised news programmes now feature multiple video streams, split-screen displays, composites of graphics and text – a welter of media that is meant to make the news more perspicuous to us.

What is remarkable is that these seemingly contradictory logics not only coexist in digital media today but are mutually dependent. Immediacy depends upon hypermediacy. In the effort to create a seamless moving image, filmmakers combine live-action footage with computer compositing and two- and three-dimensional computer graphics. In the effort to be up to the minute and complete, television news producers assemble on the screen ribbons of text, photographs, graphics and even audio without a video signal when necessary (as was the case during the Persian Gulf War). At the same time, even the most hypermediated productions strive for a kind of immediacy. So, for example, music videos rely on multiple media and elaborate editing to create an immediate and apparently spontaneous style. The desire for immediacy leads to a process of appropriation and critique by which digital media reshape or 'remediate' one another and their analogue predecessors such as film, television and photography. […]

Marshall McLuhan remarked that 'the "content" of any medium is always another medium. The content of writing is speech, just as the written word is the content of print, and print is the content of the telegraph.'[1] As his problematic examples suggest, McLuhan was not thinking of simple repurposing, but perhaps of a more complex kind of borrowing, in which one medium is itself incorporated or represented in another medium. Dutch painters incorporated maps, globes, inscriptions, letters and mirrors in their works. All our examples of hypermediacy are characterized by this kind of borrowing, as is also ancient and modern *ekphrasis*, the literary description of works of visual art, which W.J.T. Mitchell defines as 'the verbal representation of visual representation'.[2] Again, we call the representation of one medium in another 'remediation', and we argue that remediation is a defining characteristic of the new digital media. What might seem at first to be an esoteric practice is so widespread that we can identify a spectrum of different ways in which digital media remediate their predecessors, a spectrum depending upon the degree of perceived competition or rivalry between the new media and the old. […]

1   [footnote 40 in source] Marshall McLuhan, *Understanding Media: The Extensions of Man* (New York: McGraw-Hill, 1964) 23–4.

2   [41] W.J.T. Mitchell, *Picture Theory* (Chicago: University of Chicago Press, 1994) 151–2.

J. David Bolter and Richard Grisin, extracts from 'Remediation', *Configurations*, vol. 4, no. 3 (1996) 311–14, 339.

Pipilotti Rist
In Conversation with Michele Robecchi//2007

Michele Robecchi [...] They used to say that your work was subversive. There was this big thing about MTV and how you were commenting on the media culture, when, as a matter of fact, I think you were actually more influenced by experimental cinema.

Pipilotti Rist When I started I didn't know about MTV. Music films were already there. They weren't invented by MTV. MTV just created a market by putting them on TV 24/7. But that was in the 1980s. Now there are so many shows you're lucky if you see a music video at all. I don't know why they do it. Did they really find out that people prefer that to music clips? Maybe I should write them a letter. I read that the chief of MTV Europe likes my work. I didn't expect that she would know me.

Robecchi I think you should. It's also way too compartmentalized now.

Rist It is. It was completely mixed before. It shows you again the paradox of keeping completely separated those trends that are supposed to group people together. Each has its own codes, its own development, its own history, in a way. This is also because they are so brutally everywhere that they are accessible all the time. Not to mention that people are very well educated in symbols, styles and movements now. [...]

Robecchi I understand you are a John Waters fan. What do you like about him?

Rist He can talk as well as he can make films – unlike me! (*laughs*) Do you know his books? They're short stories, they're very good. *Pink Flamingos* (1972), is actually close to the subject I'm also dealing with: conventions and rules, the image of a woman and a man and how he turns them upside down to take a different viewpoint. What they do in his film could probably be true but not with that intensity. It often looks like things have been this way forever but that's not true. They always make us believe that the way men are today is down to natural development, but it could have been slightly different and that's what I like about Waters, that he gives these perspectives.

Robecchi Tell me about your feature film [*Pepperminta*, released in 2009].

Rist My subject is a girl, or a woman, or a human being if you like, who inherits a dream from her grandmother to free herself and the world from unnecessary fears. Not only to overcome unnecessary fears but to propose new rituals. Today we also have the luck that so many conventions have gone away, but we don't fill them with new ones so on the one hand we feel too restricted and on the other hand we are lost. And she tries to bring about new rituals and also to overcome the fears of being laughed at or excluded from a group. Sometimes she succeeds, sometimes she doesn't. She then goes looking for friends to spread 'health' in the world. She's completely fearless.

Robecchi What's her name in the film?

Rist Pepperminta. Like the character in *Homo Sapiens Sapiens* (2005). It's also the same main actor and performer – Ewelina Guzik from Krakau in Poland.

Robecchi You said you see this as a step forward. Is it because you are bringing your view to a different audience?

Rist It's both a different audience and a different ritual to watch. Prior to every installation I have to know everything about the space where it will be shown – the size of the room, the history of that institution … the whole package. I see a movie theatre exactly in the same way. You go to the pictures, you sit, you pay, quite a lot, and you and all the other people in the room focus in one direction and you are not supposed to leave until the end. In an installation I cannot decide when people come in and when they leave. This gives it a completely different choreography. I'm also very interested in TV. But if you want to get film funding you cannot stress this point because film people take this ritual for granted. The challenging thing is to make a story that holds up for more than an hour. You follow the actor and you identify with him or her and say 'I would do it differently'… You go on a longer journey.

Robecchi While you were talking about TV I was thinking of *Achterbahn/das Tram ist noch nicht voll* (1998), the work you made in collaboration with Thomas Rhyner and Ian Krohn. Have you ever had the opportunity of doing something with TV?

Rist To do a show or something? No. I had a small connection with TV twice. My single channel videos were shown on national TV once and then I worked on a show for teenagers about menstruation. The footage I later used for *Blutclip* (1993) was made for that show. I feel myself more on the side of the viewer and TV is more like a magazine or a newspaper – they think to know what people want. It's a powerful institution. I work with similar materials but I am completely free. I have no chiefs, no rules, nobody to tell me what goes or doesn't go on and as long as I have such good freedom, I never fight with them. Of course there is the possibility to subvert the system from inside. But it is funny as in Zurich many people working in TV come from the eighties, from this youth demonstration culture. The loudest ones, the most political people from that time, are now working with TV. They said they were giving too much money for opera and not getting anything for themselves. Over the last twenty years this has changed a lot because of the battles in the eighties. They were fighting for more concert places, fringe theatres, and spaces for expression. And the people who fought for this, the most radical ones, now are in TV. I thought they would become politicians and instead they're mainly on TV. When I watch them, it looks like they are little cogs of a big gear.

Robecchi Cable TV is a bit more experimental in this sense. You can decide what to watch and there seems to be a bit more independence.

Rist On demand, yes. It will be seen as a huge change in the next twenty years or so as to how we consumed TV. We once had plans to do alternative shows. We thought about it but the whole thing would take so many people. It's a little bit similar to the difference between experimental video and 35mm films. Everything is dependent on the moment and it has to work. And the more are working, the more you're under pressure to make it work. And the more people you have, the more money you need, and all TV institutions are like heavy, slow machines. There's a lot of administration. It's a power game – who sits the longest until everybody else falls down. I just don't feel like being part of it. From 1986 to 1994 I worked in different video studios. I know the structures and how it works. [...]

Robecchi You covered Chris Isaak's 'Wicked Game' in *Sip My Ocean* (1996). A lot of people talk about feminism when they discuss that work. Rochelle Steiner wrote that *I'm Not the Girl Who Misses Much* (1986) and *Sip My Ocean* were a response to these very macho songs with a female perspective. Do you agree with that?

Rist Both try to show hysteria in a positive light. Maybe they overlap a bit. Hysteria is associated with the idea of falling apart – it's got a very negative connotation. Trying to put it in another light, not with words but with actions, songs or pictures, helps more than if you say, 'we should not read hysteria so negatively.' That doesn't help so much, but if you exorcise it, I think it does. [...]

Pipilotti Rist and Michele Robecchi, extracts from 'Interview: Pipilotti Rist', *Contemporary*, no. 92 (May 2007). (www.contemporary-magazines.com)

Kenneth Goldsmith
In Conversation with Joanne McNeil//2011

Joanne McNeil How would you describe the work that shows up on UbuWeb?

Kenneth Goldsmith I would say it falls under the general rubric of avant-garde, but I'm not sure what avant-garde is. It's always changing. One thing that all the works in Ubu have in common is they are not worth anything monetarily. Nothing on the site ever made money. Nothing on the site probably ever will make money. So you have an inversion of the market. You've got Marcel Duchamp's music instead of his objects. A lot of painters too, but with the odd LPs that they make. Kind of the inverse of what we usually think of as important.

McNeil Is it a conscious decision not to include pictures of paintings or sculptures?

Goldsmith There are some images of paintings in the *Aspen* magazine section, but they are really bad – lousy reproductions from the Powers' Collection. Painting doesn't look so good on the web. It looks better in life. Sculpture looks better in life. What you end up with is just a reproduction. Whereas with film or with sound or with poetry, you get the deep primary experience not the secondary experience. The web delivers those primary experiences very well.

McNeil And the site is not on Google?

Goldsmith I removed it from Google. I didn't want to deal with copyright-holder mania.

McNeil But the Twitter stream is accessible through Google.

Goldsmith I'm very careful about that. There's a lot of stuff that doesn't go out on the Twitter stream. I also killed the RSS feed from the site because it was going into Google. And I killed a mirror. I need to be more controlled about what goes out and doesn't. [...]

McNeil Do you get requests for better picture quality?

Goldsmith I like bad quality. It shouldn't be too good, because then you should go out and support organizations such as Anthology Film Archives or EAI [Electronic Arts Intermix]. Ubu doesn't challenge that. It should be a sketch of the real thing. But unfortunately for many people it really is the real thing, because they don't live in a place with Anthology down the street showing Stan Brakhage films every night. [...]

McNeil Are you finding remixes of UbuWeb material?

Goldsmith You've heard of Kurt Schwitters but most people have no idea. Some kids are like, 'check out these weird sounds!' They get thrown into dance mixes! I've heard from people in Zurich who were on a dance floor and suddenly some sound poetry comes into it from Ubu. [...]

McNeil Sometimes I'll have three open tabs of Ubu videos and watch them all at once.

Goldsmith An editor on Ubu, Danny Snelson, actually did that. He curated it to balance beautifully. And isn't that the avant-garde cinema? Isn't that *Chelsea Girls* (1966)? Here Warhol becomes very predictive again. Warhol would watch two televisions at a time. [...] It's about divided attention as a new strategy of attention. I'm not being a cyber-futurist, every idea here can be found in the twentieth century history of avant-garde art. Whether it's concrete poetry and the web or split screens and divided attention coming from Warhol, that's what Ubu's all about. [...]

Kenneth Goldsmith and Joanna McNeil, extracts from 'An Interview with the founder of UbuWeb' (20 April 2011), *frieze*. (www.frieze.com)

Iwona Blazwick
In a Cinema Near You//2015

Is it the hard scrabble of artists' lives that has led to such a rich profusion of moving image work – this one-stop-shop medium that can combine sound, performance, photography and drawing? Certainly most artists are unencumbered by film crews, producers, investors or distributors. Their studio may be the kitchen table. Their camera may be a phone. Artists from Kabul to Tangiers, Buenos Aires to Hanoi are deploying film to create works that, often with the minimum of means, open new vistas of intellectual and visual enquiry. Moving deftly between analogue and digital technologies, they are equally adept at weaving through genres, at fusing the archival with the fictional, the documentary with the carnivalesque. Their films may last 30 seconds or 24 hours. And on the whole, they are to be screened, not in the cinema, on terrestrial or digital channels, but in the physical space of the gallery.

Here there is no need for star, plot and yield on investment. Galleries and museums are still spaces where artists can reveal unpalatable and urgent political realities, or reflect on the hidden and the obscure. If darkness and electricity can be provided, the white cube presents a spatial, temporal environment where film becomes phenomenology. Established art institutions – be they artists' spaces or museums – also carry with them their exhibition histories. Whether they are aware of the context of what has gone before or not, the public for moving image work brings an expectation of aesthetic invention. Unlike the formal predictability of mainstream cinema, broadcasting or gaming, artists' film leaves no convention unquestioned or reimagined.

How does it find its audience? Much moving image work can be accessed through the internet. But here it can often lie in a deep sleep. To be awoken works must be known, talked about, reviewed. By selecting and staging, curators act as messengers and champions.

In 2007 the Whitechapel Gallery decided to transform its auditorium – by night a stage for debate – by day, into a cinema. We had the space and the audience. We had knowledge of the UK scene, itself supported by spaces like Liverpool's FACT or London's Chisenhale Gallery; or events like the Jarman Award. Backed by public funding agency Film London, this annual prize, named after the pioneering filmmaker Derek Jarman, draws on nominations from across Britain to shortlist and screen ten outstanding works by artists living and working in the UK. But we were also intent on reflecting global developments. The question was, how could we discover, evaluate and bring to London work from around the world without increasing the art world's already substantial carbon footprint?

We decided to trust local knowledge. We gave over the programming to a network of curators whose work has sent out signals from locations around the globe. Each runs or has access to a black box space. Together we formed a network, a curatorial consortium. Perhaps predictably it started in Europe and America with two curatorial partners – Giacinto Pietroantonio, director of the GAMec in Bergamo and Fairfax Dorn, founder of the Marfa Ballroom in Marfa, Texas. But through chance conversations and serendipitous introductions, the idea gained momentum and began to spread incrementally – to Wellington, New Zealand and then Oslo, to Beijing and Buenos Aires. Each curator nominates one local artist – everyone in the consortium then presents that work to their local audience. No crates, no shipping and insurance, no airfares. The works were at first dispatched as DVDs and since 2012 have been sent electronically as digital files.

At the Whitechapel Gallery the lights in the Zilkha Auditorium go down, the projector is switched on and the programme runs all day for up to three months, reaching around 100,000 visitors. A project like Yto Barrada's Cinema Tangiers, however, had one-off screenings for a small but dedicated crowd. As the consortium has grown to 15 partners, films are compiled in themes. Works by artists from different geographies and cultures are put in dialogue.

Sometimes local conditions make participation impossible. Partners have had to face social unrest, withdrawal of funding or simply a paucity of work. For these participants, an advantage of the consortium framework is that they can re-enter at any point, as local conditions allow.

The result has been exposure for artists, from every continent, in every continent. A small collective from Afghanistan finds a global audience. An audience in Istanbul can view films hailing from Poland to Hong Kong. The postcolonial geopolitics of West versus East, the hegemony of Northern over Southern hemispheres is not only transcended but dissolved.

Iwona Blazwick, programme statement, Whitechapel Gallery, London, May 2015

Jacolby Satterwhite
In Conversation with Kei Kreutler//2014

Kei Kreutler Your video *The Country Ball* (1989–2012) incorporates traces of your mother's drawings in a computer-generated landscape, accompanied by footage from one of your family's cook-outs in the 1980s. The family video has a frenetic energy, which infects the piece. There is a moment, however, in which the work seems to slow down – when tracings of figures from your mother's drawings leave the din of the family video behind – that I found very interesting. It felt similar to that sensation of leaving a show, leaving a mass of huddled bodies, where it's too loud but you don't notice until you leave, your ears ringing slightly. 3D animation seems to incorporate these changes in rhythm and narrative particularly well, so I was wondering how it influences the pacing, the loose narrative points, of your works.

Jacolby Satterwhite The visual pace in my videos varies based on what motif or idea I am trying to assert. In *Country Ball*, I wanted to present a beginning, middle, that gradates. It begins with deadpan repetitive orchestra, full of folly and recreation, and a very slow camera. It evolves and collapses into an apocalyptic display of objectum-sexuality, where cumshots spew out of towering cakes, dance rituals erect trees, and ATM machines inseminate a middle class family into a giant. The camera in those scenes tends to be more erratic. I have a Walt Disney sensibility when it comes to object-perversion, animism and anthropomorphism.

Kreutler Speaking of object-perversion: the *Reifying Desire* project takes your mother's drawings as starting points for a series of six videos in which you perform in front of chroma-keyed 3D animations. One of the videos in the series, shown as part of 'The Matriarch's Rhapsody' exhibition at Monya Rowe Gallery, *Reifying Desire 5*, incorporates your mother's drawing *Pussy Power*, which provides written instructions for the elimination of feminine odour. What role do you think these forms and regimens of self-care – physically intimate and yet more or less culturally proscribed – play in your work, and how do they affect us?

Satterwhite One thing I often cite as one of my subconscious platforms of inspiration is the concept of body trauma, disease and metamorphosis of form as the consequence of a sexual act. I pick objects to work with and set up surrealist scenarios that will make their use necessary. The usage of the pussy power bottle felt necessary because I was using the Picasso painting *Les Demoiselles d'Avignon* as the conceptual departure point. I asked myself: what would prostitutes in a bathhouse need to begin their daily ritual? 'For Pussy Power, pour bubble bath into the bathtub into the water and soak for a while to turn the smell of pussy off.' I think the idea of self-care provides a vehicle for continuity. When something's preserved it can move onward to the next stage.

Kreutler In Sara Ahmed's *Queer Phenomenology: Orientations, Objects, Others,* she writes extensively on 'inherited proximities' of the body and how 'spaces acquire the shape of the bodies that inhabit them'. With the *Reifying Desire* project at large, what do you see being brought into being with these works? What are the spaces you create in them, and what, if anything, is reified in them? Finally, what role do contemporary animation technologies play in the creation of these spaces?

Satterwhite Contemporary animation technologies have an infinite range of possibilities, therefore my interest in reification or making abstraction concrete stems from having access to an unlimited terrain of visual possibility. The visual restraint lies within my body of archives, ranging from collected movements by myself and other performers to my mother's drawings and my stock photos collected from the internet. Merging them together into a dense crystal of information results in the reification of process, a concrete time-based visual system bleeding formal, philosophical and political ideas.

Kreutler There's Walt Disney, Picasso, and of course your mother's drawings – I'm curious as to your other influences, whether animators, painters, family, or others outside of traditional art history.

Satterwhite Janet Jackson was the first pop star I discovered when I was a baby, and I watched her video anthology on VHS tape every day when I got home from school. I always hoped I'd be able to make a serial body of work like hers that included surrealism and dance. Music videos (i.e. Deee Lite, Björk, Janet, Chemical Brothers, Prodigy, Michael Jackson, Madonna, etc.) structured my aesthetic, as well as gaming; I owned every console from Game Gear, Sega Genesis, SNES, 32X, Nintendo 64, Sega Saturn, Sony Playstation, and it was quite an escapist zone for me. I went to Miami Basel last week, and when I went swimming at the beach, the only thing my memory could register was Wave Race 64 on Nintendo 64. Lately I've been thinking of Beyoncé's *B'Day Anthology Video Album*, Madonna's *Erotica* and *Bedtime Stories* era, her interviews from that era, and the *Sex Book*. Lyle Ashton Harris, David Wojnarowicz, Mapplethorpe, Wolfgang Tillmans, Isaac Julien, Michael Clark, Warhol, Nauman and Beuys have been on my mind as well ...

Kreutler With your references based in the pop, art historical and gaming worlds – which are more self-consciously converging today – what do you take with you when you perform in front of a green screen in your studio? Is Wave Race 64 with you when you're not swimming down in Miami?

Satterwhite My green screen performances are all triggered by language prompts and isolated objects that I'm interested in stringing together narratively. Whether I'm performing a violent wrestling act with another model, a sexual act, or a banal miming gesture articulated through dance, the result is always a marriage between disparate languages, objects and performed acts. I take surprises away from the green screen every time.

Kreutler Coming from a painting background, I was wondering how the rhythm of your work has changed? In terms of your production, as well – the difference in productive speed between sitting behind a screen or painting or performing.

Satterwhite I used to spend a month or two on each painting, and I tend to do the same with my videos, except my latest. My latest video has taken me over six months. I keep scrapping it and starting over. I am negotiating the exact same problems that I did when I was painting as I am in my animation. The computer allows me to resolve palettes, compositions, textures, planes and frames in a much more dynamic way. Having a time-based composition, colour palette and surface variation is much more expansive. I've been getting closer to my painting days by working on static images in 3D animation. Their final form are large scale C-Prints. They act as my storyboard. My challenge is to make the 10 hyper-detailed and ambitious images congruent narratively, forcing them to animate into each other. That method allows me to have my performance/painting/gaming cake and eat it too!

Jacolby Satterwhite and Kei Kreutler, 'Artist Profile: Jacolby Satterwhite', *Rhizome* (9 January 2014). (rhizome.org)

Yuri Ancarani
In Conversation with Emanuela Mazzonis//2015

[...] *Yuri Ancarani goes beyond the boundaries of video art to produce short films that blend documentary cinema and contemporary art. In his research he sets out to explore regions of daily life that are not very visible, situations into which he ventures in person in order to cross unexplored thresholds, to enter territories that are often risky but so stimulating that they constitute a personal and professional challenge. His latest project is a trilogy –* Il Capo *(The Foreman, 2010),* Piattaforma Luna *(Luna Platform, 2011) and* Da Vinci *(2012) – devoted to the theme of work, or rather to those extreme, unusual and little discussed occupations that are carried out in fascinating and difficult settings, on the edge of survival.* [...]

Emanuela Mazzonis How do you make your works? Do you have a team working for you?

Yuri Ancarani I work with a mini-crew made up of five people. I don't feel like a director because I don't direct anyone: the director works with actors, while my actors are real people who I leave free to act in a natural way. I start making my film with great humility and put myself on the same level as the person I'm working with: a workman, a technician or whoever. Then, as the project gradually takes shape, I start to talk about myself and what I'm doing. Until I arrive at the presentation of the film, when I explain that we have worked together on the creation of a work of art.

Mazzonis In your stories it is as if at a certain point a shift takes place from a simple account to a hidden, invisible side of the events. How are your films born?

Ancarani I start out from stories told me by friends, by people I meet in the street, at the bar. Often they are strange stories, about little-known things. The stories become intuitions and the intuitions in turn make me imagine situations. I rely a great deal on my relationship with people, on what I discover by observing them. My method is based on images, and when you hear voices it is because they are significant as a source of information, as in *Piattaforma Luna*, where the characters have the nasal tone of voice that comes from breathing helium, which it was important to hear. It is hard to work like this, but I have imposed very strict rules on myself, I move within a veritable cage of rules. The fact is that as soon as you start to make the account explicit you get caught up in the mechanism of TV and the viewer becomes passive, whereas what interests me is that the viewer has a real experience and thinks about what he is seeing to the point where he 'takes the work home' with him.

Mazzonis In the collection *Ricordi per moderni* (*Memories for Moderns*), which presents fourteen videos made between 2000 and 2009, you speak of industrial zones, vacation spots, airplanes, sex, children, gambling, money. You try to reveal the hidden side of each aspect, to show what is known, but often not visible. Can you talk to us about this production?

Ancarani The beauty of *Ricordi per moderni* is that there is fiction, there is performance, there is reality, and at a certain point it is no longer clear what is true and what is false. They are stories that come from my own experience, or from what I have seen or been told, or something that I have just imagined. They are videos that I made separately, but when I united them in a single collection I saw that together they had a life of their own. The occasion was provided by an exhibition at the Museo Marino Marini in Florence in 2012, where I created an installation with fourteen videos projected in three sequences on a set of four screens hung side by side. A fifteen metre-long bench in front of the screens allowed people to have a vision of the whole thing and at the same time to watch each video individually. […]

Mazzonis The trilogy formed by *Il Capo*, *Piattaforma Luna* and *Da Vinci* investigates the relations between man and machine. What attracted you to the world of work?

Ancarani Just as for the other videos, the idea for these three films came from real stories, told me by people I met. For *Il Capo*, it was a photographer friend of mine who told me about a marble quarry that was really worth visiting. For *Piattaforma Luna*, the stories of divers overheard in a bar near the port of Ravenna were decisive. As for *Da Vinci*, the idea came to me both from conversations with a friend who is a biomedical engineer and from thinking about my mother's work as a nurse. […]

Mazzonis *Piattaforma Luna* recounts the experiences of six divers on the Luna A platform in the Ionian Sea, which works on the extraction of natural gas under extreme conditions, because of the high pressure underwater and the atmosphere filled with helium. How were you able to shoot these scenes?

Ancarani The length of time I worked on *Piattaforma Luna* was very different from *Il Capo*, for obvious reasons connected with permits and the material conditions in which the filming was done. I shot it all in seven days: three days of filming in the hyperbaric chamber and four outside it. It was a tough, difficult experience, you can't perform miracles in three days. And in the end I understood that the platform is a really dangerous place. [...]

Mazzonis Your trilogy turns ordinary people into 'mythic men', heroes to be remembered. Who for you is the hero in today's world?

Ancarani I'd say that in the trilogy heroes are present chiefly in *Il Capo* and *Piattaforma Luna*, while in *Da Vinci* it is the machine that prevails, overshadowing the human being and coming out on top. Apart from this, the theme of the hero is a very important one. These days we live in a work of fiction where a bogus vision of the hero predominates, something that is conveyed in particular by television. Instead we ought to be talking about the people who do their jobs, often dangerous ones, every day with passion. Some know that they are risking their lives, but don't want to change, and for this reason too are real heroes. The interesting thing, though, is that these 'mythic' figures often have figures from TV dramas as their own heroes. The divers in *Piattaforma Luna*, for example, are clones of Fabrizio Corona [an Italian TV personality currently serving a jail sentence for blackmail]: he is a continual source of inspiration for them. Or at least he was: when they saw themselves in my film, they realized the unique value of their own personalities.

Yuri Ancarani and Emanuela Mazzonis, extracts from 'Men at Work Interview', *Klatmagazine* (January 2015). (www.klatmagazine.com)

Travis Jeppesen
Exploding the Frame: Ryan Trecartin's Bad Language//2012

The Reality TV script is, by now, formulaic, easy enough to decode by nearly anyone. It's been around for a generation, the youngest among us has known no other function of television other than constructing and presenting a mediated form of reality. Ryan Trecartin's work, and in particular his film *I-Be Area*, is both an amplification and distortion of that script. Reality TV changes our whole perception of reality; reality is now something that you watch on a screen. In *I-Be Area*, we get screen upon screen upon screen upon endless screen. The screen is both filter and transmitter of heavily performed and heavily edited reality. Although there are many different settings, the entire action of the film occurs within a single zone, which is both RealityTV amplified and Reality© amplified, a space where all interactions are heavily scripted in order to orchestrate the illusion of chaos and a natural collusion of conflicting wills, a locale controlled by a god whose iterability manifests itself in a total situationality that is occluded by the all-recording digitalized presence. Affectation and gesture become just as important as the text being deployed by the participants in these multiproliferatory screens; they become the emotive norms that encase the seemingly random collage of words and ideas that form the script – thoughts melting into one another linguistically because one thought can never be completed: a New Real Order.

There are many different ways of watching *I-Be Area*. It's like taking a different ride each time: there is the participatory way, wherein you join the party, projecting your own zone of being and becoming into the 'total minimal situation' that the film proclaims; the narrative engulfment, in which you attempt to navigate the 'multilinear' (Kevin McGarry) pathways that the plot entails; the linguistico-linear tributary, immersing yourself in the piece's pure language stream, finding the sense in the seeming nonsense; imagistic engulfment, giving yourself over to the sensory overload in the piece's manic cuts, the repeated strains of neon colour, the detailed visual anarchy of the sets and costumes; the energo-intensive path, wherein affectation becomes your beaming guide; the elemental way, in which you attempt to sort out the millions of parts that form the spectral collage of the whole.

In all likelihood, however, your way of taking in *I-Be Area* will combine all or many of these methods, thus putting you in a schizo delirium that may repel or enliven you, depending on your openness towards destabilization and the manic mediation that forms the fabric of RTV and R©. All of your impulses become amplified, the aim of your desires is no longer certain, stable identity becomes a joke. It can be a discomfiting ride to take, which makes it all the more worthwhile.

It should be noted, however, that there can be no characterological way of watching *I-Be Area*, because in a utopia where identity is so fluid, there can be nothing so solid as character – thus there is no such thing as a standard linear narrative. Rather, the triumph of simultaneity – both the multiplicity inherent in being and in situationality. (In one of Trecartin's subsequent films from the *Any Ever* series, a character suggests re-writing the US Constitution and replacing the word 'God' with 'Internet' and 'people' with 'situations'.)

If the film can be said to be 'about' anything (this 'about' is always the worst thing anyone could ask of an artist – though we often do), then it is the dissolution of identity into a sort of digital being – a hallmark of the New Real Order. Don't like your identity? Buy a new one online, pay with plastic. Don't react; redact! 'Sometimes I feel like a prequel to a horrible person', says one persona early on in the film. This embrace of becoming – a multiplicity of selves (every one is different people, different genders) – is certainly a generational influence; an abundance of youth marks every Trecartin statement. Despite the current shadows looming over the civilized West, we must keep in mind that the RTV generation was reared into an attitude reflecting an overload of confidence, unafraid of the consequences of taking risks – unafraid of appearing stupid. It is this latter fact that allows for so much of the vileness of Reality TV, and which *I-Be Area* subtly mocks. 'What will I be when I grow up?' asks I-Be after he has been transformed into a new avatarial persona, Oliver. 'A production company!' he/she answers. Media and the means of mediation are newly morphed into one with technology's showboating and accessibility; not only is everything shot in HD, the cameras are often visible and frequently held by the speaking persona. Nearly every line of dialogue in the film is spoken directly to the camera, reflecting a consciousness of the process of mediation, a demolition of the fourth wall borrowed from the theatre, which RTV typically attempts to avoid, in its artificial framing of 'authenticity'.

Departing from the recurring concept of adoption – of babies, but also, by extension, implying the incorporative becoming of new selves – individuals drift into new personae readily and without hesitation. Everything is temporary, and so the heavy burden of ontological meaning is absent. An avatar can become 'a toxic bisexual wearing unstable flip flops' before finding her/himself a living, walking meme. In this zone, everything is temporary. Dialects and personalities can be picked up and discarded alongside wigs and make-up. Tangible is intangible and vice versa. Interactions are pure – no psychology, just a super-psychology, overburdened with mediated emotions. 'Major' and 'minor' – events, personae, substance, objects – become equal and are thus no longer worthwhile distinguishing.

The loss of agency this process entails is not necessarily a bad thing. In the film's 'Moms' scene, in which a group of mothers gathers together in a middle-class suburban living room in order to vote one of the mothers off the show that the film has suddenly become, the excluded mother proclaims, 'I can't believe New Jersey happened to me. It was like writing a book I had no control over.' Instead, in such an equalized universe, a realm where agency is absent or altered, in which subjectivity is therefore spectral and momentary, it all comes down to mattering. 'That will be a good day', shouts the excluded mom: 'When it won't matter!'

Projectile bodies mattering all over the supra-mediated normvoid.
'Do you know what your dad is?

'My dad is a building that we lit on fire.'

Just as you begin to think it's all like a high school drama improv class gone totally haywire, the setting shifts and enters into … well, what appears to be a high school drama improv class. While narrative shifts occur all the time throughout *I-Be Area*, in keeping with the multi-linearity that is the underlying aura of the piece, a major shift nonetheless can be detected about an hour into the film. Or, perhaps: a shift of realms. This new realm is a classroom compound overruled by a pregnant authoritarian teacher, Jamie, and her muse, Ramada Omar. Jamie sits with her legs spread wide open and squats constantly while standing, always about to give birth. Ramada Omar rolls around on the floor, squealing 'This is my favorite interactive!'

'It's not phone you person go call yourself!', responds Jamie.

How does all this mattering come to resolve itself in the light of the total minimal situation? Perception, after all, can also be a physical object in these heightened terms. Saying is an object; so is this gesture. 'No symbols where none intended', Beckett famously wrote at the end of his novel *Watt*, but how to read in the absence of symbols? Do reading and being become intertwined through projection and participation? How does the frame manage to function when its contents' aim is to completely decimate the material structure of its container?

We have to see the RTV zone for the metaphysical failure that it is. Just as, say, human laws cannot physically prevent someone from committing a crime, our own physical containers can no longer contain us, if they ever did. *I-Be Area* is the drama of this failed containment, a literal and ritual purging of the frame. Don't tell me what something is; rather, inhabit it.

In the end, the personae trapped in the zone that *I-Be Area* inhabits are desperate to get out of it, to bust it up. They are constantly picking up hammers, breaking glass, destroying the set, fueling the increasingly frenzied chaos that is the artificial guise of their inhabited voidosphere.

Where to go once one finally manages to escape? Escaping is never about re-location – it is about the very act of escaping. The answer is never 'there', more like 'there-ing'. Perhaps it's too unsettling, this sudden cognizance that there is no final destination, only constant movement in store. If there is any true reality, then it is in the machinic nature of shifty becomings, the drive to escape the inescapable. Perhaps the right attitude is best expressed by one of Trecartin's all-too-'real' personae: 'Fuck you and sign out.'

Travis Jeppesen, 'Exploding the Frame: Ryan Trecartin's Bad Language' (2012). (disorientations.com)

Biographical Notes

Basel Abbas is a Cyprus-born, Palestinian artist who works collaboratively with Ruanne Abou-Rahme, based in Palestine and New York.

Ruanne Abou-Rahme is an American-born, Palestinian artist who works collaboratively with Basel Abbas, based in Palestine and New York.

Francis Alÿs is a Belgian-born artist based in Mexico City.

Yuri Ancarani is an Italian artist and filmmaker based in Milan.

Ed Atkins is a British artist based in London.

Jeremy Bailey is a Canadian artist based in Toronto.

Erika Balsom is Lecturer in Film Studies and Liberal Arts, King's College London.

George Barber is a Guyanese-born artist based in London.

Judith Barry is an American artist based in New York and Berlin.

Robert Bird is Associate Professor, Department of Slavic Languages and Literatures and Department of Cinema and Media Studies, University of Chicago.

Dara Birnbaum is an American artist based in New York.

Claire Bishop is Professor of Contemporary Art, The Graduate Center, City University of New York.

Iwona Blazwick is Director of Whitechapel Gallery, London.

Christa Blümlinger is Professor of Film Studies, Université Paris 8.

J. David Bolter is Wesley Chair of New Media and a professor in the School of Literature, Media and Communication, Georgia Institute of Technology.

Brad Butler is a British artist based in London, who works collaboratively with Karen Mirza.

Rebecca Comay is Professor of Philosophy and Comparative Literature, University of Toronto.

Jonathan Crary is Meyer Schapiro Professor of Modern Art and Theory, Columbia University.

Edith Decker is a writer and curator based in Mönchengladbach, Germany.

T.J. Demos is Professor of History of Art and Visual Culture, University of California at Santa Cruz.

Jean Fisher is a writer on contemporary art and post-coloniality, based in London.

Morgan Fisher is an American artist based in California.

Hollis Frampton (1936–1984) was an American artist based in Buffalo, New York.

Jean-Michel Frodon is a French writer, critic and professor at Sciences Po, Paris.

Peter L. Galison is Joseph Pellegrino University Professor, Department of Physics, Harvard University.

Melanie Gilligan is a Canadian artist based in London and New York.

Mark Godfrey is Curator of International Art at Tate.

Kenneth Goldsmith is an American poet and teaches Poetics and Poetic Practice at the University of Pennsylvania.

Kim Gordon is an American artist and musician based in Northampton, New York, and Los Angeles.

Tim Griffin is Executive Director and Chief Curator at The Kitchen, New York.

Andrew Grossman is a writer and editor on film and queer issues based in Fairfax, Virginia.

Richard Grusin is Professor of English and Director for 21st-Century Studies, University of Wisconsin-Milwaukee.

Félix Guattari (1930-92) was a French philosopher, psychiatrist and activist.

Ed Halter is an American critic and curator based in New York.

John G. Hanhardt is Consulting Senior Curator of Film and Media Arts at the Smithsonian American Art Museum.

Gary Hill is an American artist based in Seattle.

Susan Hiller is an American-born artist based in London.

Travis Jeppesen is a writer based in Berlin.

Shanay Jhaveri is a curator based in Mumbai and London.

Stanya Kahn is an American artist based in Los Angeles.

William Kentridge is a South African artist based in Johannesburg.

Jacob King is a freelance writer and curator based in New York.

Anja Kirschner is a German artist based in London.

George Kuchar (1942–2011) was an American artist and film director based in San Francisco.

Pip Laurenson is Head of Collection Care Research, Tate.

Jay Leyda (1910–1988) was an American avant-garde filmmaker and film historian.

Kate Linker is an American critic and activist based in New York.

Susan Lord is Head of Department and Associate Professor in the Department of Film and Media, Queen's University, Ontario.

Sven Lütticken is a writer and curator and teaches at the Vrije Universiteit, Amsterdam.

Chris McCormack is a writer on art and Assistant Editor at Art Monthly.

Steve McQueen is a British artist based in Amsterdam and London.

Francesco Manacorda is Artistic Director at Tate Liverpool.

Jumana Manna is an American-born Palestinian artist based in Berlin.

Janine Marchessault is Professor, Department of Film, and Canada Research Chair: Art, Digital Media and Globalization, York University, Toronto.

H.G. Masters is a writer and editor-at-large for Art Asia Pacific.

Karen Mirza is a British artist based in London who works collaboratively with Brad Butler.

Kate Mondloch is Associate Professor, Department of History of Art and Architecture, University of Oregon.

Rob Mullender is a sound artist and composer based in London.

Michael Newman is Professor of Art Writing, Goldsmiths, University of London.

Nam June Paik (1932–2006) was a Korean-American video and media artist.

Johan Pijnappel is an art historian and curator based in Amsterdam.

Luther Price is an American artist based in Massachusetts.

Yvonne Rainer is an American choreographer and filmmaker based in California and New York.

R.V. Ramani is an Indian filmmaker based in Chennai.

Steve Reinke is a Canadian-born artist and writer and Associate Professor of Art Theory and Practice, Northwestern University, Evanston.

Ben Rivers is a British artist based in London.

Pipilotti Rist is a Swiss artist based in Zurich and the Swiss mountains.

Ken Saylor is founding principal of Saylor + Sirola, a New York-based architecture, art and design consultancy.

Jacolby Satterwhite is an American artist based in New York.

Roddy Schrock is an American sound artist and composer based in New York.

Jason Simon is an American artist based in New York.

Vivian Sobchack is Professor Emerita in the Department of Film, Television and Digital Media at UCLA.

Hito Steyerl is a German artist, filmmaker, writer and Professor of New Media Art, Berlin University of the Arts.

Ryan Trecartin is an American artist and filmmaker based in Los Angeles.

Trinh T. Minh-ha is a filmmaker and Professor of Rhetoric, Gender and Women's Studies, University of California at Berkeley.

Marcia Tucker (1940–2006) was a curator and founding director of the New Museum, New York.

Andrew V. Uroskie is Associate Professor and MA/PhD Graduate Program Director in the Art Department, Stony Brook University.

Woody Vasulka is a Czech-born artist and collaborator with Steina Vasulka, based in Buffalo, New York.

Bill Viola is an American artist based in California.

Ian White (1971–2013) was a London and Berlin-based artist and writer on artist's film and video, and Curator of film at Whitechapel Gallery.

Kaelen Wilson-Goldie is a writer and critic based in Beirut.

Akram Zaatari is a Lebanese artist based in Beirut.

Thomas Zummer is a philosopher, media theorist, curator and artist based in New York.

Bibliography

Agamben, Giorgio, 'What is an Apparatus' (2006), *What is an Apparatus? And Other Essays* (Stanford: Stanford University Press, 2009)

Alÿs, Francis, and Anna Dezeuze, 'Walking the Line: Francis Alÿs interviewed by Anna Dezeuze', *Art Monthly*, no. 323 (February 2009)

Ancarani, Yuri, and Emanuela Mazzonis, 'Men at Work Interview', *Klatmagazine* (January 2015)

Atkins, Ed, Melanie Gilligan, Anja Kirschner, Ben Rivers, Dan Kidner, 'More than a Feeling', *frieze*, no. 142 (October 2011)

Bailey, Jeremy, 'Performance for the Computer' (April 2006) (www.jeremybailey.net)

Balsom, Erika, 'Original Copies: How Film and Video Became Art Objects', *Cinema Journal*, vol. 53, no. 1 (Fall 2013)

Balsom, Erika, *Exhibiting Cinema in Contemporary Art (Film Culture in Transition)* (Amsterdam: Amsterdam University Press, 2014)

Barber, George, 'Scratch and After: Edit Suite Technology and the Determination of Style in Video Art', in *Culture, Technology and Creativity in the Late Twentieth Century*, ed. Phillip Hayward (London: John Libbey, 1990)

Barry, Judith, *Public Fantasy: An Anthology of Critical Essays, Fictions and Project Descriptions*, ed. Iwona Blazwick (London: Institute of Contemporary Arts, 1991)

Bazin, André, *What is Cinema?* (1962) (Berkeley and Los Angeles: University of California Press, 2004)

Bellour, Raymond, *Between-the-Images* (1990/1999) (Dijon: Les Presses du Réel, 2011)

Bird, Robert, 'Mundane Virtuosity: Olga Chernysheva's Work on Video', *Afterall*, no. 35 (Spring 2014)

Birnbaum, Dara, and Nicolás Guagnini, 'Cable TV's Failed Utopian Vision: An Interview with Dara Birnbaum', *Cabinet*, no. 9 (Winter 2002–3)

Bishop, Claire, and Francesco Manacorda, 'The Producer as Artist', in *Phil Collins: yeah ... you, baby you*, ed. Sinisa Mitrovic (Milton Keynes: Milton Keynes Gallery/Shady Lane Publications, 2005)

Blümlinger, Christa, 'Was bei Farockis "Parallel" auf dem Spiel steht/What's at Play in Harun Farocki's Parallel', *Berlin Documentary 3* (Berlin: Haus der Kulturen der Welt, 2014)

Bode, Steven, 'From Video Art to Artists' Video', in *FACTORS* (Liverpool: Video Positive Festival, 1995) J. David Bolter and Richard Grisin, 'Remediation', *Configurations*, vol. 4, no. 3 (1996)

Broegger, Andreas, and Omar Kholeif, eds, *Vision, Memory and Media* (Liverpool: Liverpool University Press/Chicago: University of Chicago Press, 2010)

Comay, Rebecca, and Michael Newman, 'Ghostly Medium: James Coleman's *Charon (MIT Project)*', in *James Coleman* (Madrid: Centro de Arte Museu Nacional Reina Sofía, 2012)

Comer, Stuart, ed., *Film and Video Art* (London: Tate Publishing, 2008)

Connolly, Maeve, *The Place of Artists' Cinema Space, Site and Screen* (London: Intellect Books, 2009)

Crary, Jonathan, *Techniques of the Observer: On Vision and Modernity in the Nineteenth Century* (Cambridge, Massachusetts: The MIT Press, 1992)

Crary, Jonathan, 'Olafur Eliasson: Visionary Events', in *Olafur Eliasson* (Basel: Kunsthalle Basel, 1997)

Crary, Jonathan, *24/7: Late Capitalism and the Ends of Sleep* (London and New York: Verso, 2014) de Lauretis, Teresa, and Stephen Heath, eds, *The Cinematic Apparatus* (London: Macmillan, 1980).

Deleuze, Gilles, *Cinema I: The Movement Image* and *Cinema 2: The Time Image* (1983); trans. Hugh Tomlinson and Barbara Habberjam (London: Athlone Press, 1992)

Demos, T.J., 'The Unfinished Revolution: Oreet Ashery's Party for Freedom', in *Oreet Ashery: Party for Freedom* (London: Artangel, 2013)

Doane, Mary Ann, 'Remembering Women: Psychical and Historical Constructions in Film Theory', in E. Ann Kaplan, ed., *Psychoanalysis and Cinema* (London and New York: Routledge, 1990)

Ferguson, Russell, ed., *Art and Film Since 1945: Hall of Mirrors* (Los Angeles: The Museum of Contemporary Art/New York: The Monacelli Press, 1996)

Fisher, Jean, 'In Living Memory: Archive and Testimony in the Films of the Black Audio Film Collective', in *The Ghosts of Songs: The Film Art of Black Audio Film Collective 1982–1998* (Liverpool: Liverpool University Press, 2007)

Fisher, Jean, 'Minerva Cuevas and the Art of Para-sitic Intervention', *Afterall*, no. 27 (Summer 2011).

Fisher, Morgan, in *Morgan Fisher: Writings*, ed. Sabine Folie and Susanne Titz (Cologne: Verlag der Buchhandlung Walther König, 2012)

Flaxman, Gregory, *The Brain is the Screen: Deleuze and the Philosophy of Cinema*, ed. Gregory Flaxman (Minneapolis: University of Minnesota Press, 2000)

Frampton, Hollis: *On the Camera Arts and Consecutive Matters: The Writings of Hollis Frampton*, ed. Bruce Jenkins (Cambridge, Massachusetts: The MIT Press, 2009)

Frodon, Jean-Michel, 'From Films to Cinema: Entering the Life of Traces', in Joana Hadjithomas and Khalil Joreige, ed. Clément Dirie and Michele Theriault (Zurich: JRP/Ringier, 2013)

Gale, Peggy and Lisa Steele, eds, 'Video Has Captured Our Imagination', *Video re/View* (Toronto; Art Metropole/VTape, 1996)

Gidal, Peter, 'Theory and Definition of Structural/Materialist Film' (1975), in Gidal, ed., *Structural Film Anthology* (London: British Film Institute, 1976)

Godfrey, Mark, 'Making History: Omer Fast', *frieze*, no. 97 (March 2006)

Goldsmith, Kenneth, and Joanna McNeil, 'An Interview with the Founder of UbuWeb' (20 April 2011), *frieze* (www.frieze.com)

Gordon, Kim, *Performing/Guzzling* (New York: Rizzoli, 2009)

Griffin, Tim, 'On Multiple Screens', in *Gretchen Bender: Tracking the Thrill* (New York: The Kitchen, 2013)

Grossman, Andrew, 'Finger Envy: A Glimpse into the Short Films of VALIE EXPORT' (30 April 2012) (brightlightsfilm.com)

Guattari, Félix, 'Towards a Post-Media Era' (1990); trans. Alya Sebti and Clemens Apprich, in *Provocative Alloys: A Post-Media Anthology*, ed. Clemens Apprich, et al. (London: Mute/PML Books, 2013)

Halter, Ed, 'The Matter of Electronics', in *Playlist: Playing Games, Music, Art* (Gijón: LABoral Centro de Arte y Creación, 2009)

Hill, Gary, 'Inter-view', in *Gary Hill* (Paris: Centre Pompidou/Amsterdam: Stedelijk Museum, 1993)

Hiller, Susan, *Thinking about Art: Conversations with Susan Hiller*, ed. Barbara Einzig (Manchester: Manchester University Press, 1996)

Iles, Chrissie, ed., *Into the Light: The Projected Image in American Art 1964–1977* (New York: Whitney

Museum of American Art/Harry N. Abrams, 2001)

Jeppesen, Travis, 'Exploding the Frame: Ryan Trecartin's Bad Language' (2012) (disorientations.com)

Jhaveri, Shanay, 'Shared Senses of Inquietude: Communists Like Us' (2011), in *The Otolith Group: Thoughtform* (Milan: Mousse Publishing, 2011)

Kahn, Stanya, and Grant Wahlquist, 'Interview with Grant Wahlquist', *2010 California Biennial* (Newport Beach: Orange County Museum of Art, 2010)

Kaplan, E. Ann, ed., *Psychoanalysis and Cinema* (London and New York: Routledge, 1990)

Kentridge, William, Peter L. Galison and Margaret K. Koerner, 'Death, Time, Soup: A Conversation with William Kentridge and Peter Galison', *The New York Review of Books* (30 June 2012)

King, Jacob, and Jason Simon, 'Before and After UbuWeb: A Conversation about Artists' Film and Video Distribution', *Rhizome* (20 February 2014) (rhizome.org)

Klein, Norman M., 'Cross-embedded Media: An Introduction', in Andreas Broegger and Omar Kholeif, eds, *Vision, Memory and Media*, op. cit.

Krauss, Rosalind, 'Video: The Aesthetics of Narcissism', *October*, no. 1 (Spring 1976)

Kuchar, George, and Charles Bernstein, 'George Kuchar with Charles Bernstein on Close Listening (2009)', in *Whitney Biennial 2012* (New York: Whitney Museum of American Art, 2012)

Laurenson, Pip, 'Vulnerabilities and Contingencies in Film and Video Art', in *Film and Video Art*, ed. Stuart Comer, op. cit.

Leyda, Jay, *Films Beget Films* (London: George Allen & Unwin, 1964)

Linker, Kate, 'Cinema and Space(s) in the Art of Judith Barry', in *Judith Barry: Body without Limits* (Salamanca: Domus Artium, 2009)

Lütticken, Sven, 'Media Memories', in *Stan Douglas: Inconsolable Memories* (Vancouver: University of British Columbia Press, 2005)

McCormack, Chris, 'Moments Not Remembered', in *ars viva 2014/15* (Ostfildern–Ruit: Hatje Cantz, 2014)

McLuhan, Marshall, *Understanding Media: The Extensions of Man* (New York: McGraw-Hill, 1964)

McLuhan, Marshall, *The Medium is the Massage* (1967) (London: Penguin Books, 2008)

McQueen, Steve, and Adrian Searle, interview, in *Steve McQueen: Works* (Basel: Schaulager, 2013)

Manovich, Lev, *Soft Cinema: Navigating the Database* (Cambridge, Massachusetts: The MIT Press, 2005)

Manna, Jumana, and Omar Kholeif, interview, *frieze*, no. 164 (June–August 2014)

Marchessault, Janine, and Susan Lord, eds, *Fluid Screens, Expanded Cinema* (Toronto: University of Toronto Press, 2008)

Marks, Laura U., *Touch: Sensuous Theory and Multisensory Media* (Minneapolis: University of Minnesota Press, 2002)

Masters, H.G., 'Disembodied Perspective: Jananne Al-Ani', *Art Asia Pacific*, no. 78 (May/June 2012)

Metz, Christian, *Film Language: A Semiotics of the Cinema* (1974) (Chicago: University of Chicago, 1990)

Mirza, Karen, and Brad Butler, 'On Expanded Cinema', in *Expanded Cinema: Art, Performance, Film* (London: Tate Publishing, 2010)

Mondloch, Kate, *Screens: Viewing Media Installation Art* (Minneapolis: University of Minnesota Press, 2010)

Mullender, Rob, 'The Haptic Object', *Sequence*, no. 1 (London: no.w.here, 2010)

Mulvey, Laura, *Visual and Other Pleasures* (London: Macmillan, 1989)

Paik, Nam June: *Nam June Paik: Video Time – Video Space*, ed. Thomas Kellein and Toni Stooss (New York: Harry N. Abrams, 1993)

Price, Luther, Aaron Cutler and Mariana Shellard, 'The Hand Made Luther Price', *Idiom* (October 2012)

Rainer, Yvonne, *The Films of Yvonne Rainer* (Bloomington: Indiana University Press, 1989)

Ramani, R.V., and Pallavi Paul, interview, *Wide Screen*, vol. 5, no. 1 (February 2014)

Rees, A.L., *A History of Experimental Film and Video* (London: Palgrave Macmillan, 2011)

Rist, Pipilotti, and Michele Robecchi, 'Interview: Pipilotti Rist', *Contemporary*, no. 92 (May 2007)

Rodowick, D.N., *Reading the Figural, or Philosophy after the New Media* (Durham, North Carolina: Duke University Press, 2001)

Satterwhite, Jacolby, and Kei Kreutler, 'Artist Profile: Jacolby Satterwhite', *Rhizome* (9 January 2014)

Schrock, Roddy, 'The Internet in Our Bones' (2014) (www.rddy.im)

Sobchack, Vivian, 'Nostalgia for a Digital Object: Regrets on the Quickening of Quick Time', in *Future Cinema: The Cinematic Imaginary after Film*, ed. Jeffrey Shaw and Peter Weibel (Cambridge, Massachusetts: The MIT Press, 2003)

Steyerl, Hito, *The Wretched of the Screen*, ed. Julieta Aranda, Brian Kuan Wood, Anton Vidokle (Berlin and New York: Sternberg Press, 2012)

Trecartin, Ryan, and Cindy Sherman, 'Cindy Sherman Interviews Ryan Trecartin', in *Ryan Trecartin: Any Ever* (New York: Elizabeth Dee/Skira Rizzoli, 2011)

Trinh T. Minh-ha, *D-Passage: The Digital Way* (Durham, North Carolina: Duke University Press, 2013)

Tucker, Marcia, 'PheNAUMANology', *Artforum*, no. 9 (December 1970)

Uroskie, Andrew V., *Between the Black Box and the White Cube: Expanded Cinema and Postwar Art* (Chicago: University of Chicago Press, 2014)

van den Boomen, Marianne, Sybille Lammes, et al., *Digital Material: Tracing New Media in Everyday Life and Technology* (Amsterdam: Amsterdam University Press, 2009)

Viola, Bill, and Michael Nash, 'Bill Viola. Long Beach, California, 30 June 1990', *Journal of Contemporary Art* (www.jca-online.com)

White, Ian, and Mike Sperlinger, eds, *Kinomuseum: Towards an Artists' Cinema* (Cologne: Verlag der Buchhandlung Walther König, 2008)

Wilson-Goldie, Kaelen, 'The Body on Stage and Screen: Collaboration and the Creative Process in Rabih Mroué's Photo-Romance', *Afterall*, no. 25 (Autumn/Winter 2010)

Wollen, Peter, *Signs and Meaning in the Cinema* (Bloomington: Indiana University Press, 1969)

Zaatari, Akram, 'Scratching and Stretching Skin' (Paris: Galerie Imane Farès, 2011).

Zizek, Slavoj, 'From Virtual Reality to the Virtualization of Reality', in *Electronic Culture: Technology and Visual Representation*, ed. Tim Druckrey (New York: Aperture, 1996)

Zoller, Maxa, *The Pregnant Apparatus* (Halle, Germany: Werkleitz Media Art Festival, 2014)

Zummer, Thomas, 'Projection and Dis/embodiment: Genealogies of the Virtual', in *Into the Light: The Projected Image in American Art 1964–1977*, op. cit.

Index

Abbas, Basel 18, 192-3

Abe, Shuya 28

Abou-Rahme, Rouanne 18, 192-3

Acconci, Vito 112, 156, 201

Adorno, Theodor W. 93, 94n1-2

Agamben, Giorgio 50, 51n3, 147n4, 160, 162n6, 166, 169n2

Ahmed, Sara 218

Akerman, Chantal 183

Akomfrah, John 160

al-Ani, Jananne 16, 95-7

al-Haytham, Ibn 24

Altaf, Navjot 118

Althusser, Louis 50

Alÿs, Francis 16, 74-7

Ancarani, Yuri 18, 220-22

Anger, Kenneth 149

Arcangel, Cory 125

Arnheim, Rudolf 47, 49n2

Ashery, Oreet 16, 143-7

Atkins, Ed 16, 182, 184, 185, 186

Auguis, Reece 160

Bachchan, Amitabh 120

Bachelard, Gaston 22

Bailey, Jeremy 16, 124-7

Baldessari, John 201

Balsom, Erika 18, 19n7, 199, 203-5

Barber, George 187-9

Barker, Jennifer M. 51

Barrada, Yto 216

Barry, Iris 94

Barry, Judith 16, 59-64

Barry, Robert 84

Barthes, Roland 126

Baudrillard, Jean 28, 156, 159

Baudry, Jean-Louis 50

Bazin, André 19n4, 173, 173n4

Bellour, Raymond 12, 19n1

Bender, Gretchen 42-5

Benjamin, Walter 23, 24n3, 57, 61, 82, 85n1, 159-60, 162n1, n3, 166

Benning, Sadie 67

Benvenisti, Meron 76

Bergson, Henri 12

Berlant, Lauren 190

Beuys, Joseph 219

Beyoncé 83, 218

Bird, Robert 77-81

Birnbaum, Dara 16, 112-16

Bishop, Claire 82-6

Black Audio Film Collective 16, 159-62

Blazwick, Iwona 215-16

Blümlinger, Christa 193-5

Bode, Steven 65-7

Bolter, J. David 18, 207-10

Borden, Lizzie 201, 202

Breitz, Candice 73

Breivik, Anders 150

Brener, Aleksandr 79

Brezhnev, Leonid 79

Broodthaers, Marcel 30, 47, 48

Brown, Wendy 144, 146n2

Bryson, Norman 61, 62n10

Buchanan, Roderick 67

Burden, Chris 48

Butalia, Urvashi 119

Butler, Brad 16, 69-71

Cage, John 31, 126

Callas, Maria 158

Campbell, Colin 124

Campbell, Duncan 185

Campus, Peter 30, 125

Cardew, Cornelius 100

Carpenter, Karen 139

Castro, Fidel 90

Castelli, Leo 199, 200, 201, 202, 204

ACKNOWLEDGEMENTS

Editor's acknowledgements

I would like to thank Iwona Blazwick for this opportunity and Ian Farr for his inspiring commitment to this volume. Gratitude is due to Sofia Victorino for reading various drafts of my original proposal and to the numerous pioneers, colleagues and friends who helped shape my knowledge and passion for the moving image over the years, in particular, Karen Alexander, Rosa Barba, Judith Barry, Heather Corcoran, Ben Cook, Richard W. Dyer, Jean Fisher, Frank Gallacher, Ed Halter, Shanay Jhaveri, Mark Nash, Sarah Perks and Ian White, to whose memory this book is dedicated.

Publisher's acknowledgements

Whitechapel Gallery is grateful to all those who gave their generous permission to reproduce the listed material. Every effort has been made to secure all permissions and we apologize for any inadvertent errors or omissions. If notified, we will endeavour to correct these at the earliest opportunity. We would like to express our thanks to all who contributed to the making of this volume, especially Basel Abbas, Ruanne Abou-Rahme, Jananne Al-Ani, Yuri Ancarani, Clemens Apprich, Jeremy Bailey, Erika Balsom, Judith Barry, Charles Bernstein, Robert Bird, Claire Bishop, Christa Blümlinger, Steven Bode, Brad Butler, Rebecca Comay, Jonathan Crary, Aaron Cutler, Edith Decker-Phillips, T.J. Demos, Anna Dezeuze, Jean Fisher, Morgan Fisher, Jean-Michel Frodon, Mark Godfrey, Kenneth Goldsmith, Kim Gordon, Tim Griffin, Andrew Grossman, Nicolás Guagnini, Ed Halter, Ken Hakuta, Gary Hill, Susan Hiller, John G. Hanhardt, Shanay Jhaveri, Travis Jeppesen, Stanya Kahn, William Kentridge, Jason King, Anja Kirschner, Meg Koerner, Pip Laurenson, Kate Linker, Susan Lord, Sven Lütticken, Chris McCormack, Joanne McNeil, Steve McQueen, Francesco Manacorda, Jumana Manna, Emanuela Mazzonis, Karen Mirza, Michael Newman, Pallavi Paul, Elena Pinto Simon, R.V. Ramani, Steve Reinke, Andrew Renton, James Richards, Michele Robecchi, Alison Rowley, Jacolby Satterwhite, Ken Saylor, Roddy Schrock, Marcel Schwierin, Mariana Shellard, Jason Simon, Vivian Sobchack, Mike Sperlinger, Hito Steyerl, Marita Sturken, Ryan Trecartin, Trinh T. Minh-ha, Andrew V. Uroskie, Woody Vasulka, Bill Viola, Kaelen Wilson-Goldie, Akram Zaatari, Maxa Zoller, Thomas Zummer.

We also gratefully acknowledge the cooperation of 303 Gallery, Afterall, Artangel, Art Asia Pacific, Artforum, Art Monthly, Bortolami Gallery, Cabinet,

Callicoon Fine Arts, Carroll/Fletcher, University of Chicago Press, Thomas Dane, Frieze, Idiom, Indiana University Press, Journal of Contemporary Art, JRP/Ringier, John Libbey Publishing, Liverpool University Press, University of Minnesota Press, The MIT Press, Mousse Publishing, Mute, no.w.here, Maureen Paley, Andrea Rosen Gallery, Sprueth Magers, Sternberg Press, Tate Publishing, University of Texas Press, University of Toronto Press.

Whitechapel Gallery is supported by